JOURNEY TO **STAR WARS:** THE FORCE AWAKENS

STAR WARS

SHATTERED EMPIRE

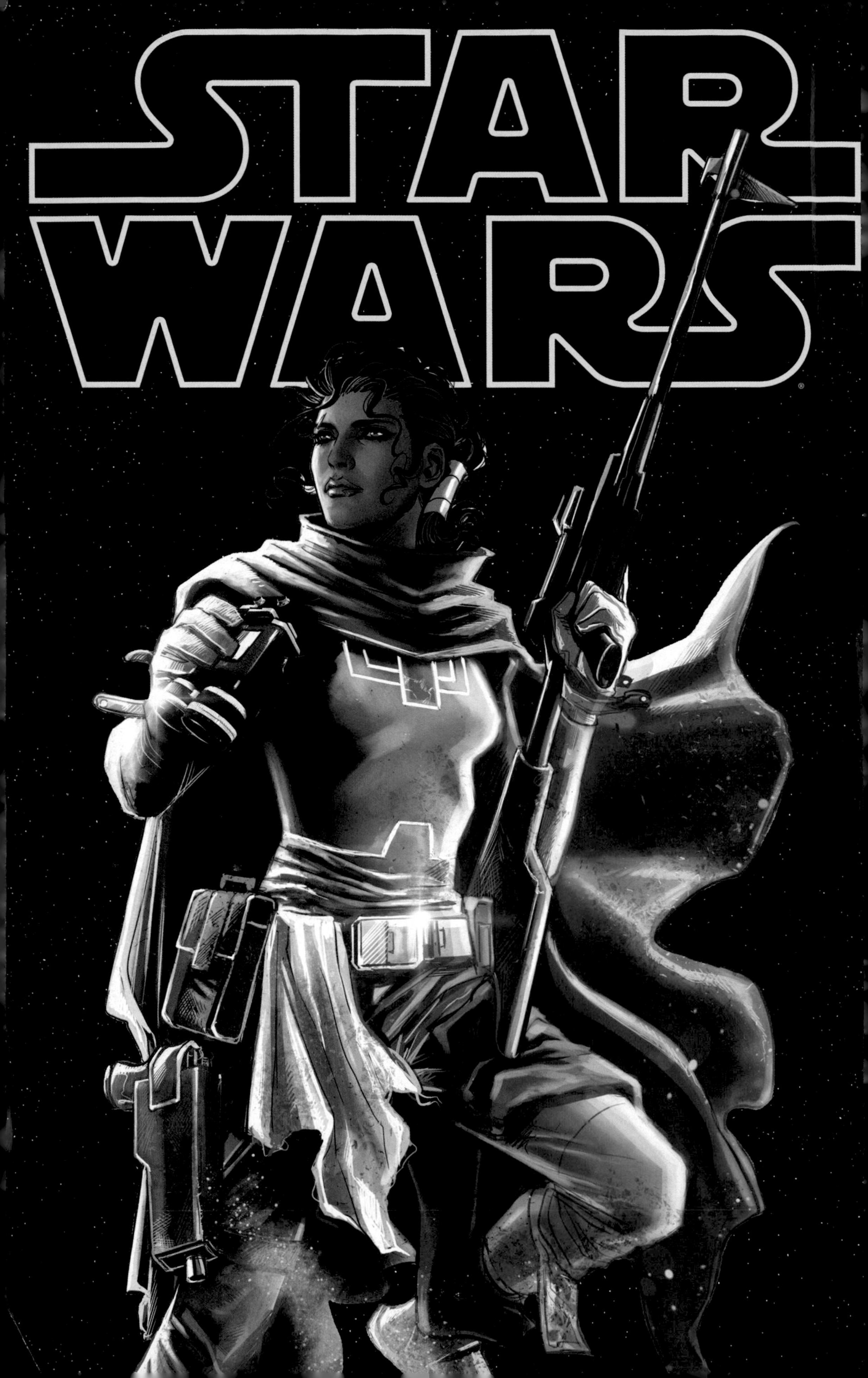
STAR WARS

JOURNEY TO **STAR WARS: THE FORCE AWAKENS**

SHATTERED EMPIRE

Writer	**GREG RUCKA**
Artists	**MARCO CHECCHETTO** (#1-4), **ANGEL UNZUETA** (#2-3) & **EMILIO LAISO** (#2)
Colorist	**ANDRES MOSSA**
Letterer	**VC's JOE CARAMAGNA**
Cover Art	**PHIL NOTO** (#1) & **MARCO CHECCHETO** (#2-4)
Assistant Editor	**HEATHER ANTOS**
Editor	**JORDAN D. WHITE**
Executive Editor	**C.B. CEBULSKI**

Editor in Chief	**AXEL ALONSO**
Chief Creative Officer	**JOE QUESADA**
Publisher	**DAN BUCKLEY**

For Lucasfilm:

Creative Director	**MICHAEL SIGLAIN**
Senior Editor	**FRANK PARISI**
Lucasfilm Story Group	**RAYNE ROBERTS, PABLO HIDALGO, LELAND CHEE**

Collection Editor	**JENNIFER GRÜNWALD**
Assistant Editor	**SARAH BRUNSTAD**
Associate Managing Editor	**ALEX STARBUCK**
Editor, Special Projects	**MARK D. BEAZLEY**
Senior Editor, Special Projects	**JEFF YOUNGQUIST**
SVP Print, Sales & Marketing	**DAVID GABRIEL**
Book Designer	**ADAM DEL RE**

STAR WARS: JOURNEY TO STAR WARS: THE FORCE AWAKENS — SHATTERED EMPIRE. Contains material originally published in magazine form as JOURNEY TO STAR WARS: THE FORCE AWAKENS — SHATTERED EMPIRE #1-4, PRINCESS LEIA #1 and STAR WARS #1. First printing 2015. ISBN# 978-0-7851-9781-2. Published by MARVEL WORLDWIDE, INC., a subsidiary of MARVEL ENTERTAINMENT, LLC. OFFICE OF PUBLICATION: 135 West 50th Street, New York, NY 10020. STAR WARS and related text and illustrations are trademarks and/or copyrights, in the United States and other countries, of Lucasfilm Ltd. and/or its affiliates. © & TM Lucasfilm Ltd. No similarity between any of the names, characters, persons, and/or institutions in this magazine with those of any living or dead person or institution is intended, and any such similarity which may exist is purely coincidental. Marvel and its logos are TM Marvel Characters, Inc. **Printed in Canada.** ALAN FINE, President, Marvel Entertainment; DAN BUCKLEY, President, TV, Publishing and Brand Management; JOE QUESADA, Chief Creative Officer; TOM BREVOORT, SVP of Publishing; DAVID BOGART, SVP of Operations & Procurement, Publishing; C.B. CEBULSKI, VP of International Development & Brand Management; DAVID GABRIEL, SVP Print, Sales & Marketing; JIM O'KEEFE, VP of Operations & Logistics; DAN CARR, Executive Director of Publishing Technology; SUSAN CRESPI, Editorial Operations Manager; ALEX MORALES, Publishing Operations Manager; STAN LEE, Chairman Emeritus. For information regarding advertising in Marvel Comics or on Marvel.com, please contact Jonathan Rheingold, VP of Custom Solutions & Ad Sales, at jrheingold@marvel.com. For Marvel subscription inquiries, please call 800-217-9158. **Manufactured between 9/11/2015 and 10/19/2015 by SOLISCO PRINTERS, SCOTT, QC, CANADA.**

10 9 8 7 6 5 4 3 2 1

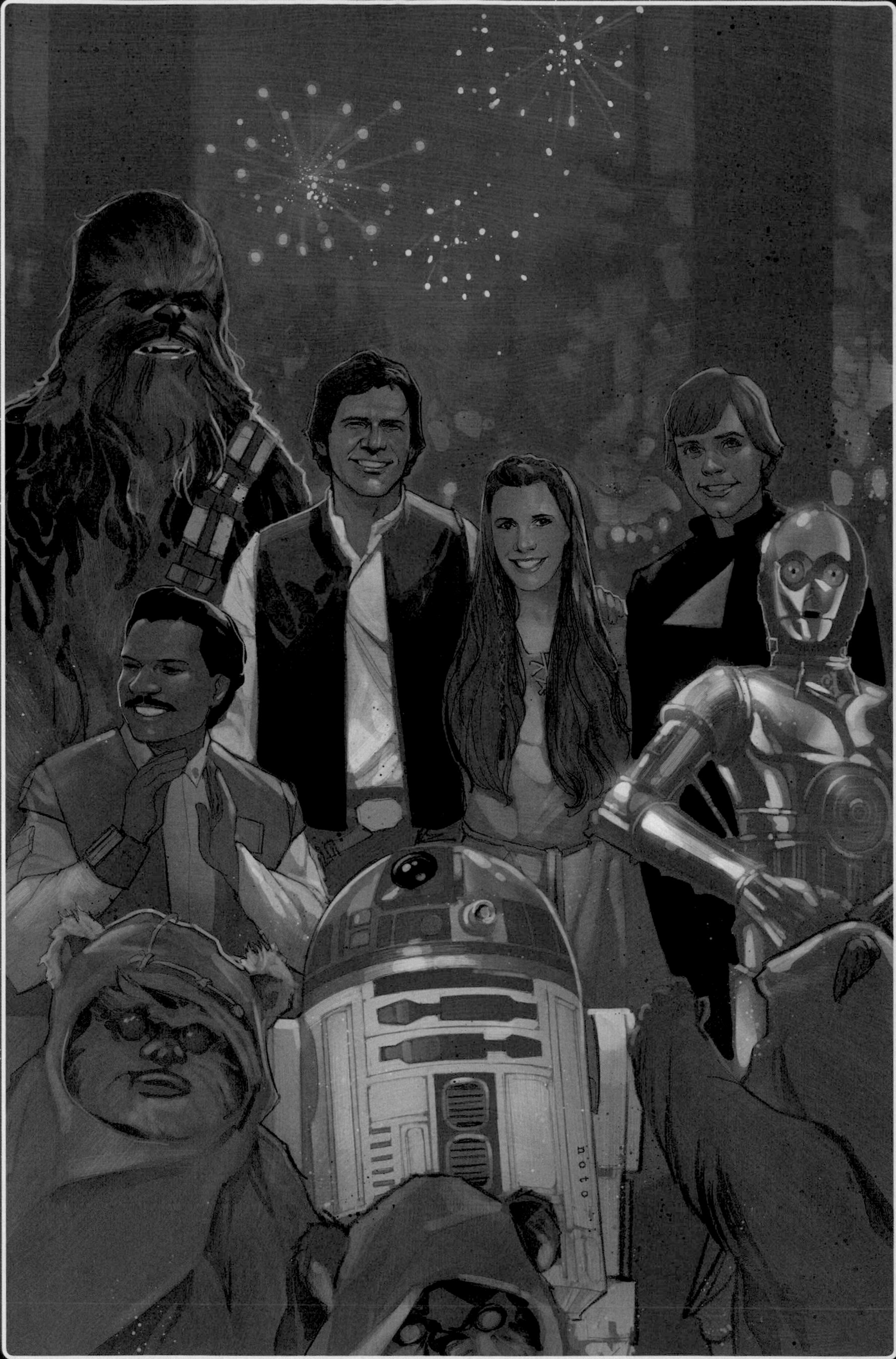
noto

1

SHATTERED EMPIRE

It is the final moments of the BATTLE OF ENDOR. Amidst the stars above the Forest Moon, Rebel forces have engaged the evil Galactic Empire in a desperate, final confrontation, hoping to end the tyrannical rule of Emperor Palpatine and bring peace to a wearied and battered galaxy.

But the Rebel Fleet has fallen into a trap. The second DEATH STAR is fully operational, and on Endor's moon, the energy shield protecting it still stands. What was to be a moment of triumph now teeters on the brink of disaster.

Now, rebel pilots have engaged Imperial forces in furious dogfights, frantically trying to protect the Rebellion's capital ships, and to buy enough time to rescue victory from the jaws of defeat....

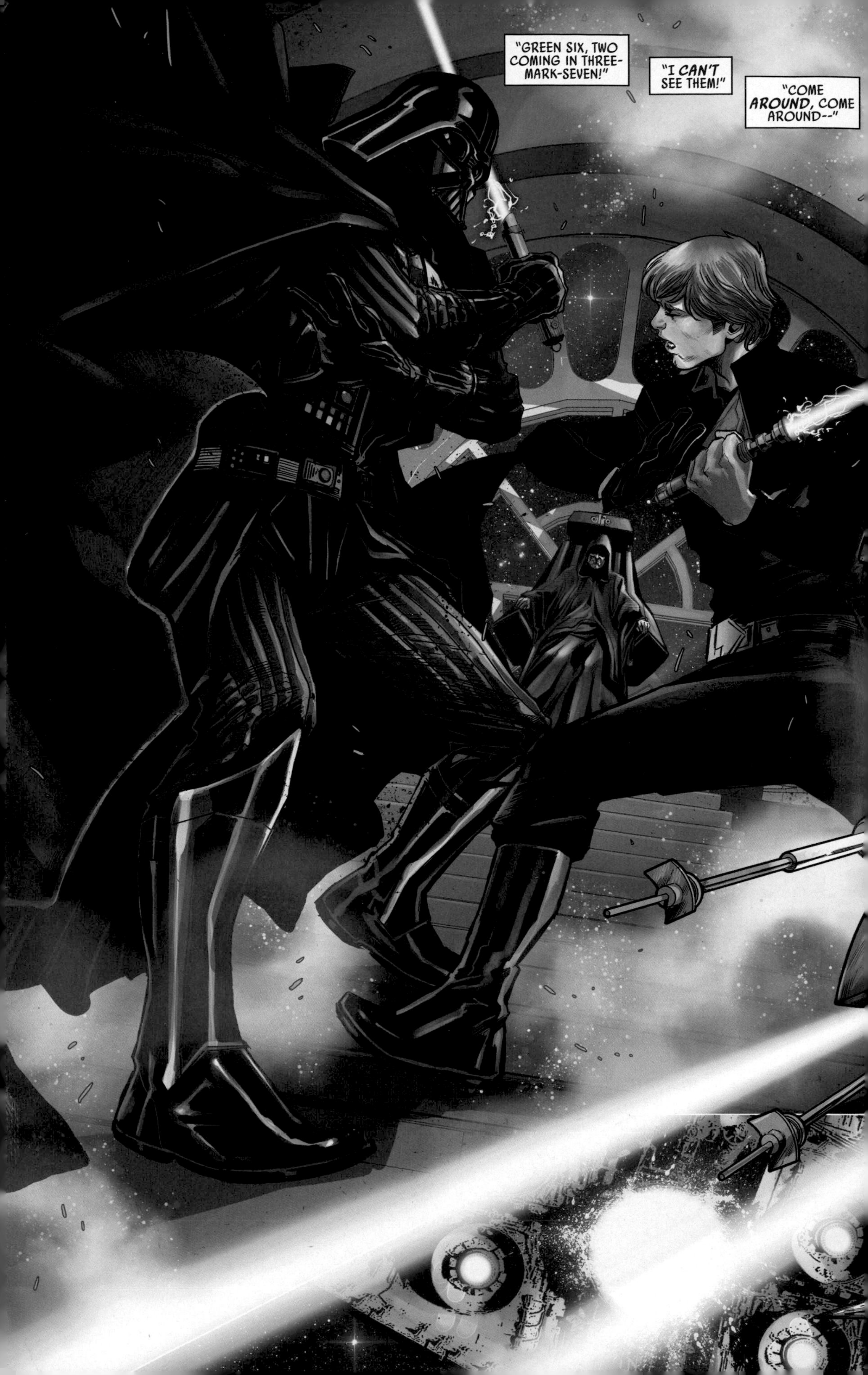
"GREEN SIX, TWO COMING IN THREE-MARK-SEVEN!"
"I CAN'T SEE THEM!"
"COME AROUND, COME AROUND--"

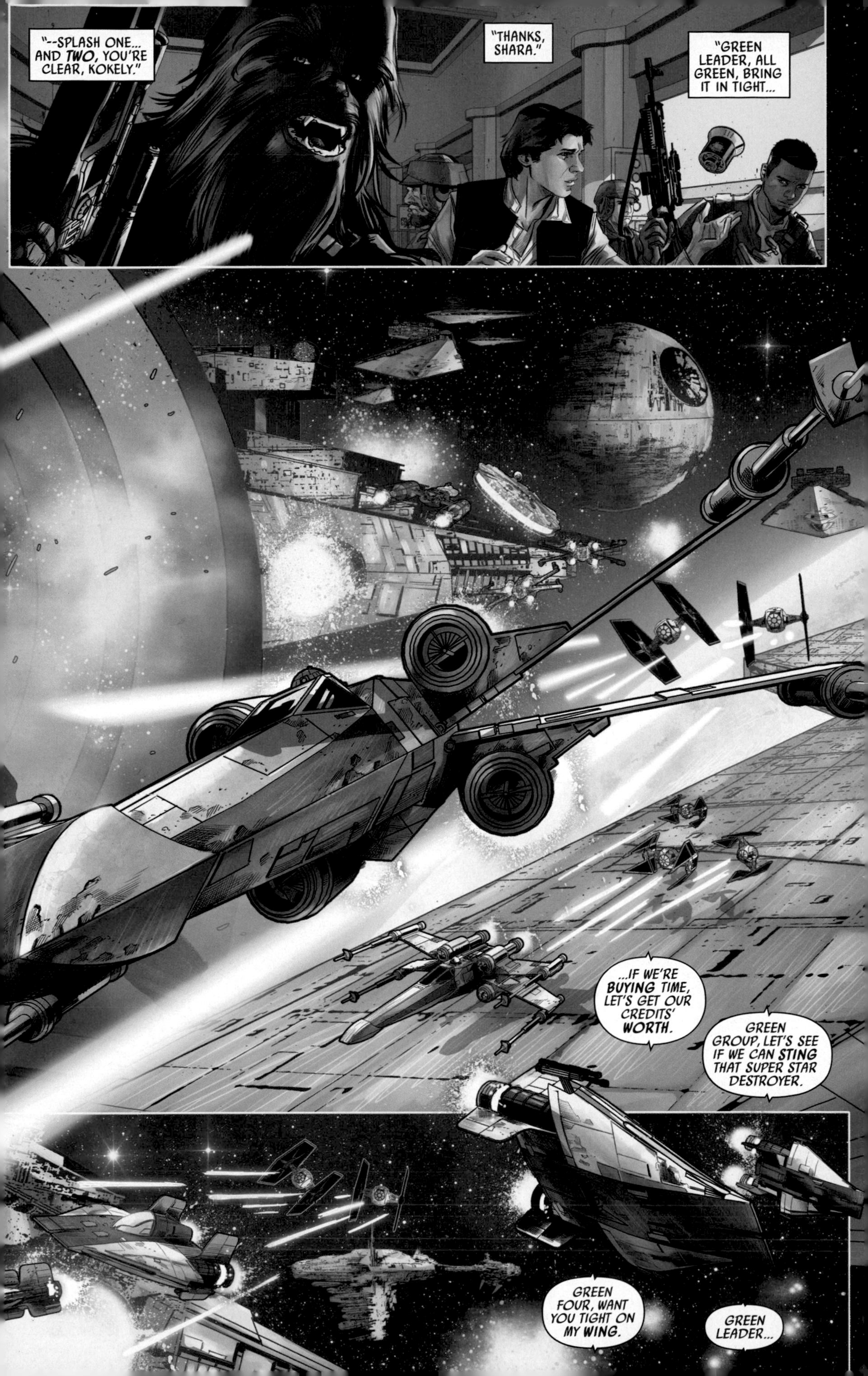
"--SPLASH ONE... AND TWO, YOU'RE CLEAR, KOKELY."
"THANKS, SHARA."
"GREEN LEADER, ALL GREEN, BRING IT IN TIGHT...
...IF WE'RE BUYING TIME, LET'S GET OUR CREDITS' WORTH.
GREEN GROUP, LET'S SEE IF WE CAN STING THAT SUPER STAR DESTROYER.
GREEN FOUR, WANT YOU TIGHT ON MY WING.
GREEN LEADER...

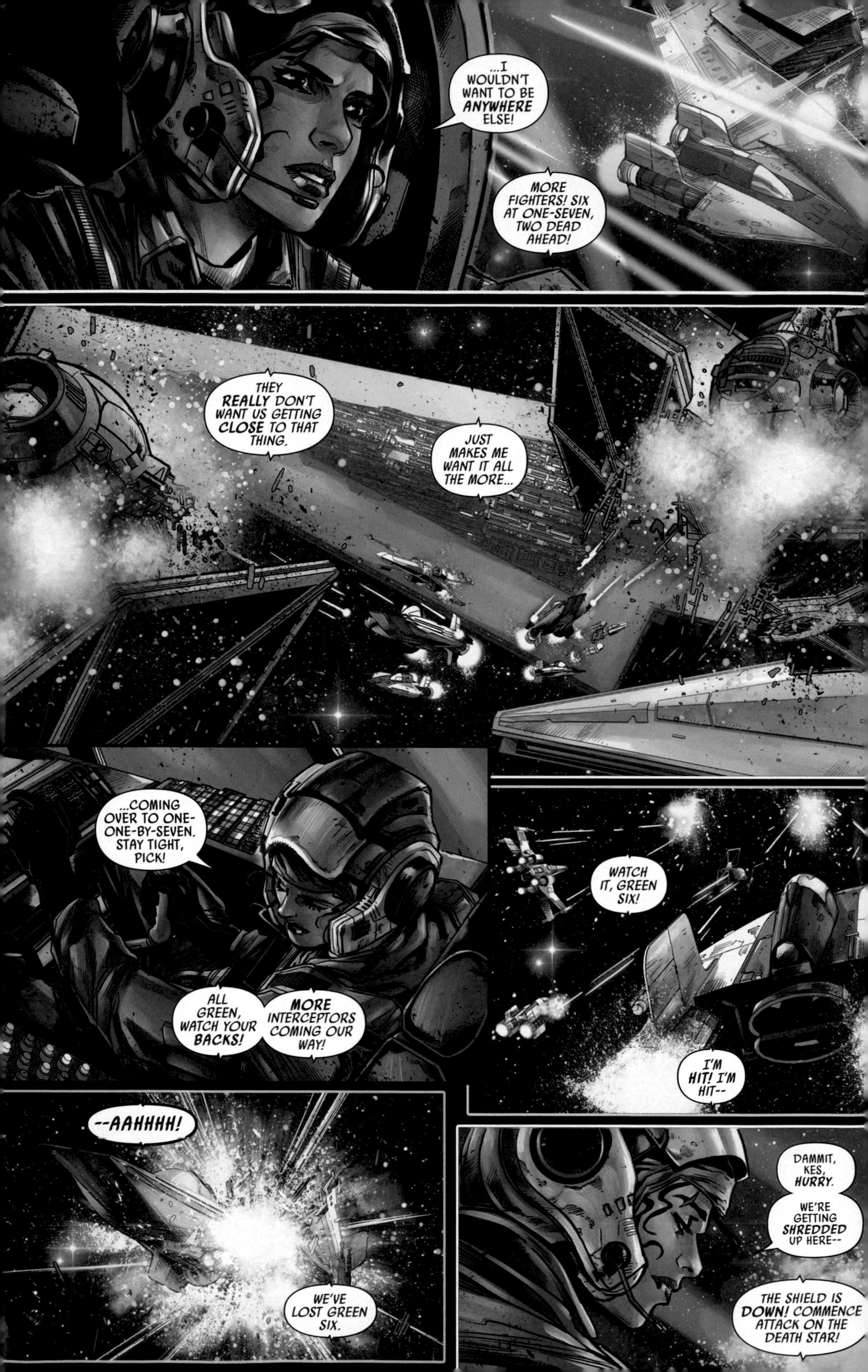
...I WOULDN'T WANT TO BE ANYWHERE ELSE!
MORE FIGHTERS! SIX AT ONE-SEVEN, TWO DEAD AHEAD!
THEY REALLY DON'T WANT US GETTING CLOSE TO THAT THING.
JUST MAKES ME WANT IT ALL THE MORE...
...COMING OVER TO ONE-ONE-BY-SEVEN. STAY TIGHT, PICK!
ALL GREEN, WATCH YOUR BACKS!
MORE INTERCEPTORS COMING OUR WAY!
WATCH IT, GREEN SIX!
I'M HIT! I'M HIT--
--AAHHHH!
WE'VE LOST GREEN SIX.
DAMMIT, KES, HURRY.
WE'RE GETTING SHREDDED UP HERE--
THE SHIELD IS DOWN! COMMENCE ATTACK ON THE DEATH STAR!

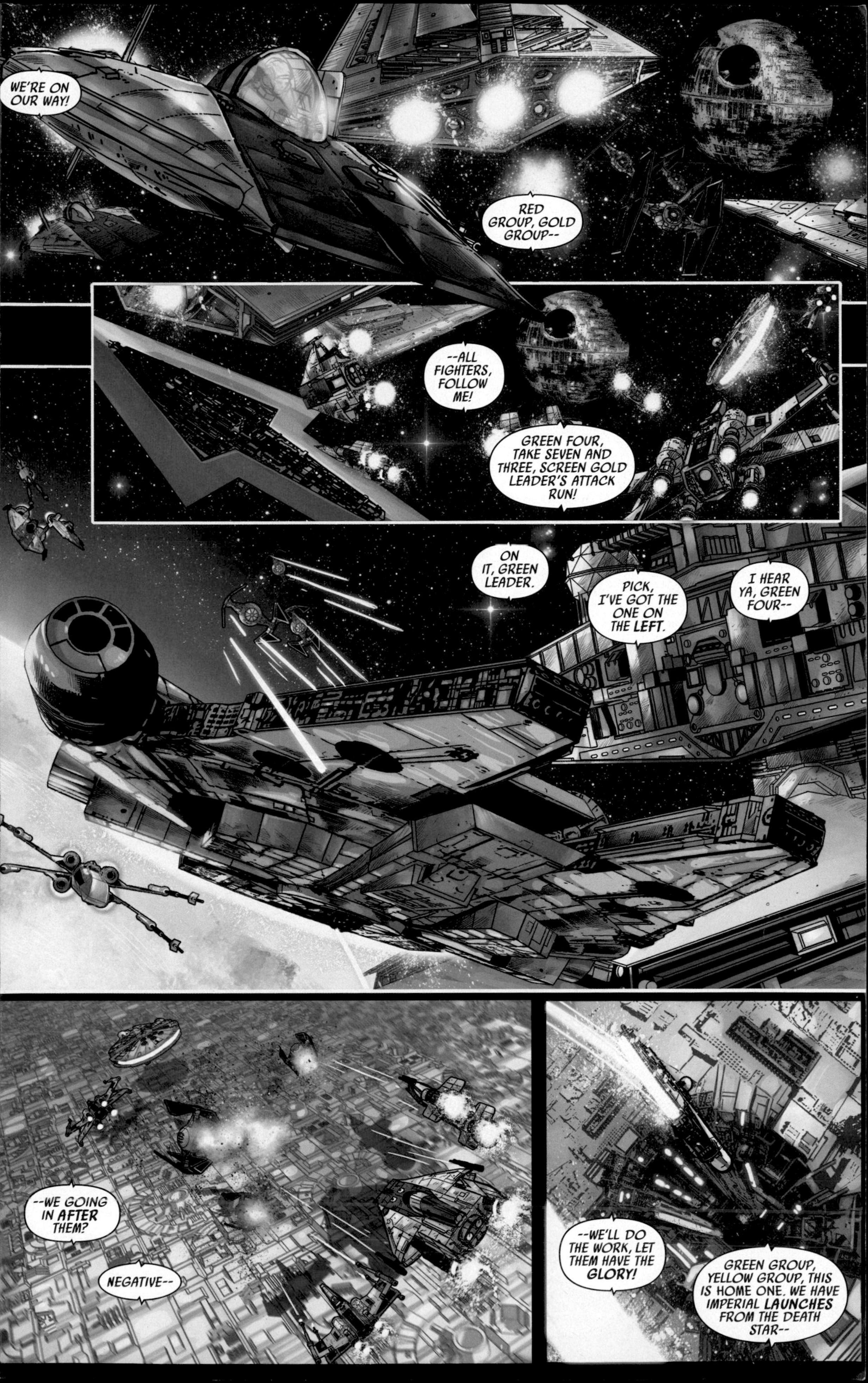
WE'RE ON OUR WAY!
RED GROUP, GOLD GROUP--
--ALL FIGHTERS, FOLLOW ME!
GREEN FOUR, TAKE SEVEN AND THREE, SCREEN GOLD LEADER'S ATTACK RUN!
ON IT, GREEN LEADER.
PICK, I'VE GOT THE ONE ON THE LEFT.
I HEAR YA, GREEN FOUR--
--WE GOING IN AFTER THEM?
NEGATIVE--
--WE'LL DO THE WORK, LET THEM HAVE THE GLORY!
GREEN GROUP, YELLOW GROUP, THIS IS HOME ONE. WE HAVE IMPERIAL LAUNCHES FROM THE DEATH STAR--

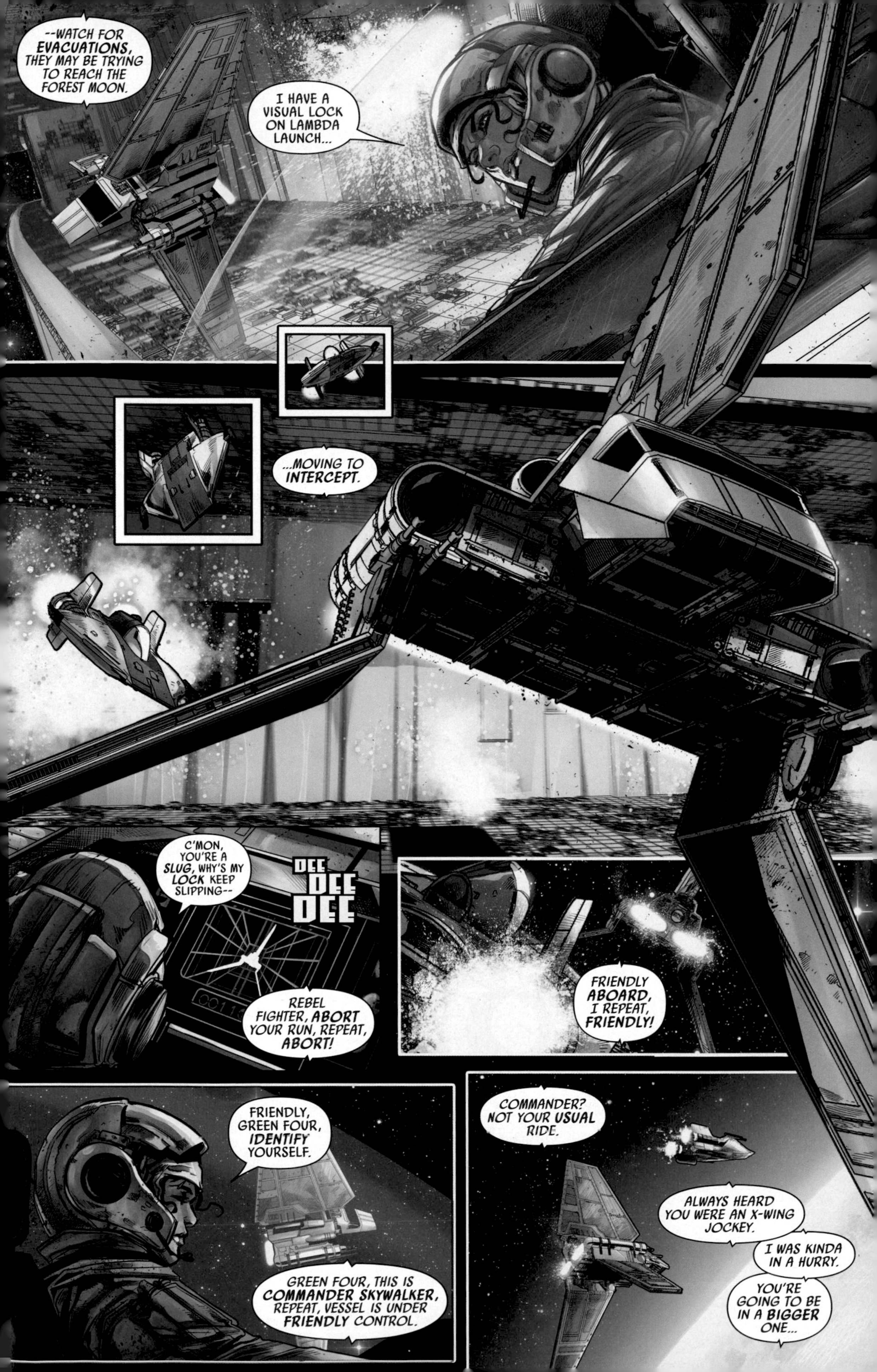

--WATCH FOR EVACUATIONS, THEY MAY BE TRYING TO REACH THE FOREST MOON.
I HAVE A VISUAL LOCK ON LAMBDA LAUNCH...
...MOVING TO INTERCEPT.
C'MON, YOU'RE A SLUG, WHY'S MY LOCK KEEP SLIPPING--
DEE DEE DEE
REBEL FIGHTER, ABORT YOUR RUN, REPEAT, ABORT!
FRIENDLY ABOARD, I REPEAT, FRIENDLY!
FRIENDLY, GREEN FOUR, IDENTIFY YOURSELF.
GREEN FOUR, THIS IS COMMANDER SKYWALKER, REPEAT, VESSEL IS UNDER FRIENDLY CONTROL.
COMMANDER? NOT YOUR USUAL RIDE.
ALWAYS HEARD YOU WERE AN X-WING JOCKEY.
I WAS KINDA IN A HURRY.
YOU'RE GOING TO BE IN A BIGGER ONE...

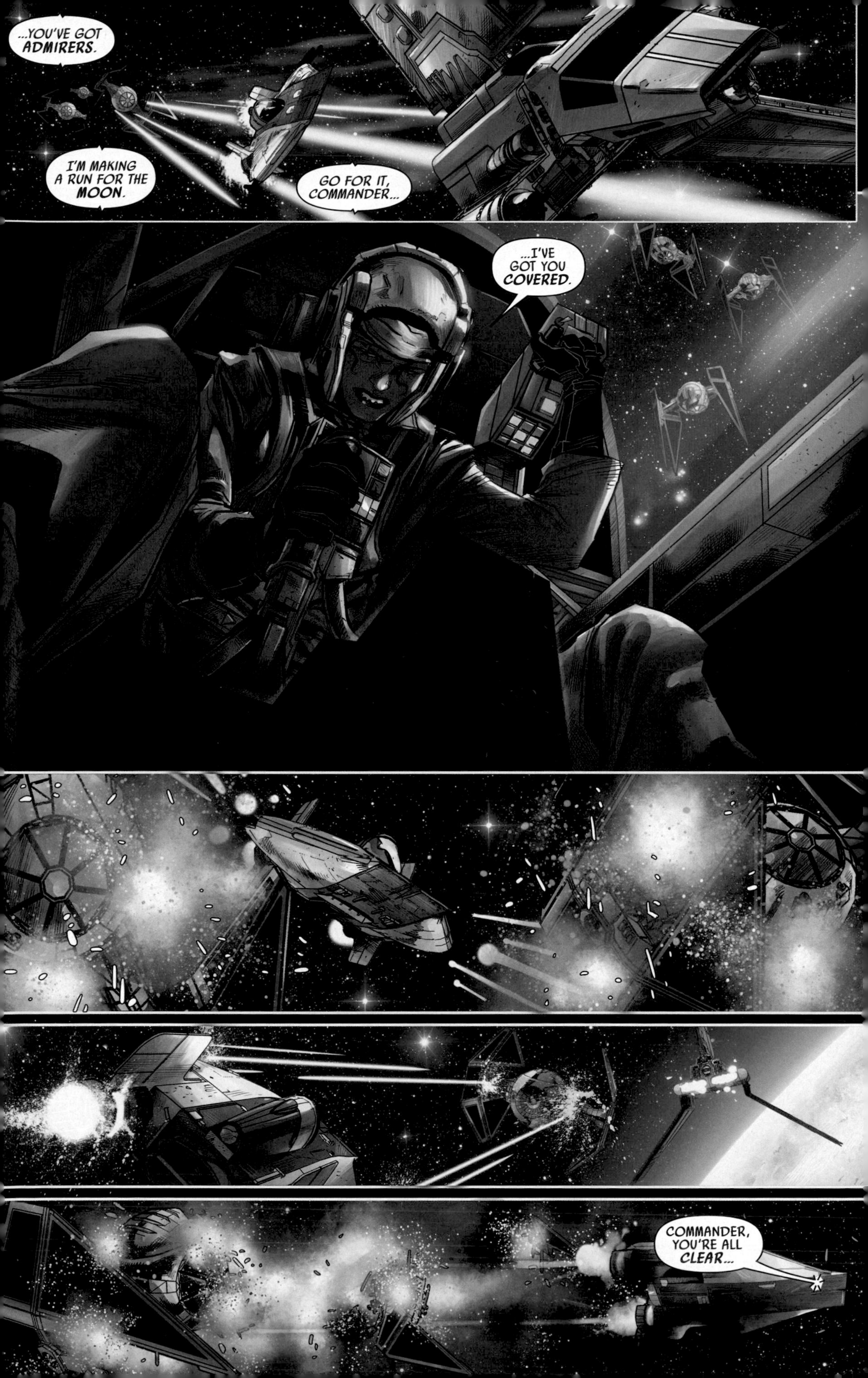
...YOU'VE GOT ADMIRERS.
I'M MAKING A RUN FOR THE MOON.
GO FOR IT, COMMANDER...
...I'VE GOT YOU COVERED.
COMMANDER, YOU'RE ALL CLEAR...

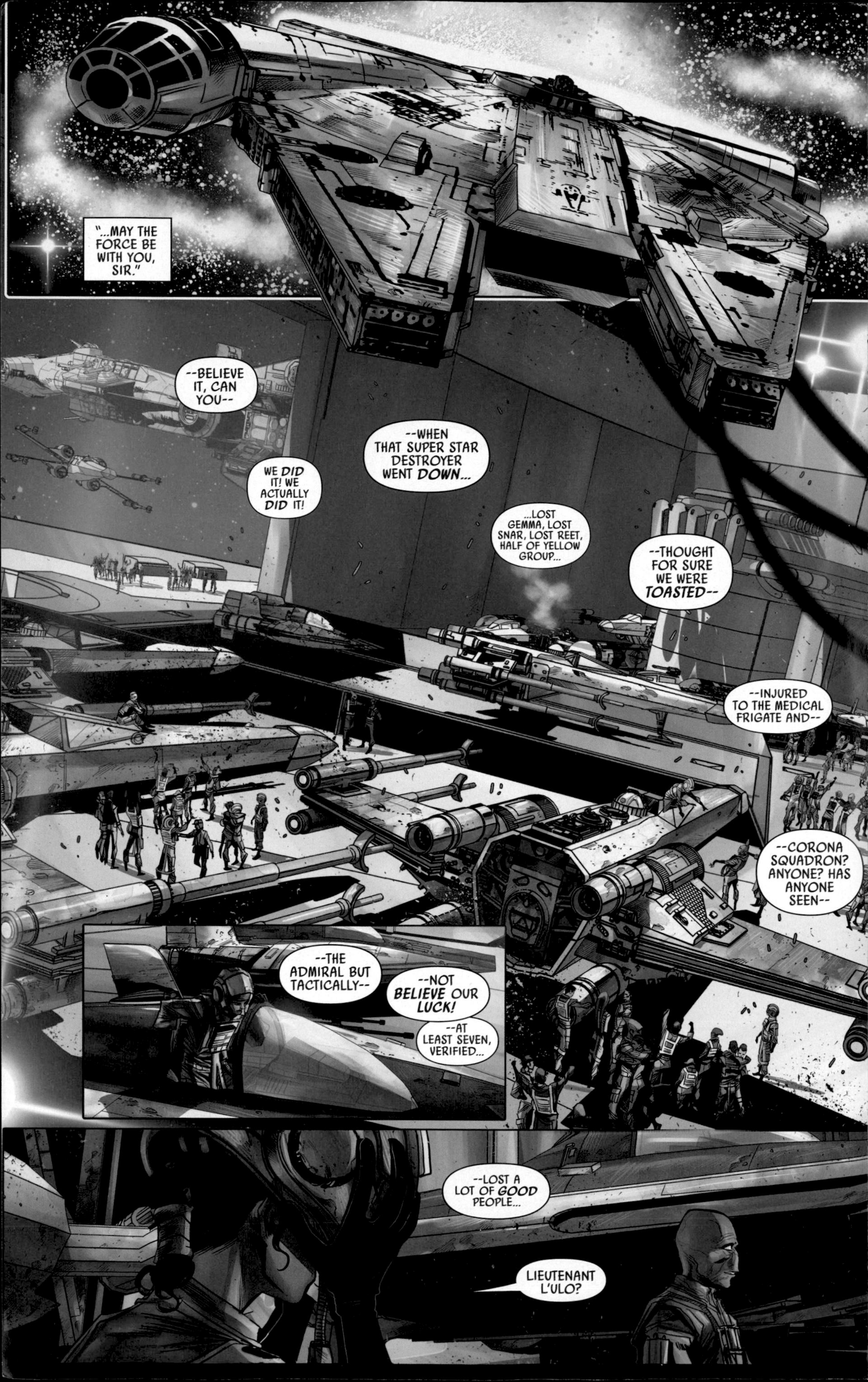
"...MAY THE FORCE BE WITH YOU, SIR."
--BELIEVE IT, CAN YOU--
WE *DID* IT! WE ACTUALLY *DID* IT!
--WHEN THAT SUPER STAR DESTROYER WENT *DOWN*...
...LOST GEMMA, LOST SNAR, LOST REET, HALF OF YELLOW GROUP...
--THOUGHT FOR SURE WE WERE *TOASTED*--
--INJURED TO THE MEDICAL FRIGATE AND--
--CORONA SQUADRON? ANYONE? HAS ANYONE SEEN--
--THE ADMIRAL BUT TACTICALLY--
--NOT *BELIEVE* OUR *LUCK!*
--AT LEAST SEVEN, VERIFIED...
--LOST A LOT OF *GOOD* PEOPLE...
LIEUTENANT L'ULO?

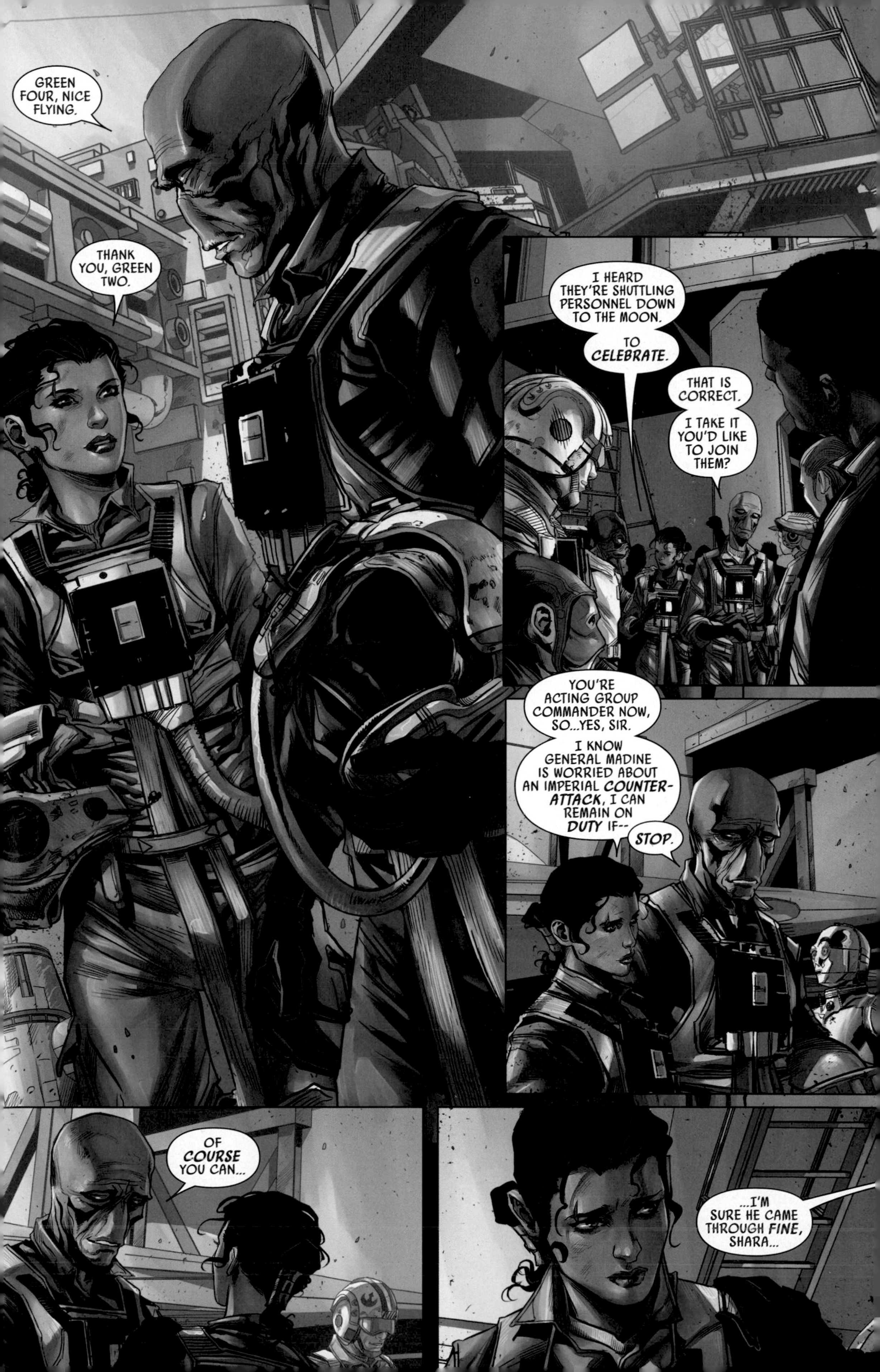
GREEN FOUR, NICE FLYING.
THANK YOU, GREEN TWO.
I HEARD THEY'RE SHUTTLING PERSONNEL DOWN TO THE MOON.
TO *CELEBRATE*.
THAT IS CORRECT.
I TAKE IT YOU'D LIKE TO JOIN THEM?
YOU'RE ACTING GROUP COMMANDER NOW, SO...YES, SIR.
I KNOW GENERAL MADINE IS WORRIED ABOUT AN IMPERIAL *COUNTER-ATTACK*, I CAN REMAIN ON *DUTY* IF--
STOP.
OF *COURSE* YOU CAN...
...I'M SURE HE CAME THROUGH *FINE*, SHARA...

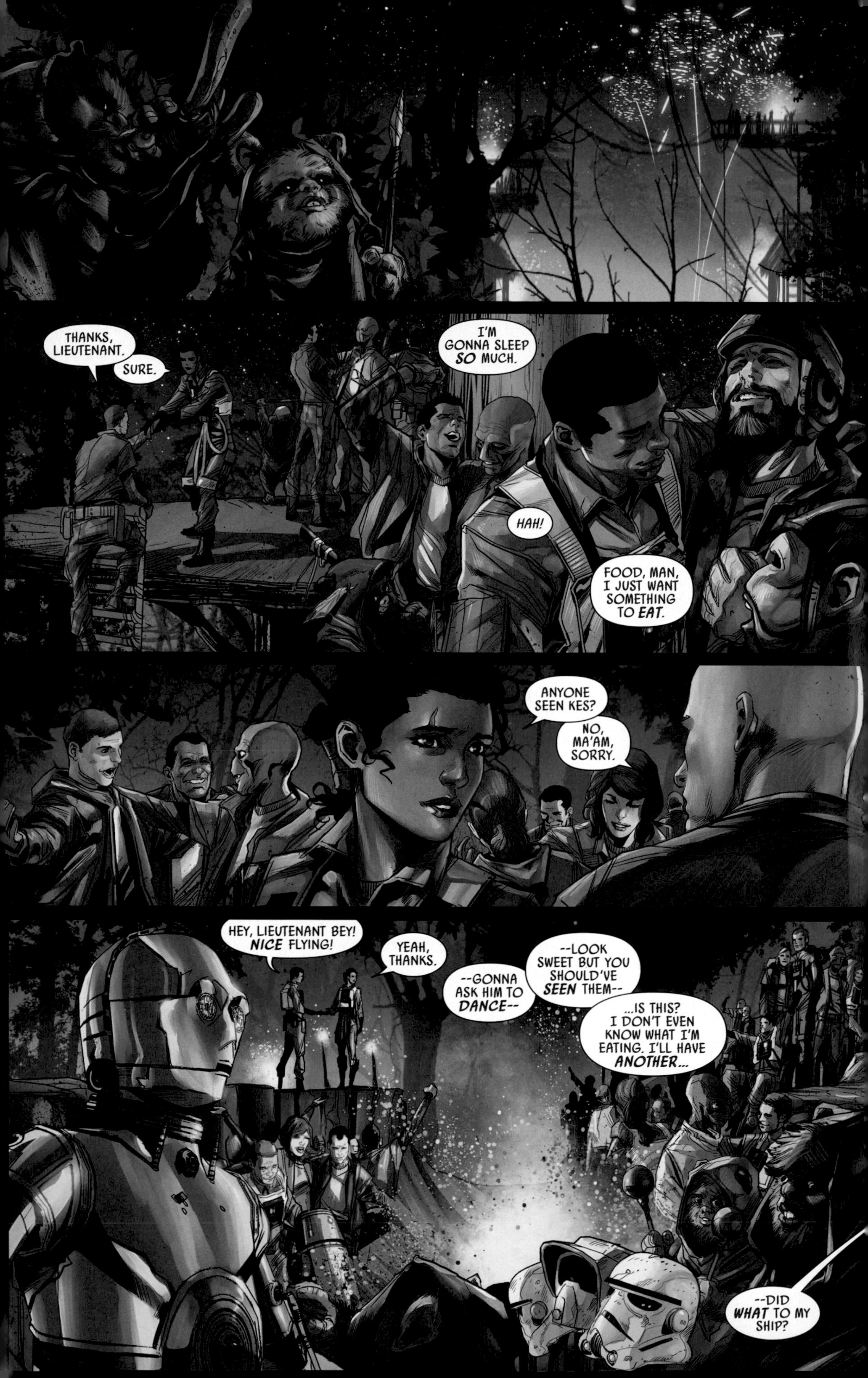
THANKS, LIEUTENANT.
SURE.
I'M GONNA SLEEP SO MUCH.
HAH!
FOOD, MAN, I JUST WANT SOMETHING TO EAT.
ANYONE SEEN KES?
NO, MA'AM, SORRY.
HEY, LIEUTENANT BEY! NICE FLYING!
YEAH, THANKS.
--GONNA ASK HIM TO DANCE--
--LOOK SWEET BUT YOU SHOULD'VE SEEN THEM--
...IS THIS? I DON'T EVEN KNOW WHAT I'M EATING. I'LL HAVE ANOTHER...
--DID WHAT TO MY SHIP?

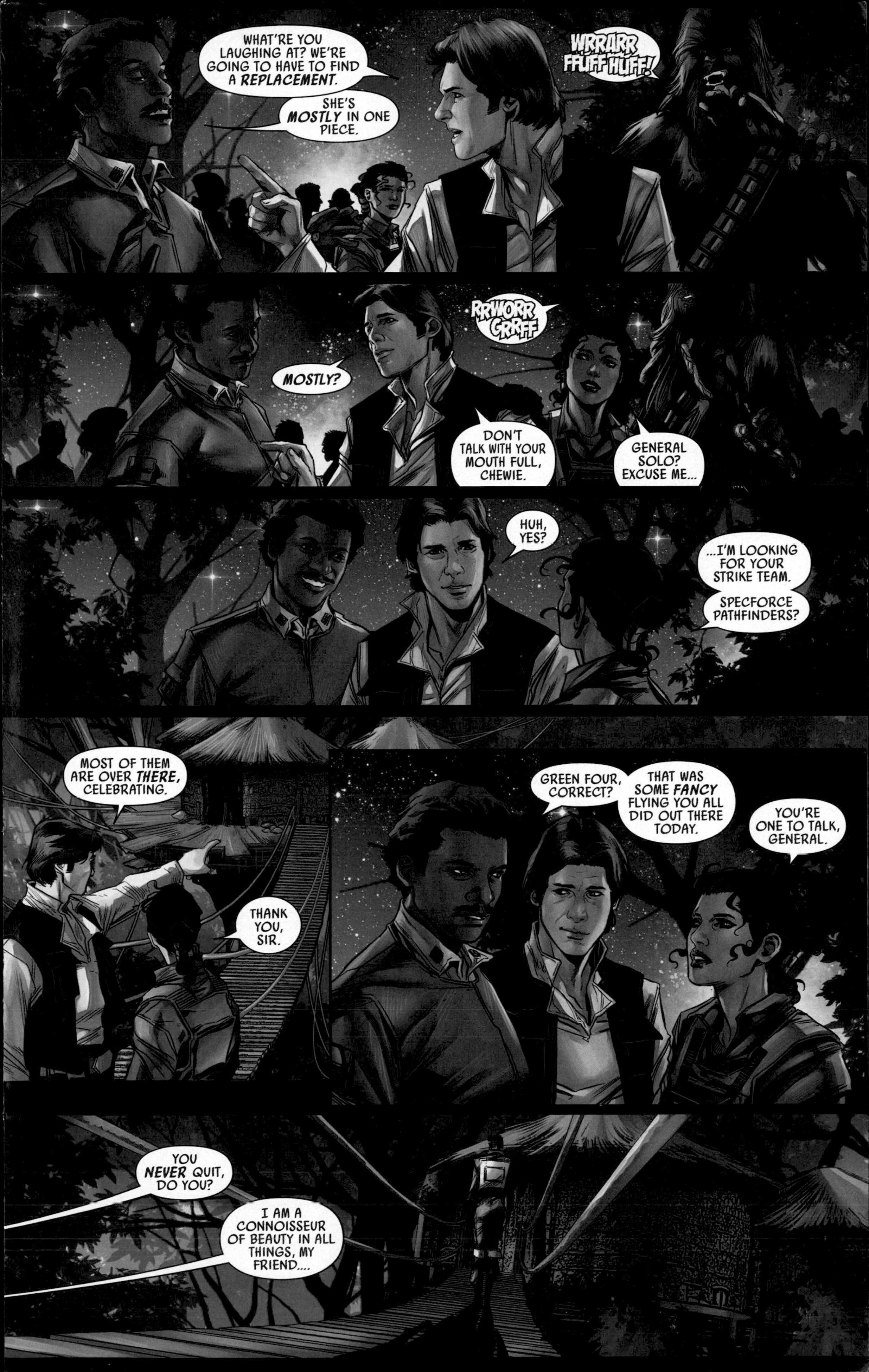
WHAT'RE YOU LAUGHING AT? WE'RE GOING TO HAVE TO FIND A REPLACEMENT.
SHE'S MOSTLY IN ONE PIECE.
WRRARR FFUFF HUFF!
MOSTLY?
RRWORR GRRFF
DON'T TALK WITH YOUR MOUTH FULL, CHEWIE.
GENERAL SOLO? EXCUSE ME...
HUH, YES?
...I'M LOOKING FOR YOUR STRIKE TEAM.
SPECFORCE PATHFINDERS?
MOST OF THEM ARE OVER THERE, CELEBRATING.
THANK YOU, SIR.
GREEN FOUR, CORRECT?
THAT WAS SOME FANCY FLYING YOU ALL DID OUT THERE TODAY.
YOU'RE ONE TO TALK, GENERAL.
YOU NEVER QUIT, DO YOU?
I AM A CONNOISSEUR OF BEAUTY IN ALL THINGS, MY FRIEND....

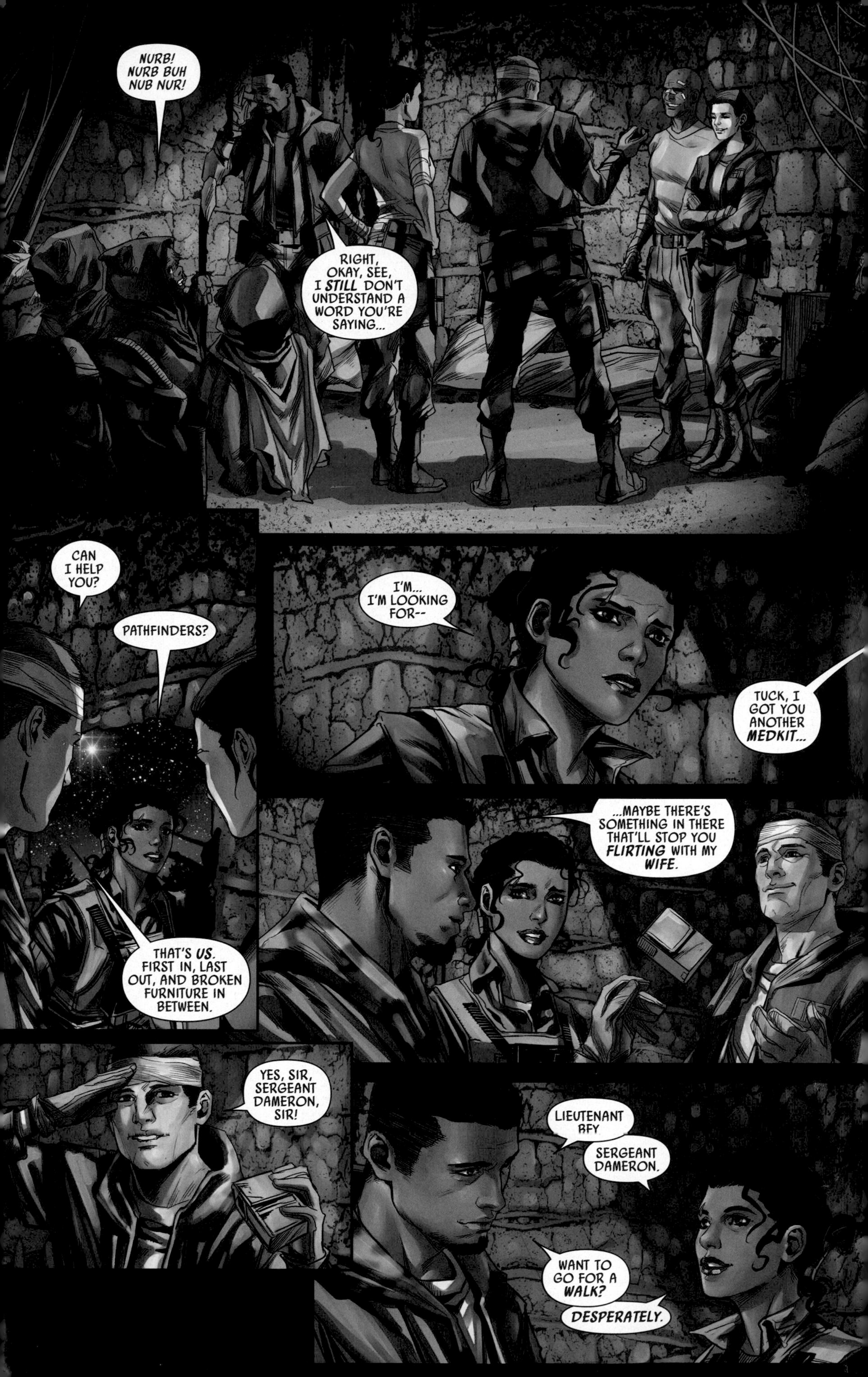
NURB! NURB BUH NUB NUR!
RIGHT, OKAY, SEE, I STILL DON'T UNDERSTAND A WORD YOU'RE SAYING...
CAN I HELP YOU?
PATHFINDERS?
THAT'S US. FIRST IN, LAST OUT, AND BROKEN FURNITURE IN BETWEEN.
I'M... I'M LOOKING FOR--
TUCK, I GOT YOU ANOTHER MEDKIT...
...MAYBE THERE'S SOMETHING IN THERE THAT'LL STOP YOU FLIRTING WITH MY WIFE.
YES, SIR, SERGEANT DAMERON, SIR!
LIEUTENANT BEY.
SERGEANT DAMERON.
WANT TO GO FOR A WALK?
DESPERATELY.

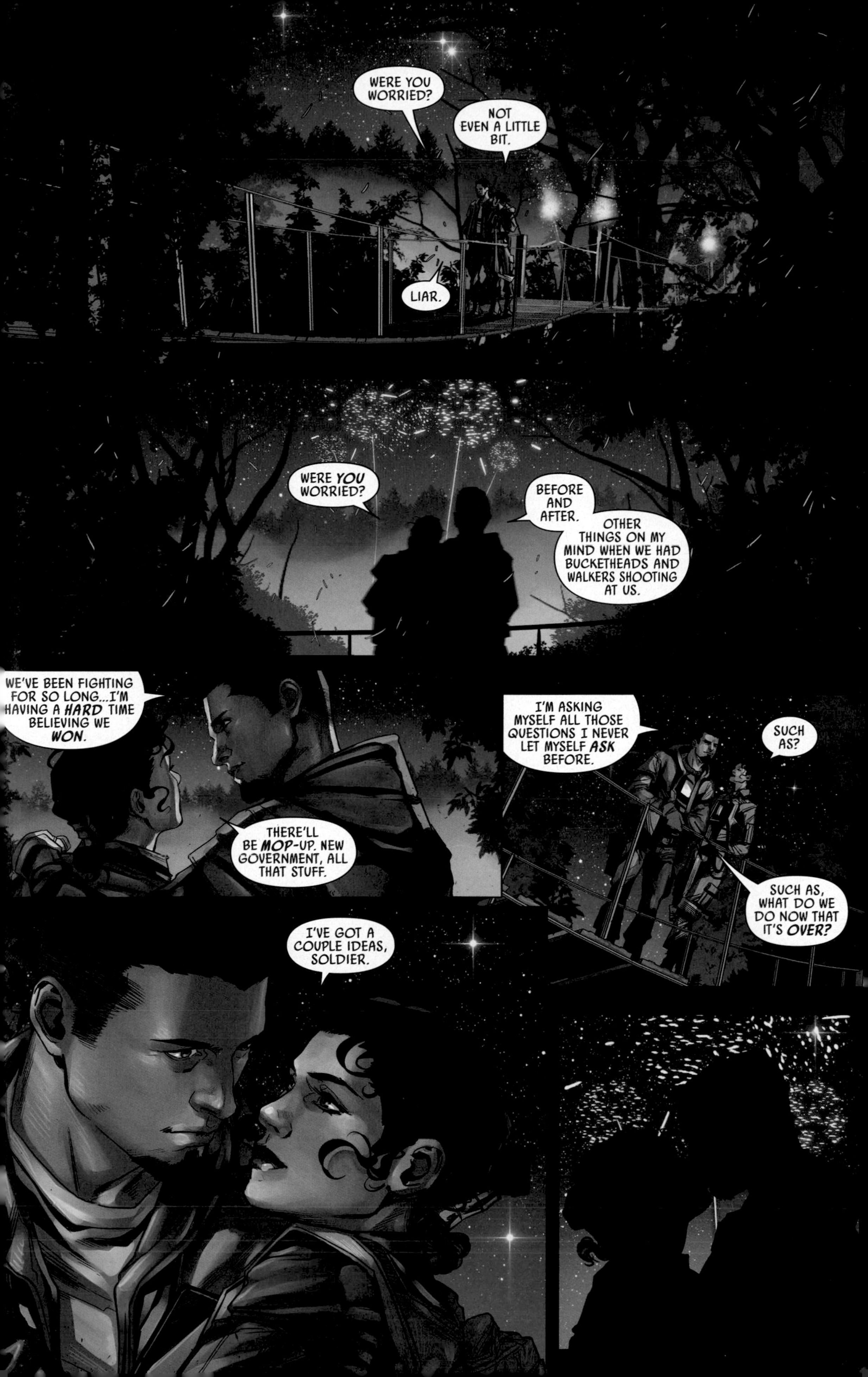
WERE YOU WORRIED?
NOT EVEN A LITTLE BIT.
LIAR.
WERE YOU WORRIED?
BEFORE AND AFTER.
OTHER THINGS ON MY MIND WHEN WE HAD BUCKETHEADS AND WALKERS SHOOTING AT US.
WE'VE BEEN FIGHTING FOR SO LONG...I'M HAVING A HARD TIME BELIEVING WE WON.
THERE'LL BE MOP-UP. NEW GOVERNMENT, ALL THAT STUFF.
I'M ASKING MYSELF ALL THOSE QUESTIONS I NEVER LET MYSELF ASK BEFORE.
SUCH AS?
SUCH AS, WHAT DO WE DO NOW THAT IT'S OVER?
I'VE GOT A COUPLE IDEAS, SOLDIER.

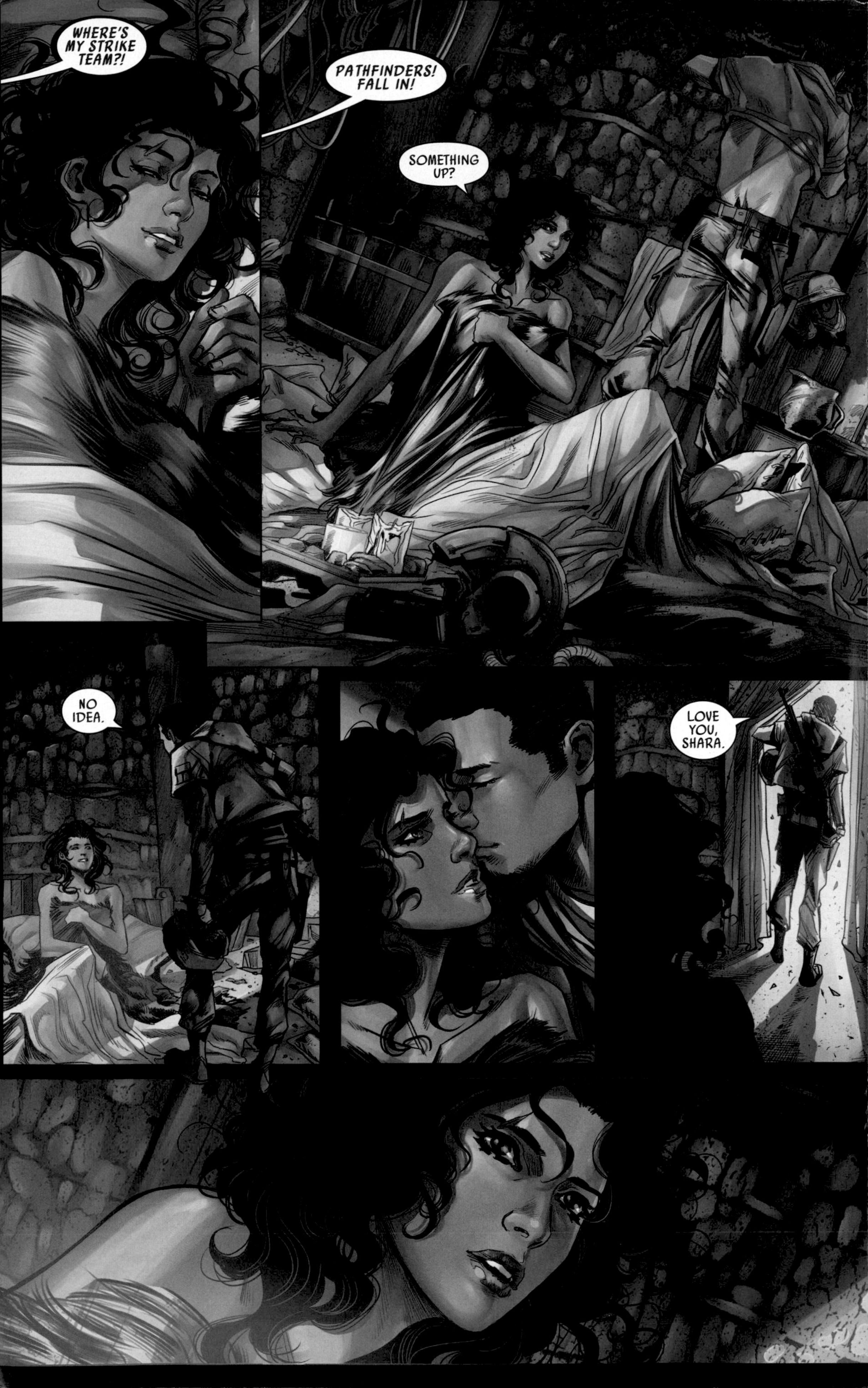
WHERE'S MY STRIKE TEAM?!
PATHFINDERS! FALL IN!
SOMETHING UP?
NO IDEA.
LOVE YOU, SHARA.

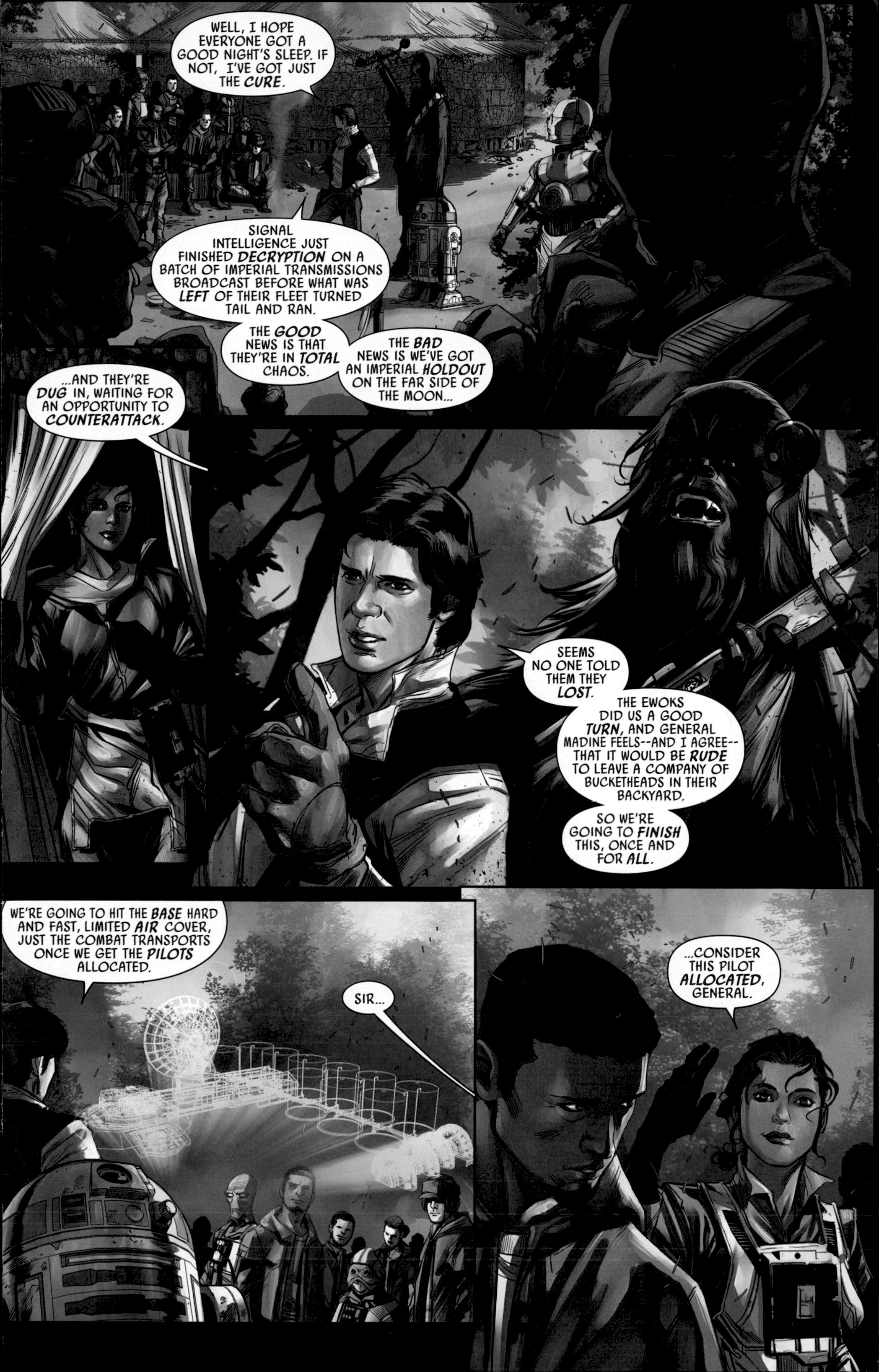
WELL, I HOPE EVERYONE GOT A GOOD NIGHT'S SLEEP. IF NOT, I'VE GOT JUST THE CURE.
SIGNAL INTELLIGENCE JUST FINISHED DECRYPTION ON A BATCH OF IMPERIAL TRANSMISSIONS BROADCAST BEFORE WHAT WAS LEFT OF THEIR FLEET TURNED TAIL AND RAN.
THE GOOD NEWS IS THAT THEY'RE IN TOTAL CHAOS.
THE BAD NEWS IS WE'VE GOT AN IMPERIAL HOLDOUT ON THE FAR SIDE OF THE MOON...
...AND THEY'RE DUG IN, WAITING FOR AN OPPORTUNITY TO COUNTERATTACK.
SEEMS NO ONE TOLD THEM THEY LOST.
THE EWOKS DID US A GOOD TURN, AND GENERAL MADINE FEELS--AND I AGREE--THAT IT WOULD BE RUDE TO LEAVE A COMPANY OF BUCKETHEADS IN THEIR BACKYARD.
SO WE'RE GOING TO FINISH THIS, ONCE AND FOR ALL.
WE'RE GOING TO HIT THE BASE HARD AND FAST, LIMITED AIR COVER, JUST THE COMBAT TRANSPORTS ONCE WE GET THE PILOTS ALLOCATED.
SIR...
...CONSIDER THIS PILOT ALLOCATED, GENERAL.

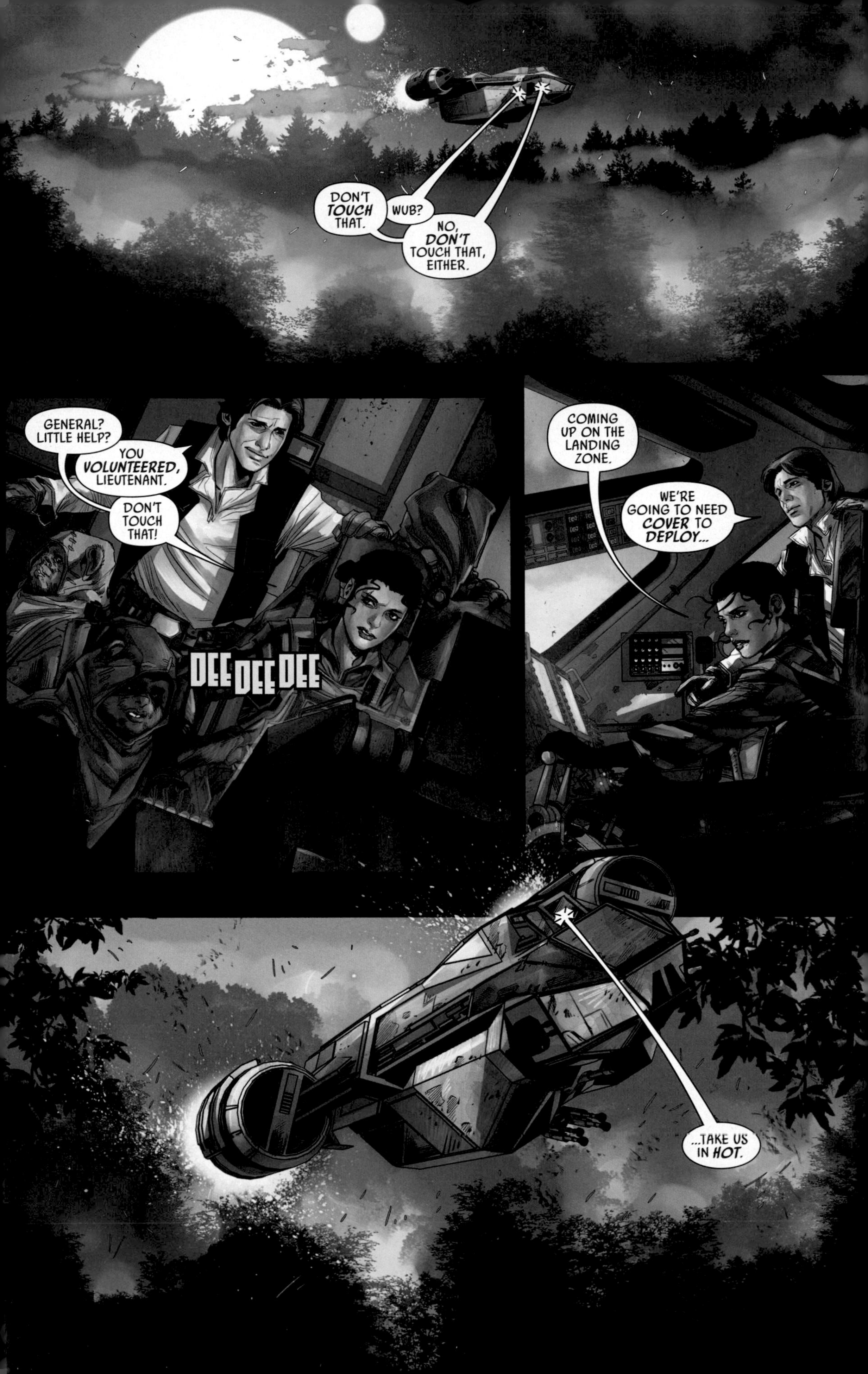
DON'T TOUCH THAT.
WUB?
NO, DON'T TOUCH THAT, EITHER.
GENERAL? LITTLE HELP?
YOU VOLUNTEERED, LIEUTENANT.
DON'T TOUCH THAT!
DEE DEE DEE
COMING UP ON THE LANDING ZONE.
WE'RE GOING TO NEED COVER TO DEPLOY...
...TAKE US IN HOT.

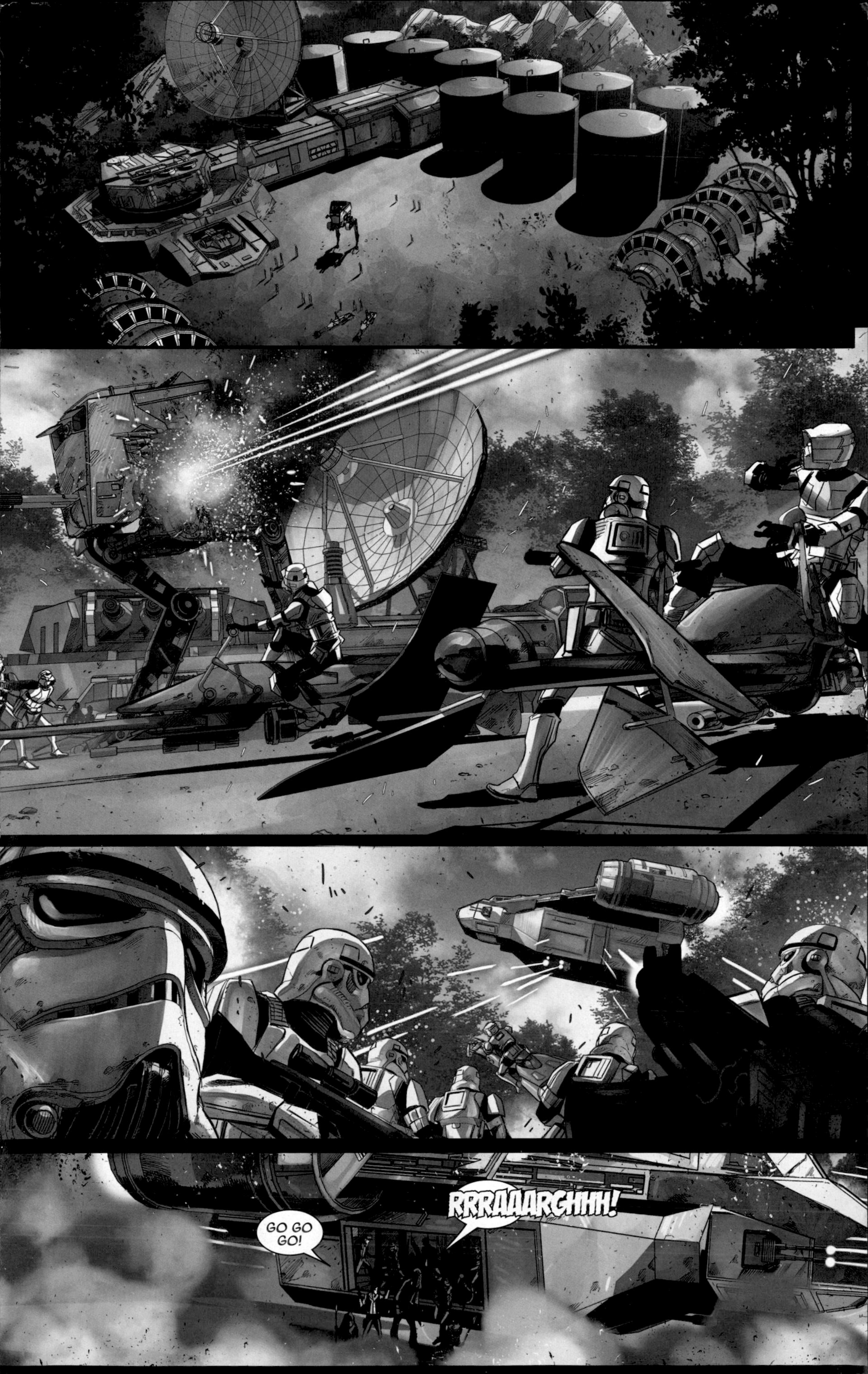

RRRAAARGHHH!
GO GO GO!

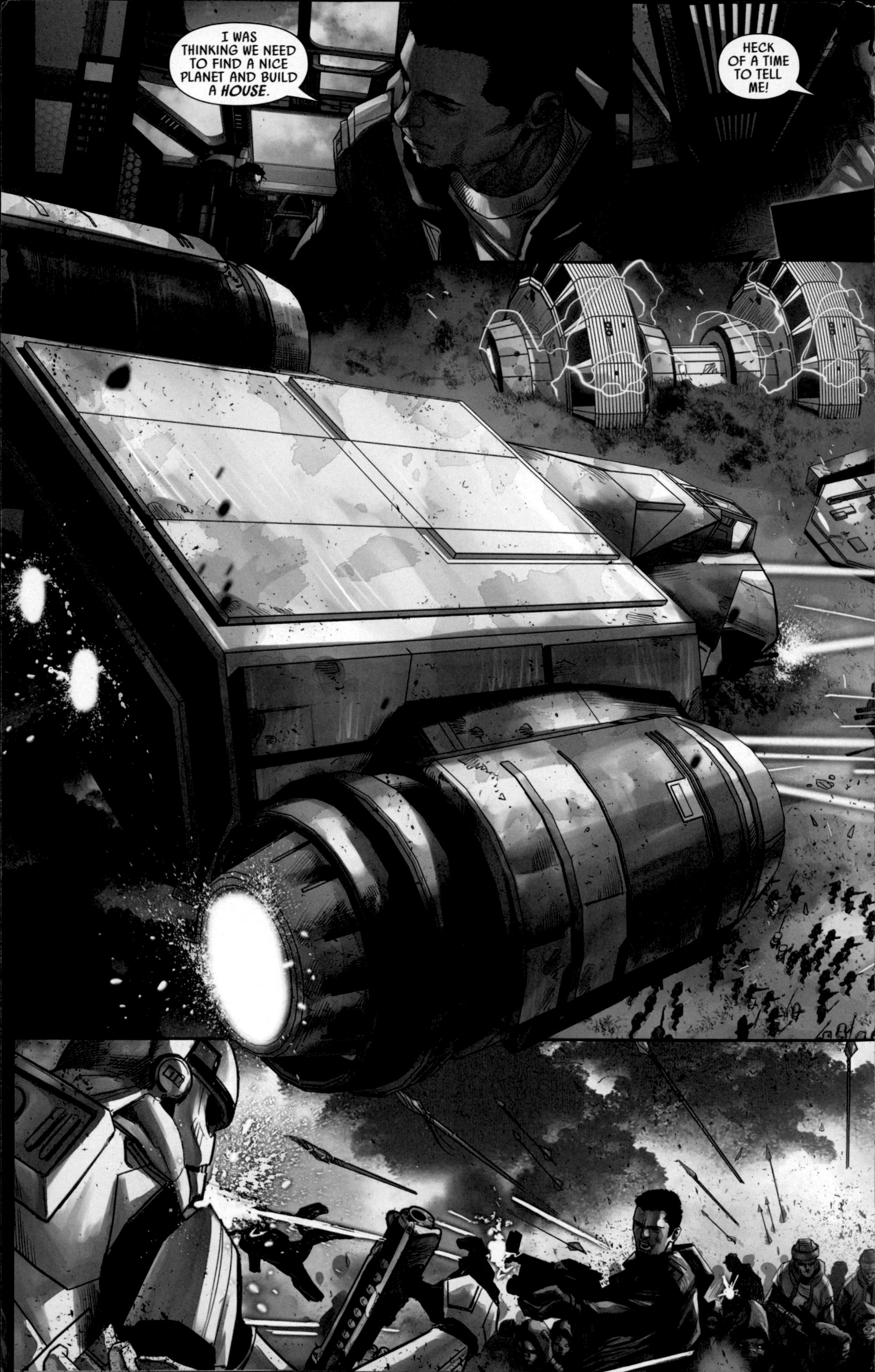
I WAS THINKING WE NEED TO FIND A NICE PLANET AND BUILD A HOUSE.
HECK OF A TIME TO TELL ME!

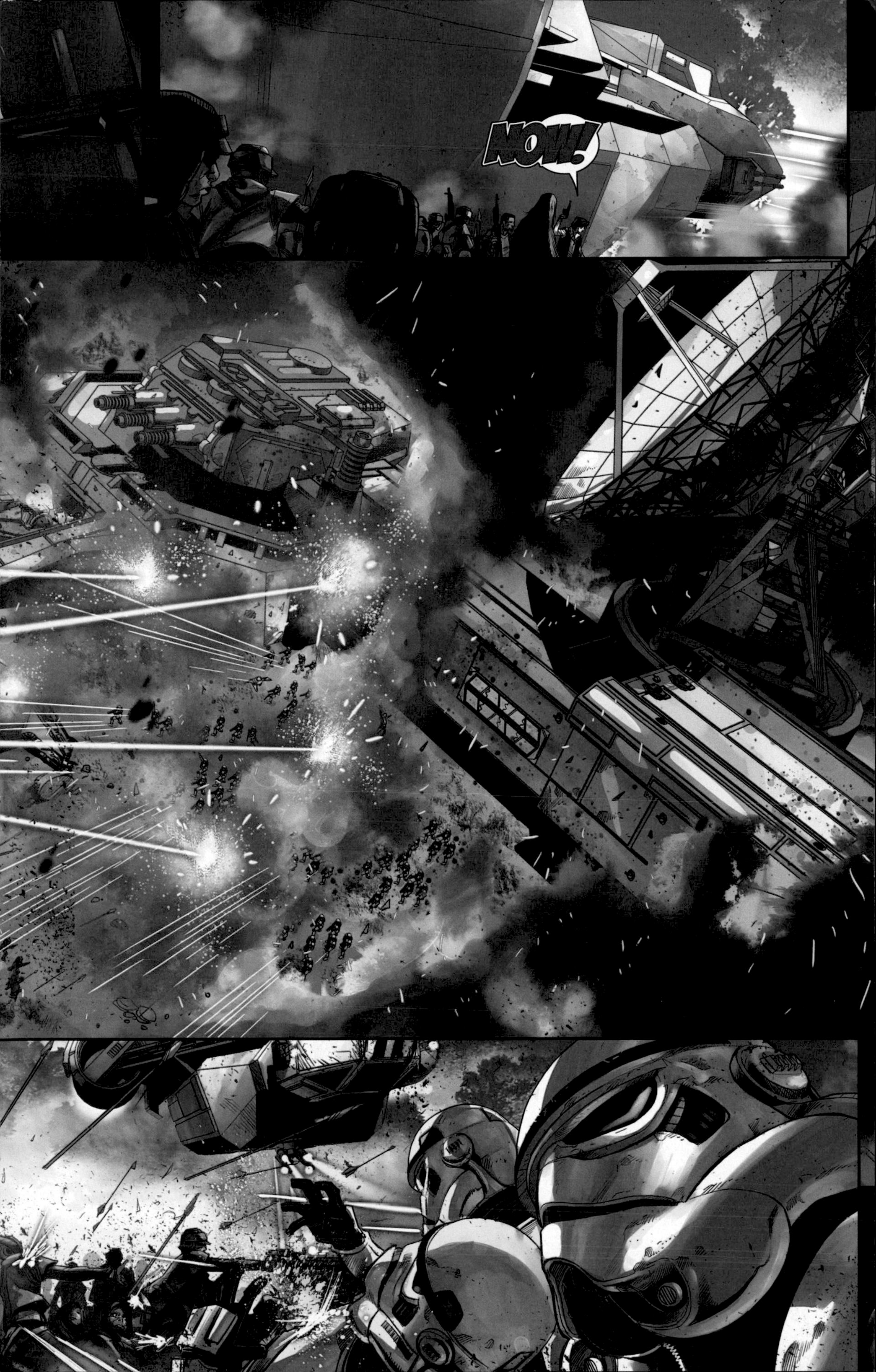
NOW!

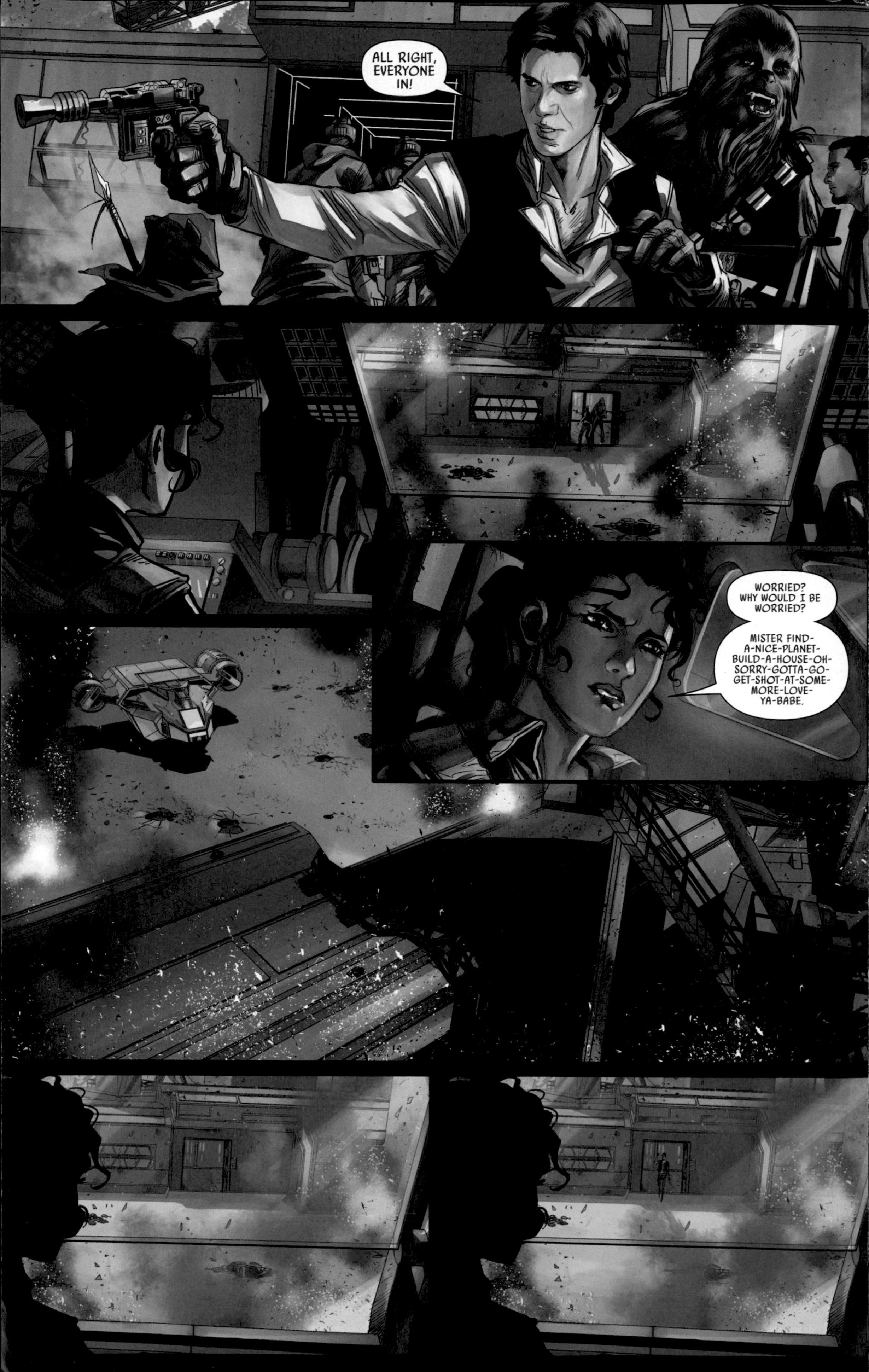
ALL RIGHT, EVERYONE IN!
WORRIED? WHY WOULD I BE WORRIED?
MISTER FIND-A-NICE-PLANET-BUILD-A-HOUSE-OH-SORRY-GOTTA-GO-GET-SHOT-AT-SOME-MORE-LOVE-YA-BABE.

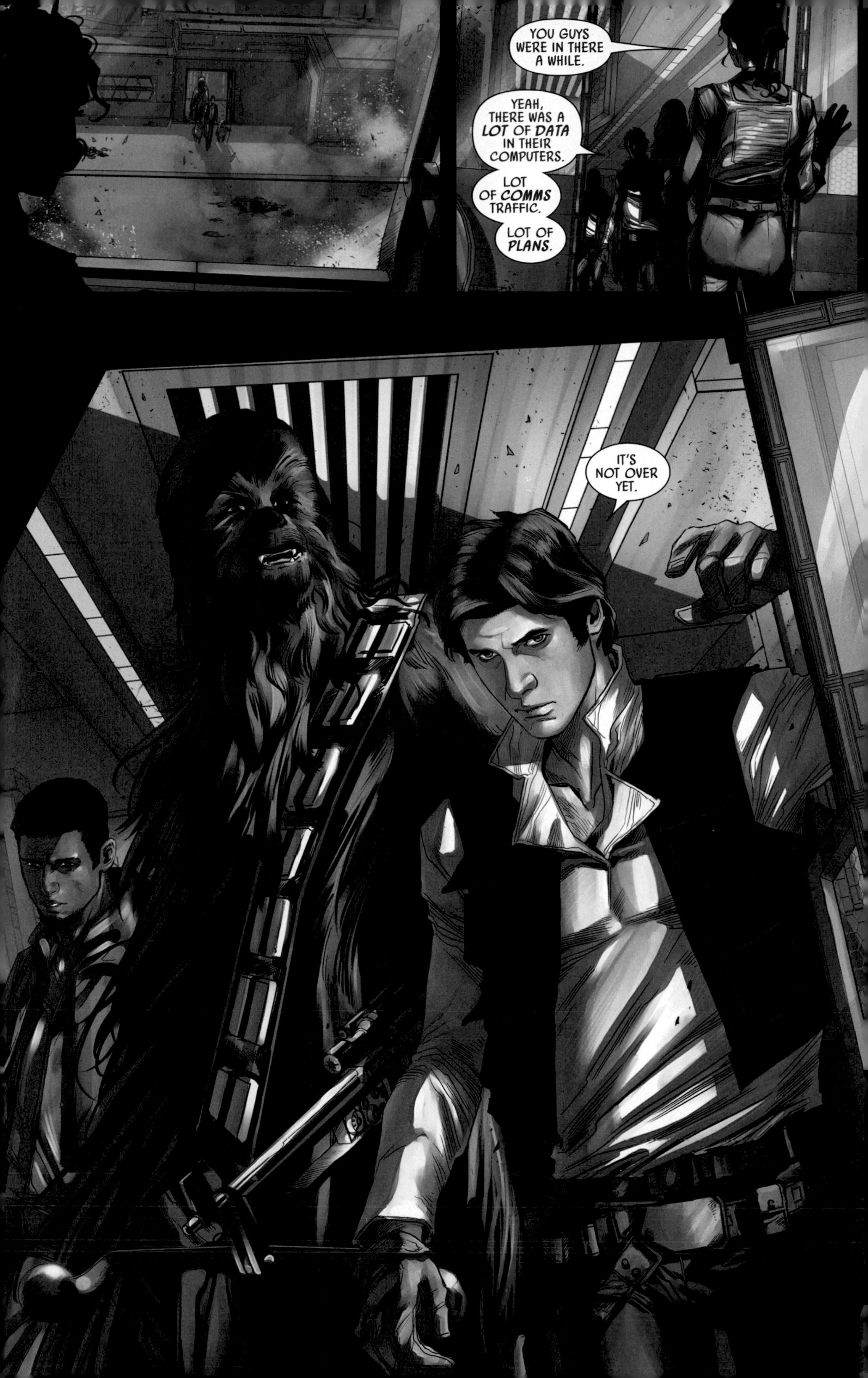
YOU GUYS WERE IN THERE A WHILE.
YEAH, THERE WAS A LOT OF DATA IN THEIR COMPUTERS.
LOT OF COMMS TRAFFIC.
LOT OF PLANS.
IT'S NOT OVER YET.

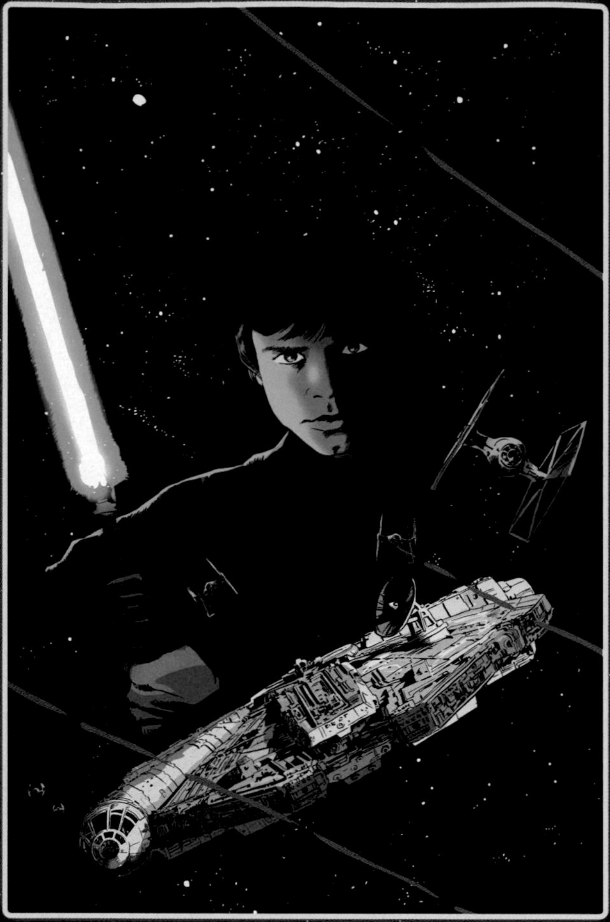

STAR WARS: SHATTERED EMPIRE #1 Variant by FRANCESCO FRANCAVILLA

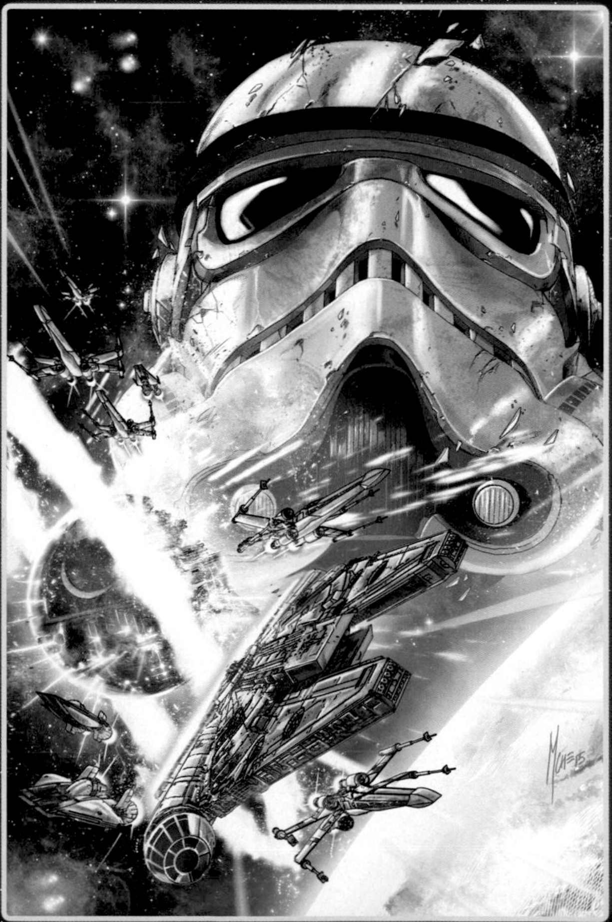

STAR WARS: SHATTERED EMPIRE #1 Variant by MARCO CHECCHETTO

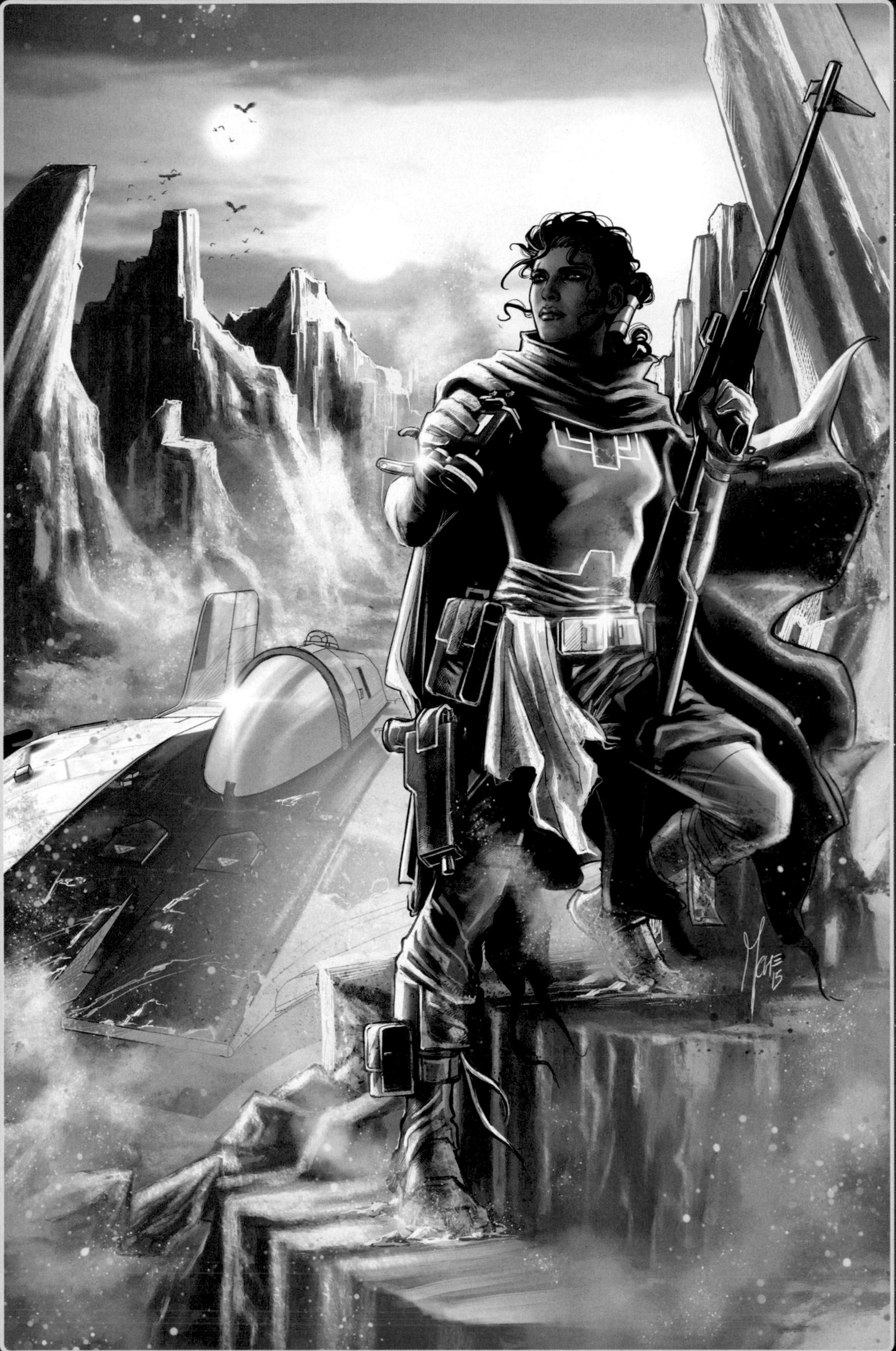

2

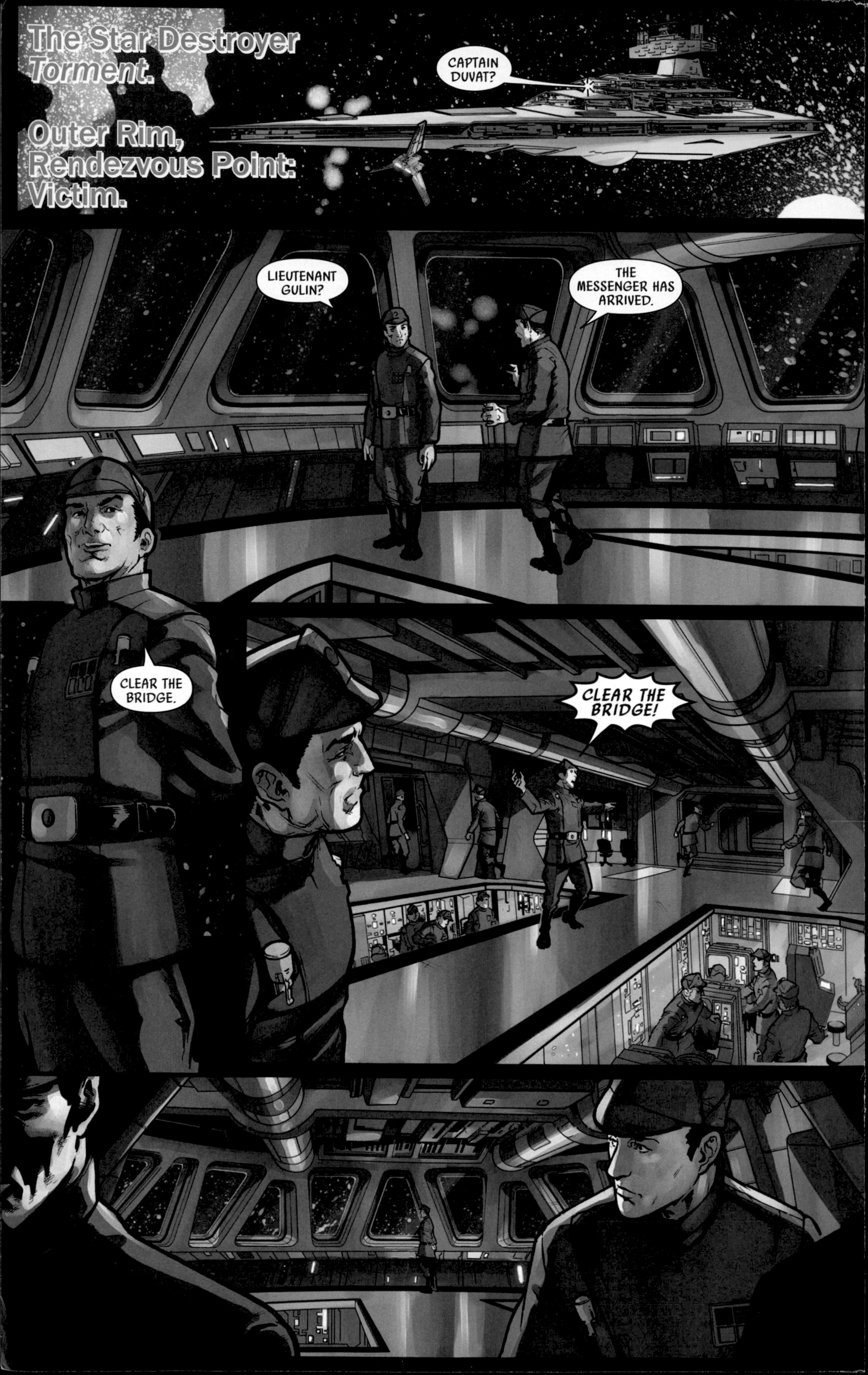
The Star Destroyer *Torment*.
Outer Rim, Rendezvous Point: Victim.
CAPTAIN DUVAT?
LIEUTENANT GULIN?
THE MESSENGER HAS ARRIVED.
CLEAR THE BRIDGE.
CLEAR THE BRIDGE!

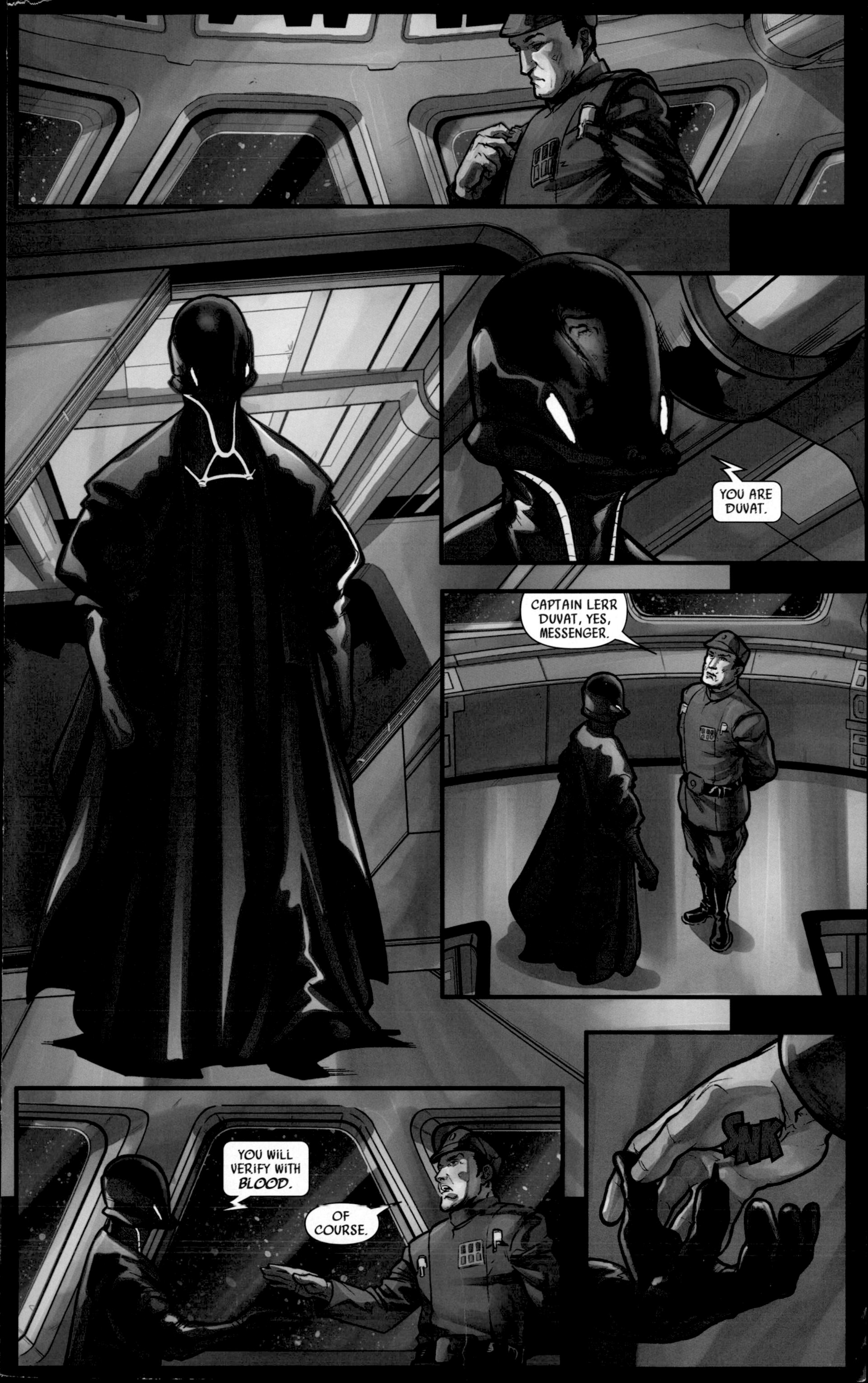
YOU ARE DUVAT.
CAPTAIN LERR DUVAT, YES, MESSENGER.
YOU WILL VERIFY WITH BLOOD.
OF COURSE.
SNK

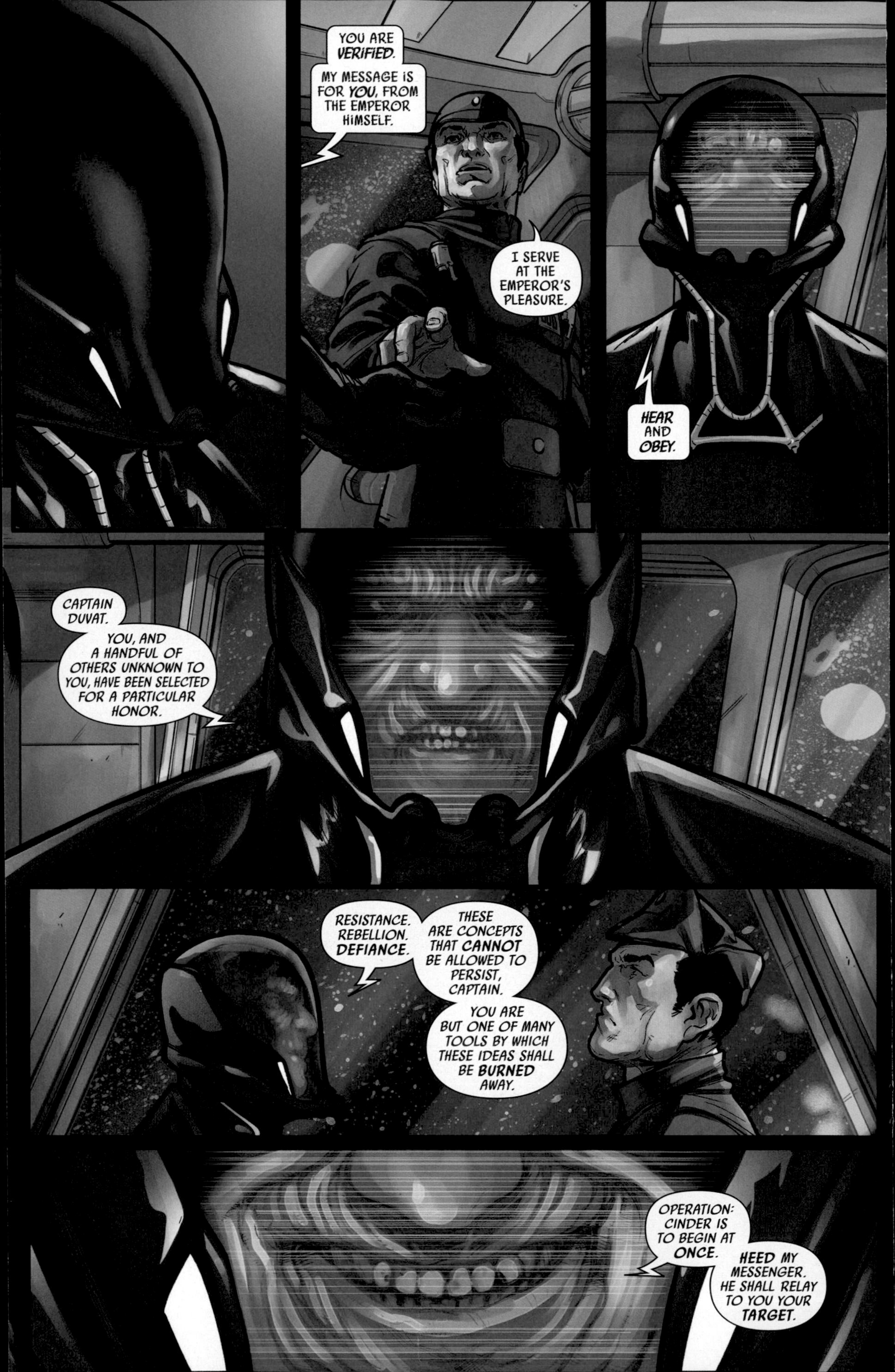
YOU ARE VERIFIED.
MY MESSAGE IS FOR YOU, FROM THE EMPEROR HIMSELF.
I SERVE AT THE EMPEROR'S PLEASURE.
HEAR AND OBEY.
CAPTAIN DUVAT.
YOU, AND A HANDFUL OF OTHERS UNKNOWN TO YOU, HAVE BEEN SELECTED FOR A PARTICULAR HONOR.
RESISTANCE. REBELLION. DEFIANCE.
THESE ARE CONCEPTS THAT CANNOT BE ALLOWED TO PERSIST, CAPTAIN.
YOU ARE BUT ONE OF MANY TOOLS BY WHICH THESE IDEAS SHALL BE BURNED AWAY.
OPERATION: CINDER IS TO BEGIN AT ONCE.
HEED MY MESSENGER. HE SHALL RELAY TO YOU YOUR TARGET.

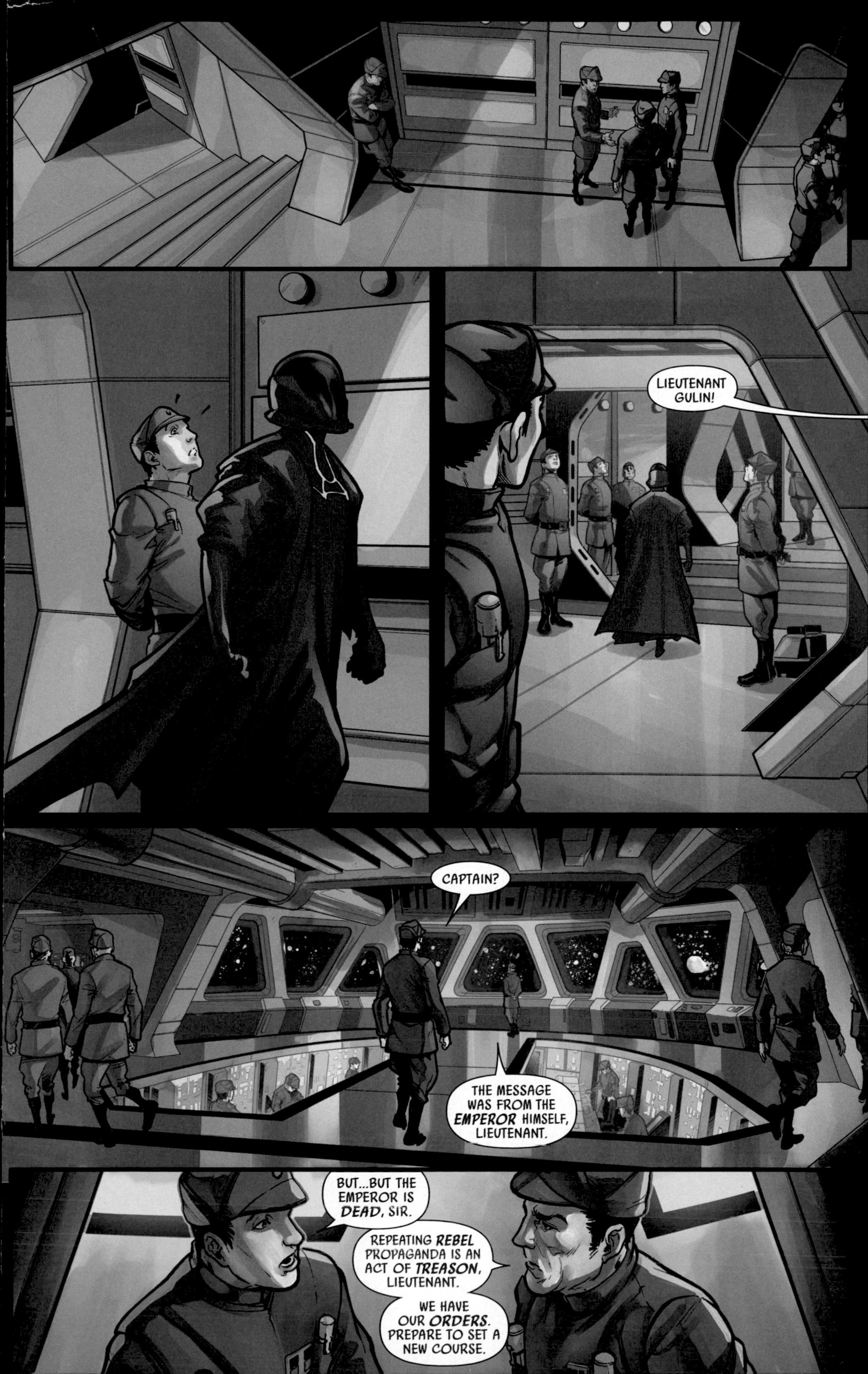
LIEUTENANT GULIN!
CAPTAIN?
THE MESSAGE WAS FROM THE EMPEROR HIMSELF, LIEUTENANT.
BUT...BUT THE EMPEROR IS DEAD, SIR.
REPEATING REBEL PROPAGANDA IS AN ACT OF TREASON, LIEUTENANT.
WE HAVE OUR ORDERS. PREPARE TO SET A NEW COURSE.

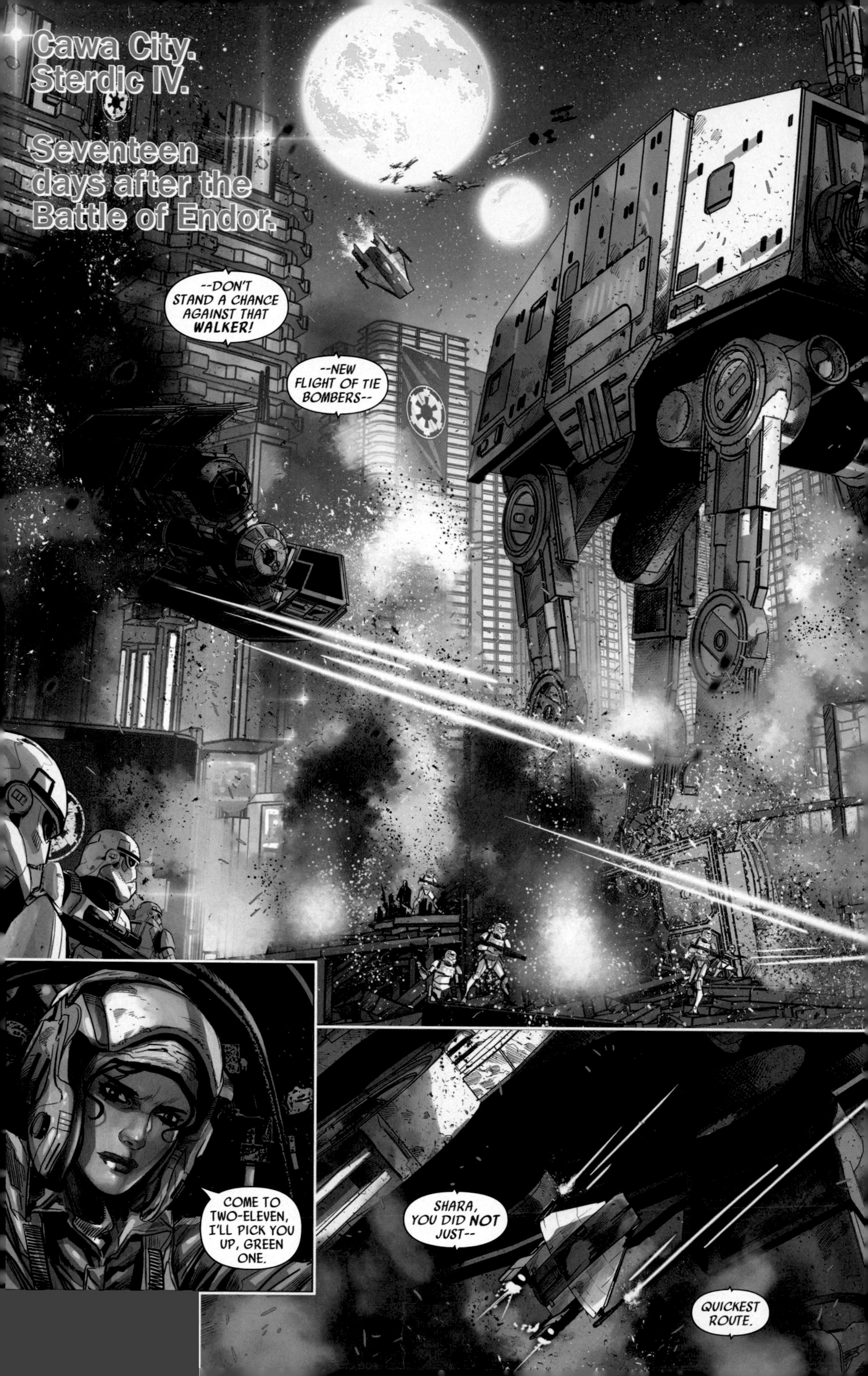

Cawa City.
Sterdic IV.
Seventeen days after the Battle of Endor.
--DON'T STAND A CHANCE AGAINST THAT WALKER!
--NEW FLIGHT OF TIE BOMBERS--
COME TO TWO-ELEVEN, I'LL PICK YOU UP, GREEN ONE.
SHARA, YOU DID NOT JUST--
QUICKEST ROUTE.

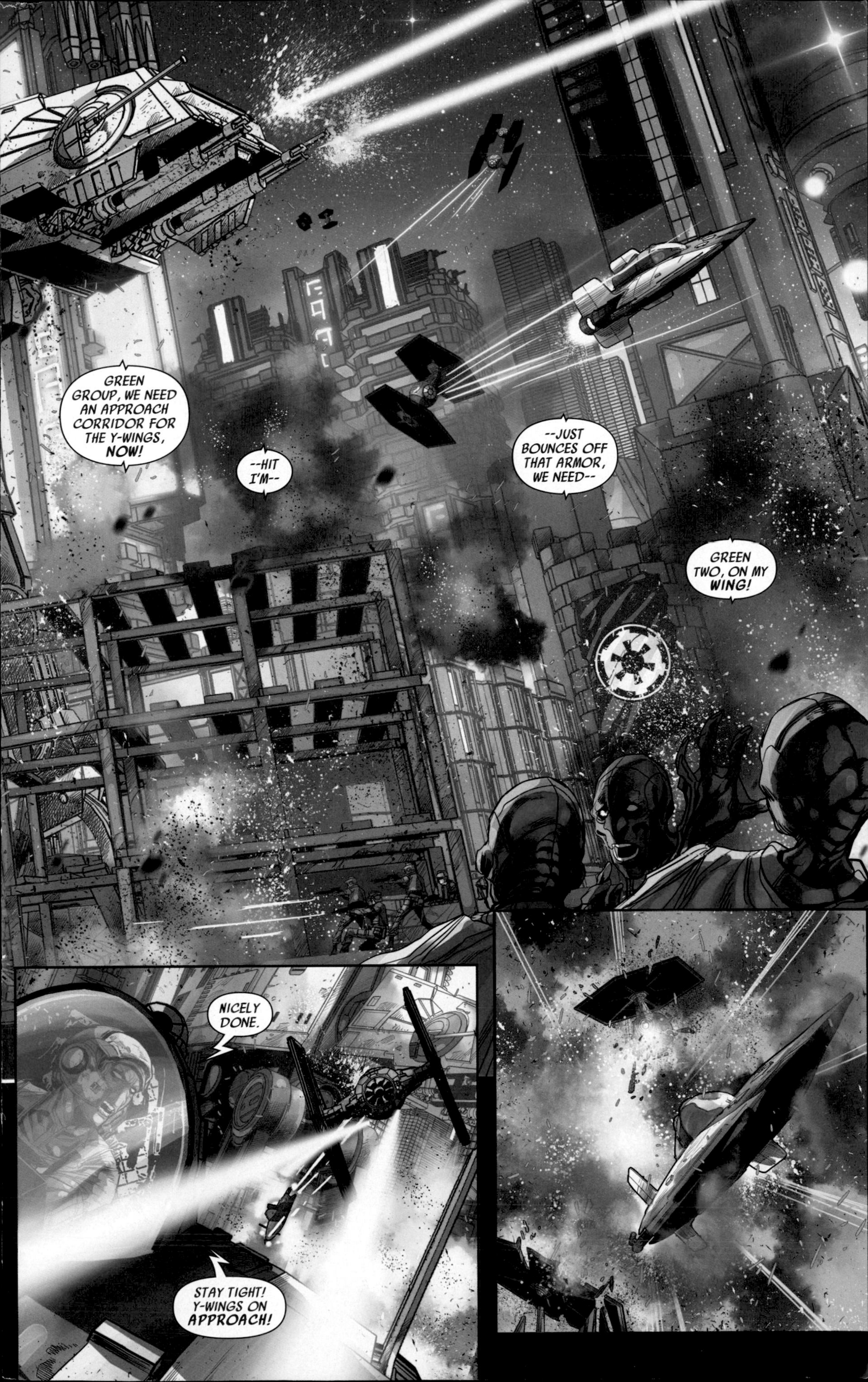
GREEN GROUP, WE NEED AN APPROACH CORRIDOR FOR THE Y-WINGS, NOW!
--HIT I'M--
--JUST BOUNCES OFF THAT ARMOR, WE NEED--
GREEN TWO, ON MY WING!
NICELY DONE.
STAY TIGHT! Y-WINGS ON APPROACH!

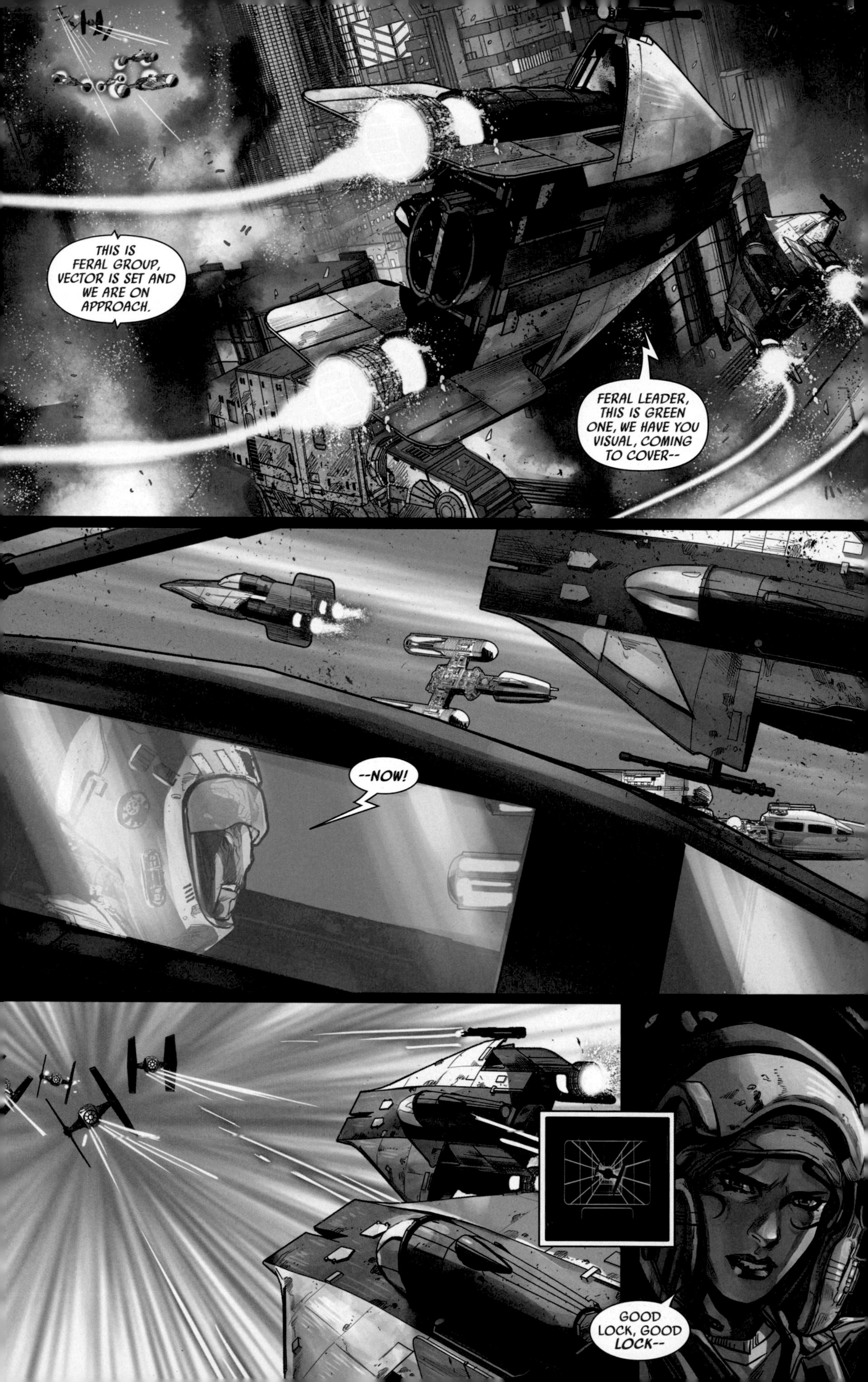
THIS IS FERAL GROUP, VECTOR IS SET AND WE ARE ON APPROACH.
FERAL LEADER, THIS IS GREEN ONE, WE HAVE YOU VISUAL, COMING TO COVER--
--NOW!
GOOD LOCK, GOOD LOCK--

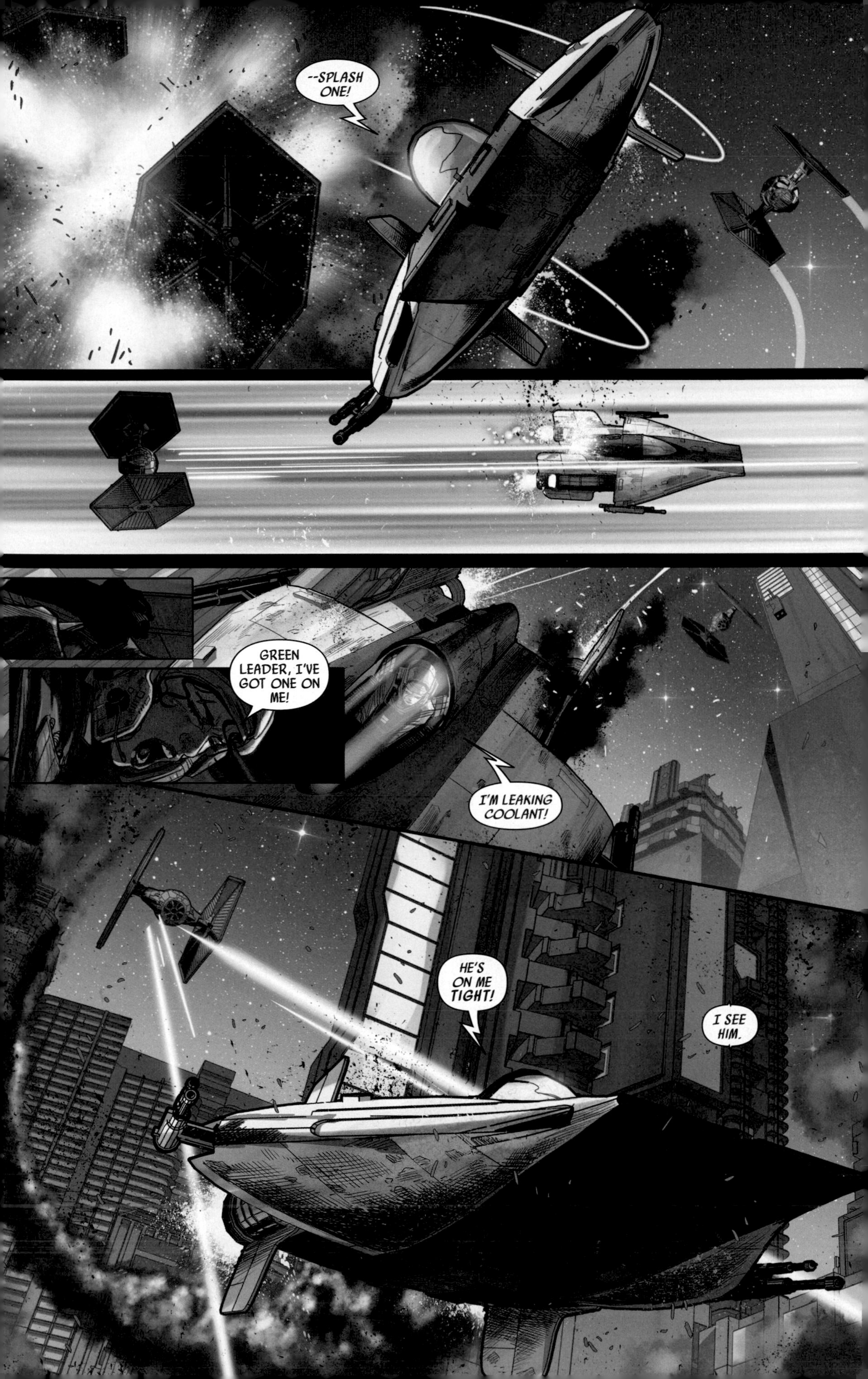
--SPLASH ONE!
GREEN LEADER, I'VE GOT ONE ON ME!
I'M LEAKING COOLANT!
HE'S ON ME TIGHT!
I SEE HIM.

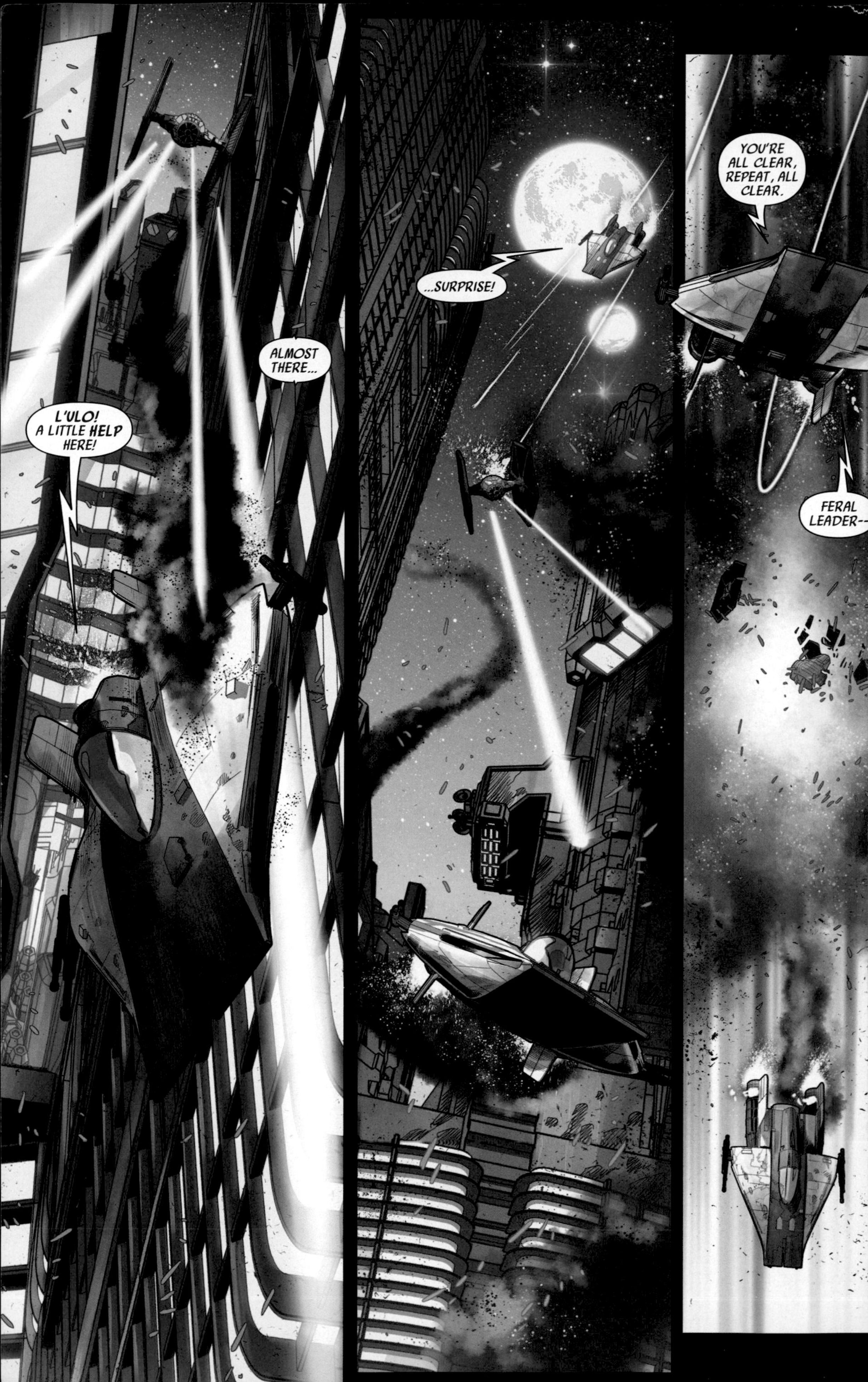
L'ULO! A LITTLE HELP HERE!
ALMOST THERE...
...SURPRISE!
YOU'RE ALL CLEAR, REPEAT, ALL CLEAR.
FERAL LEADER--

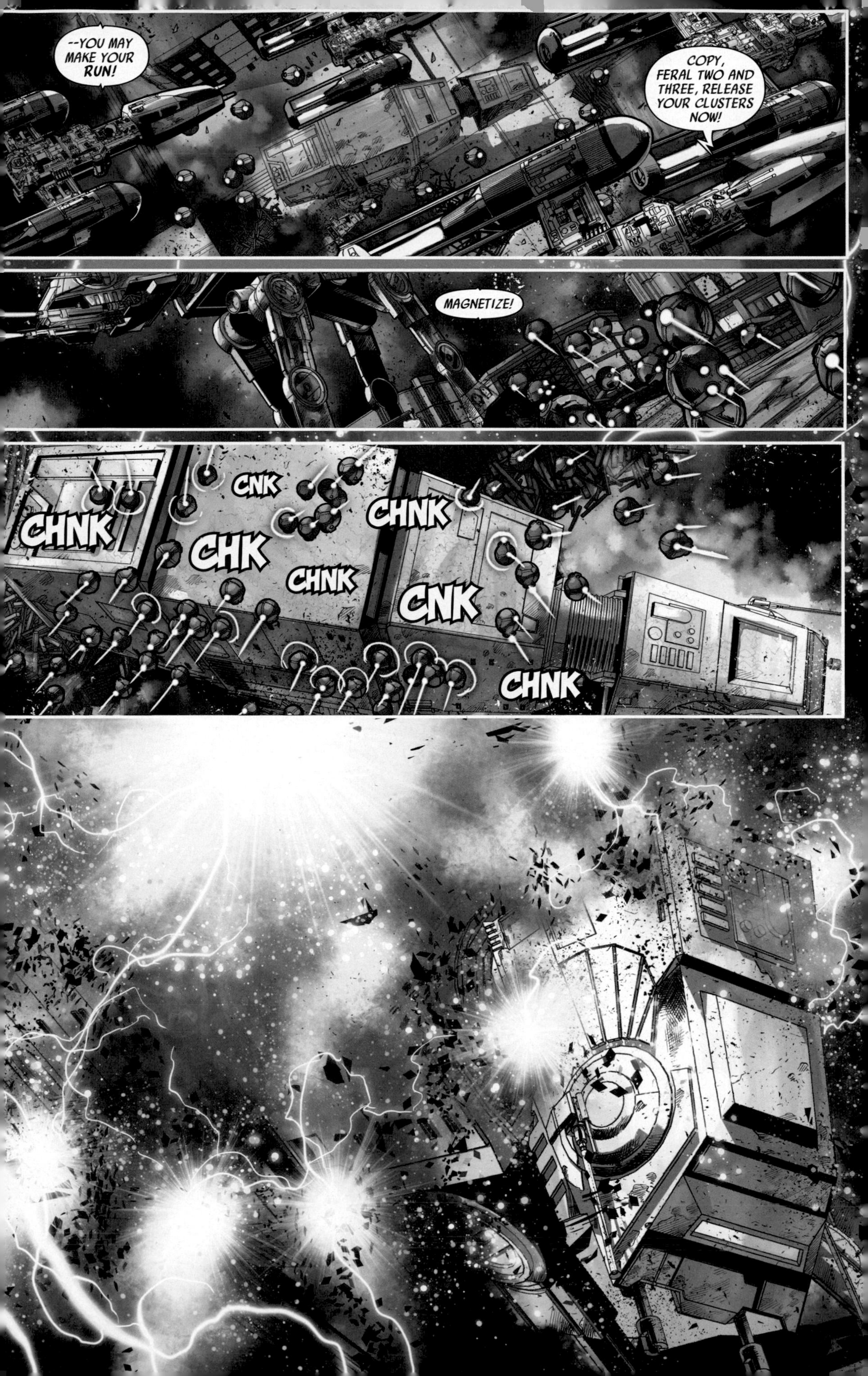
--YOU MAY MAKE YOUR RUN!
COPY, FERAL TWO AND THREE, RELEASE YOUR CLUSTERS NOW!
MAGNETIZE!
CNK
CHNK
CHNK
CHK
CHNK
CNK
CHNK
CHNK

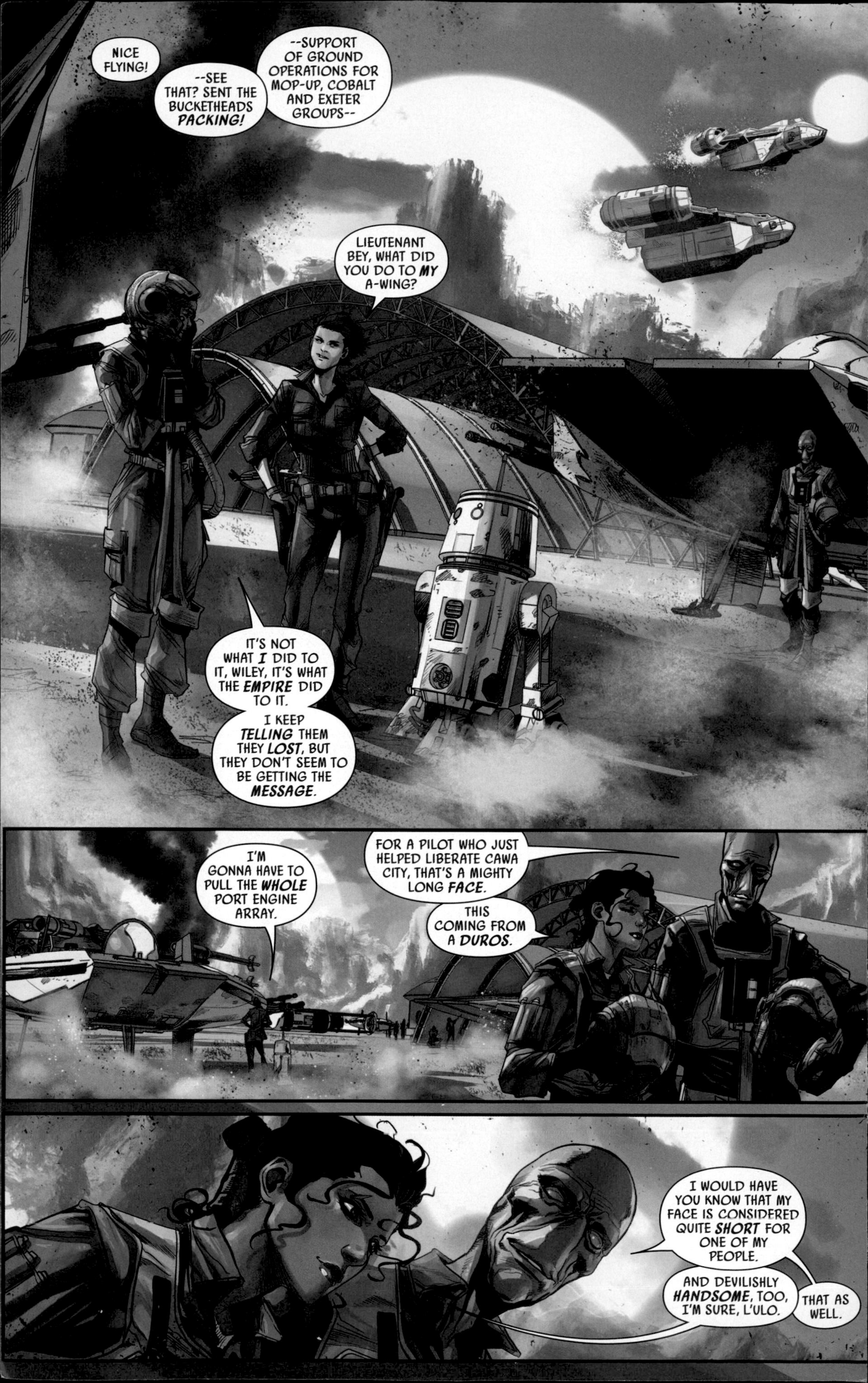
NICE FLYING!
--SEE THAT? SENT THE BUCKETHEADS PACKING!
--SUPPORT OF GROUND OPERATIONS FOR MOP-UP, COBALT AND EXETER GROUPS--
LIEUTENANT BEY, WHAT DID YOU DO TO MY A-WING?
IT'S NOT WHAT I DID TO IT, WILEY, IT'S WHAT THE EMPIRE DID TO IT.
I KEEP TELLING THEM THEY LOST, BUT THEY DON'T SEEM TO BE GETTING THE MESSAGE.
I'M GONNA HAVE TO PULL THE WHOLE PORT ENGINE ARRAY.
FOR A PILOT WHO JUST HELPED LIBERATE CAWA CITY, THAT'S A MIGHTY LONG FACE.
THIS COMING FROM A DUROS.
I WOULD HAVE YOU KNOW THAT MY FACE IS CONSIDERED QUITE SHORT FOR ONE OF MY PEOPLE.
AND DEVILISHLY HANDSOME, TOO, I'M SURE, L'ULO.
THAT AS WELL.

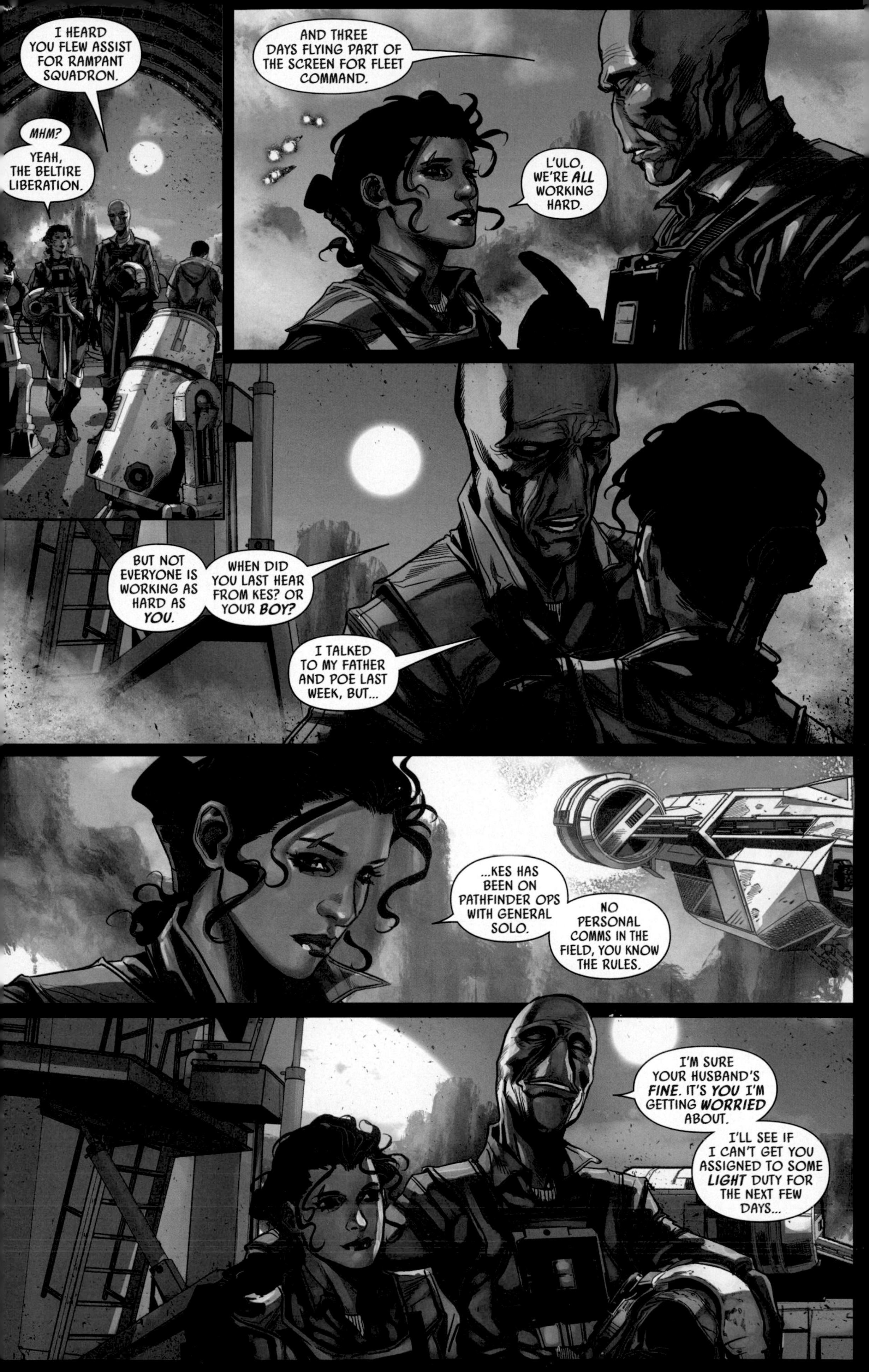
I HEARD YOU FLEW ASSIST FOR RAMPANT SQUADRON.
MHM?
YEAH, THE BELTIRE LIBERATION.
AND THREE DAYS FLYING PART OF THE SCREEN FOR FLEET COMMAND.
L'ULO, WE'RE ALL WORKING HARD.
BUT NOT EVERYONE IS WORKING AS HARD AS YOU.
WHEN DID YOU LAST HEAR FROM KES? OR YOUR BOY?
I TALKED TO MY FATHER AND POE LAST WEEK, BUT...
...KES HAS BEEN ON PATHFINDER OPS WITH GENERAL SOLO.
NO PERSONAL COMMS IN THE FIELD, YOU KNOW THE RULES.
I'M SURE YOUR HUSBAND'S FINE. IT'S YOU I'M GETTING WORRIED ABOUT.
I'LL SEE IF I CAN'T GET YOU ASSIGNED TO SOME LIGHT DUTY FOR THE NEXT FEW DAYS...

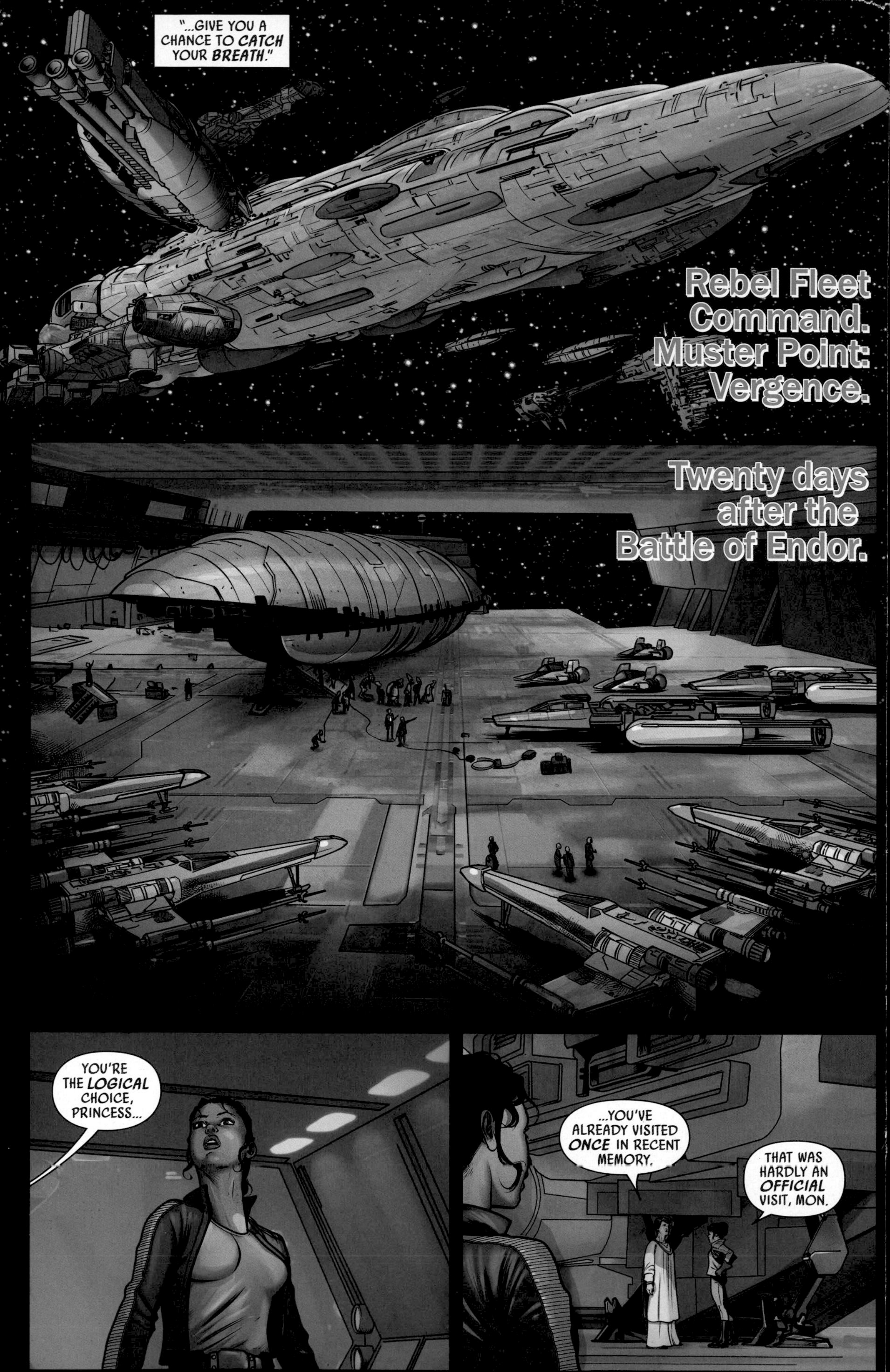
"...GIVE YOU A CHANCE TO *CATCH* YOUR *BREATH*."
Rebel Fleet Command. Muster Point: Vergence.
Twenty days after the Battle of Endor.
YOU'RE THE *LOGICAL* CHOICE, PRINCESS...
...YOU'VE ALREADY VISITED *ONCE* IN RECENT MEMORY.
THAT WAS HARDLY AN *OFFICIAL* VISIT, MON.

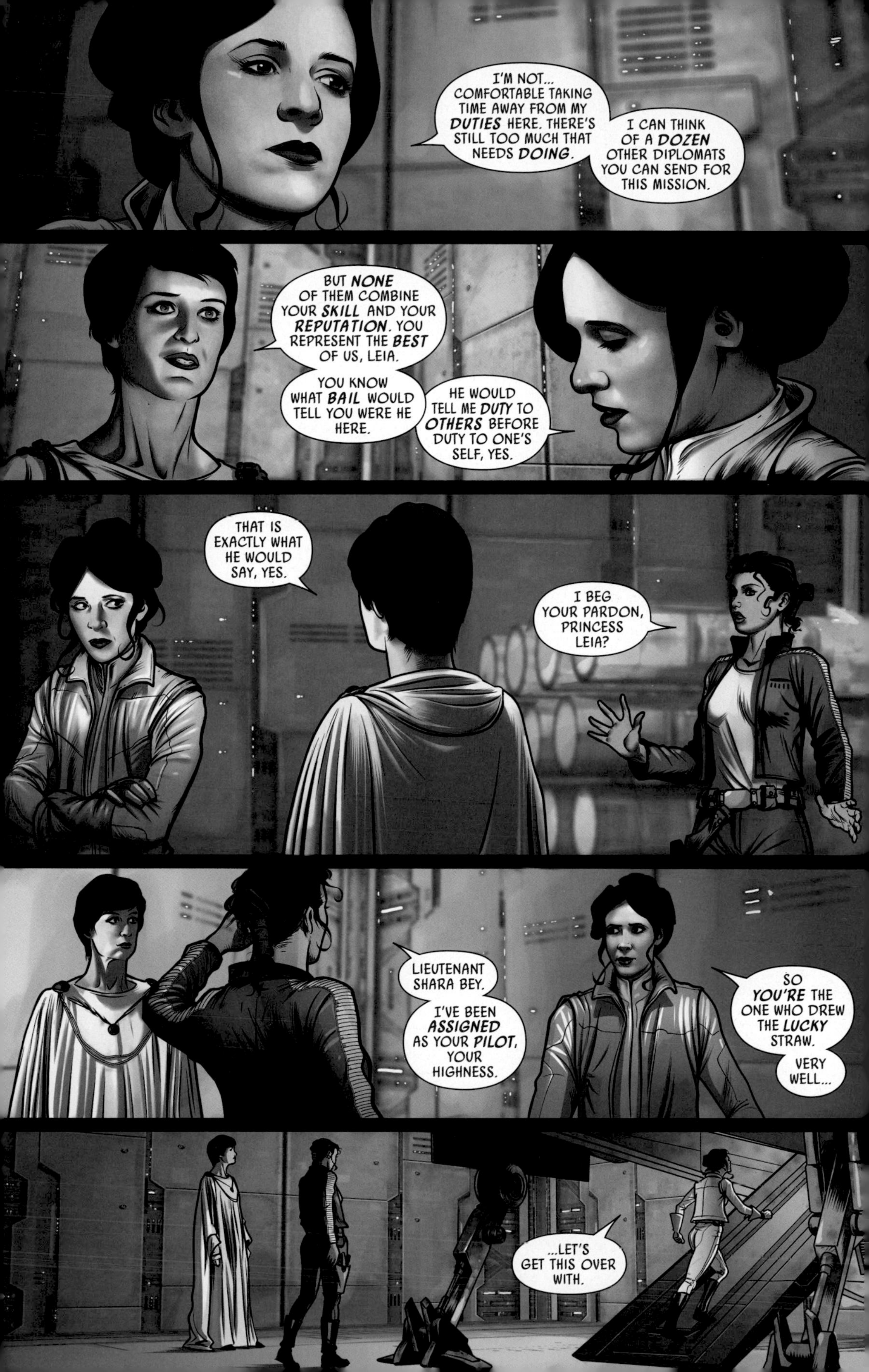
I'M NOT... COMFORTABLE TAKING TIME AWAY FROM MY DUTIES HERE. THERE'S STILL TOO MUCH THAT NEEDS DOING.
I CAN THINK OF A DOZEN OTHER DIPLOMATS YOU CAN SEND FOR THIS MISSION.
BUT NONE OF THEM COMBINE YOUR SKILL AND YOUR REPUTATION. YOU REPRESENT THE BEST OF US, LEIA.
YOU KNOW WHAT BAIL WOULD TELL YOU WERE HE HERE.
HE WOULD TELL ME DUTY TO OTHERS BEFORE DUTY TO ONE'S SELF, YES.
THAT IS EXACTLY WHAT HE WOULD SAY, YES.
I BEG YOUR PARDON, PRINCESS LEIA?
LIEUTENANT SHARA BEY.
I'VE BEEN ASSIGNED AS YOUR PILOT, YOUR HIGHNESS.
SO YOU'RE THE ONE WHO DREW THE LUCKY STRAW.
VERY WELL...
...LET'S GET THIS OVER WITH.

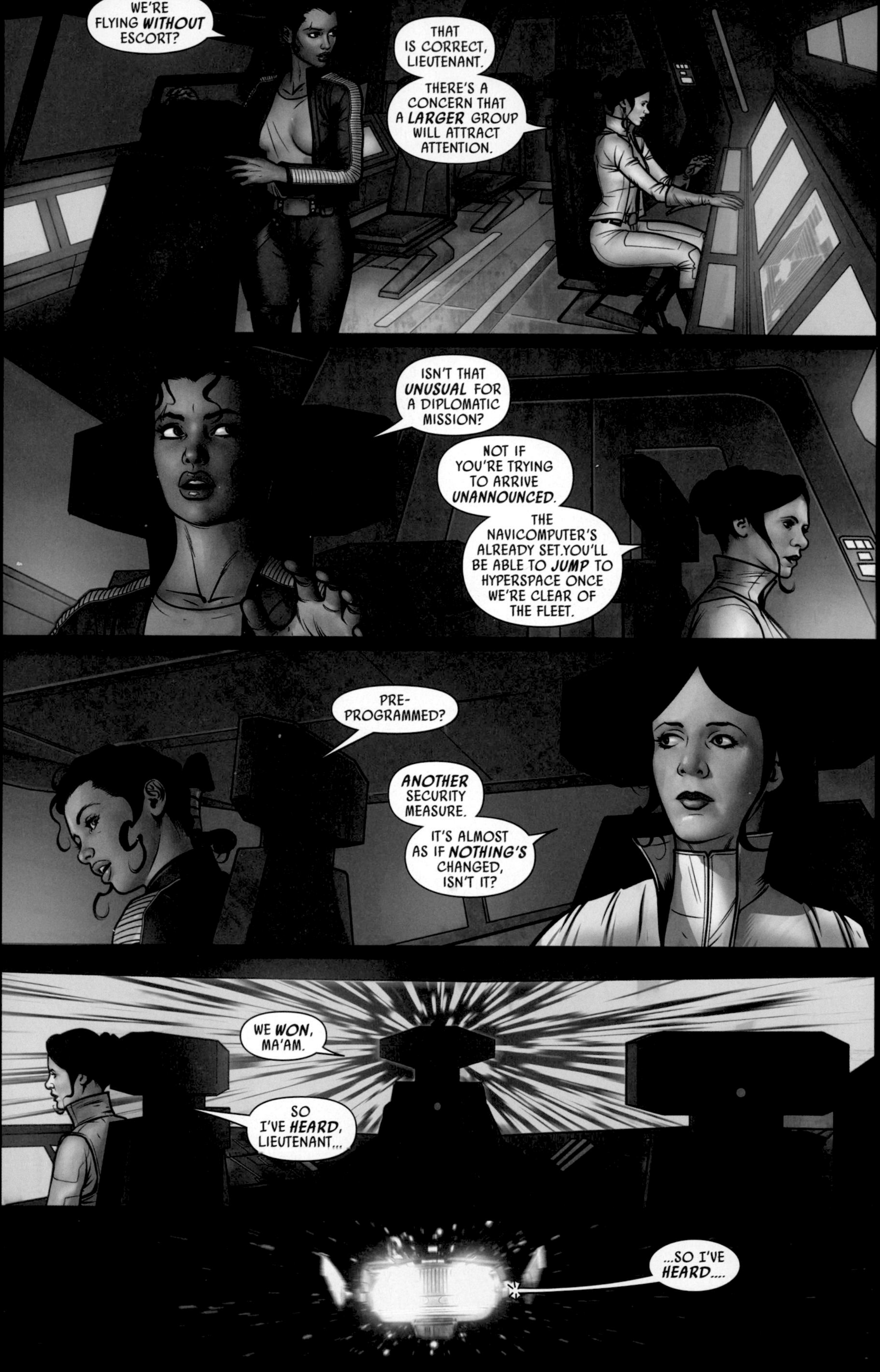
WE'RE FLYING WITHOUT ESCORT?
THAT IS CORRECT, LIEUTENANT.
THERE'S A CONCERN THAT A LARGER GROUP WILL ATTRACT ATTENTION.
ISN'T THAT UNUSUAL FOR A DIPLOMATIC MISSION?
NOT IF YOU'RE TRYING TO ARRIVE UNANNOUNCED.
THE NAVICOMPUTER'S ALREADY SET. YOU'LL BE ABLE TO JUMP TO HYPERSPACE ONCE WE'RE CLEAR OF THE FLEET.
PRE-PROGRAMMED?
ANOTHER SECURITY MEASURE.
IT'S ALMOST AS IF NOTHING'S CHANGED, ISN'T IT?
WE WON, MA'AM.
SO I'VE HEARD, LIEUTENANT...
...SO I'VE HEARD....

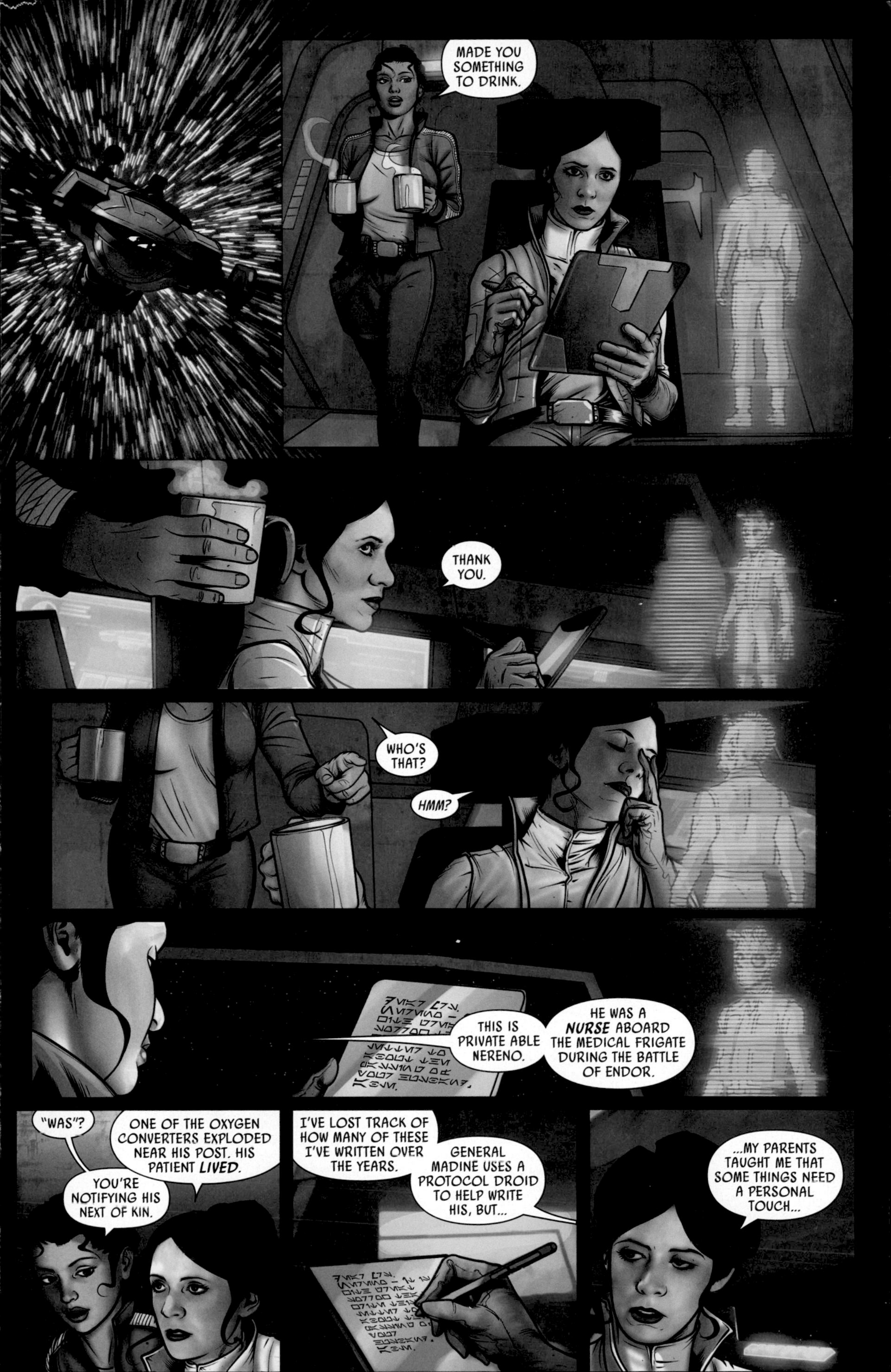
MADE YOU SOMETHING TO DRINK.
THANK YOU.
WHO'S THAT?
HMM?
THIS IS PRIVATE ABLE NERENO.
HE WAS A *NURSE* ABOARD THE MEDICAL FRIGATE DURING THE BATTLE OF ENDOR.
"WAS"?
ONE OF THE OXYGEN CONVERTERS EXPLODED NEAR HIS POST. HIS PATIENT *LIVED*.
YOU'RE NOTIFYING HIS NEXT OF KIN.
I'VE LOST TRACK OF HOW MANY OF THESE I'VE WRITTEN OVER THE YEARS.
GENERAL MADINE USES A PROTOCOL DROID TO HELP WRITE HIS, BUT...
...MY PARENTS TAUGHT ME THAT SOME THINGS NEED A PERSONAL TOUCH...

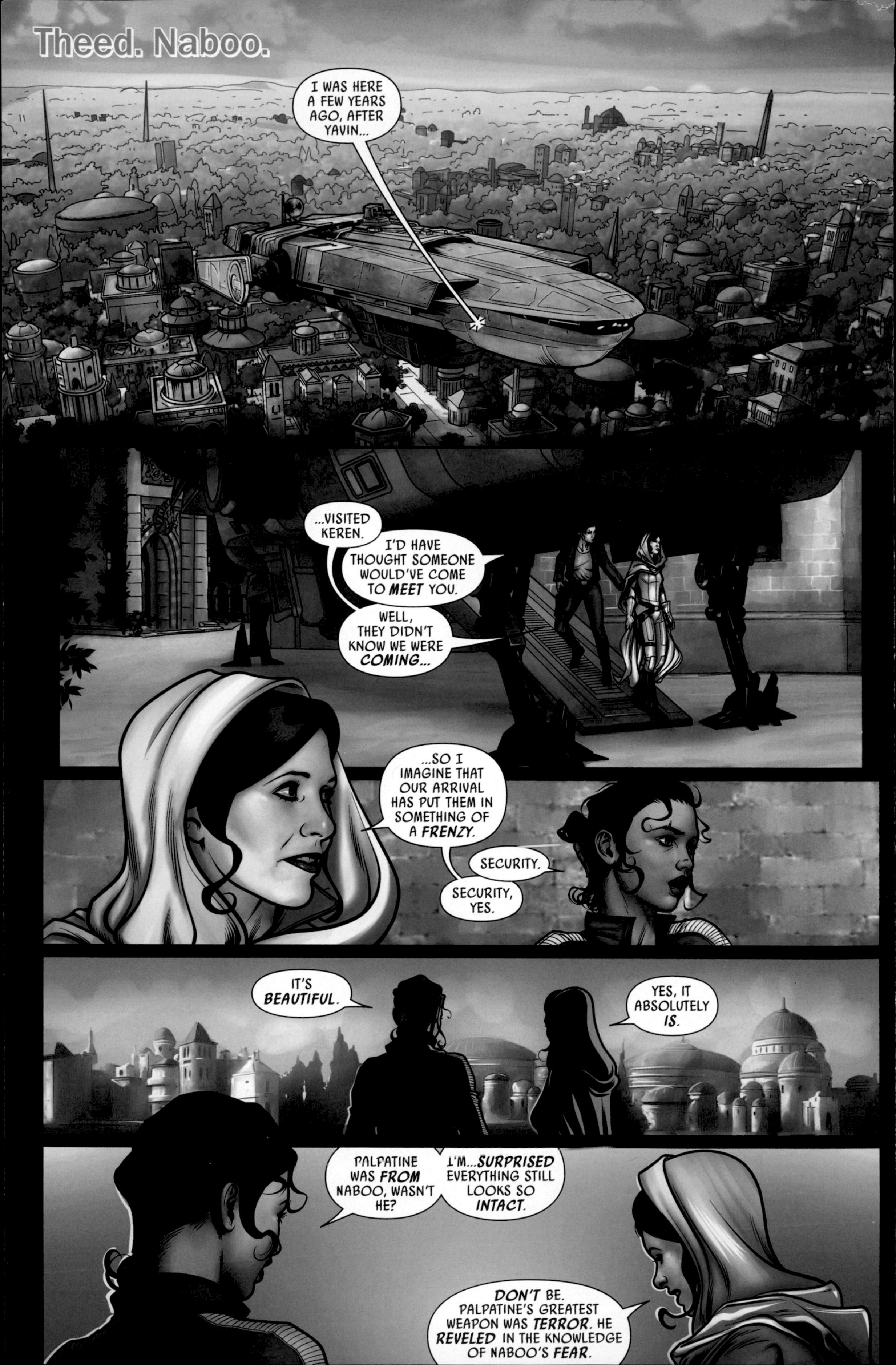
Theed. Naboo.
I WAS HERE A FEW YEARS AGO, AFTER YAVIN...
...VISITED KEREN.
I'D HAVE THOUGHT SOMEONE WOULD'VE COME TO MEET YOU.
WELL, THEY DIDN'T KNOW WE WERE COMING...
...SO I IMAGINE THAT OUR ARRIVAL HAS PUT THEM IN SOMETHING OF A FRENZY.
SECURITY.
SECURITY, YES.
IT'S BEAUTIFUL.
YES, IT ABSOLUTELY IS.
PALPATINE WAS FROM NABOO, WASN'T HE?
I'M...SURPRISED EVERYTHING STILL LOOKS SO INTACT.
DON'T BE. PALPATINE'S GREATEST WEAPON WAS TERROR. HE REVELED IN THE KNOWLEDGE OF NABOO'S FEAR.

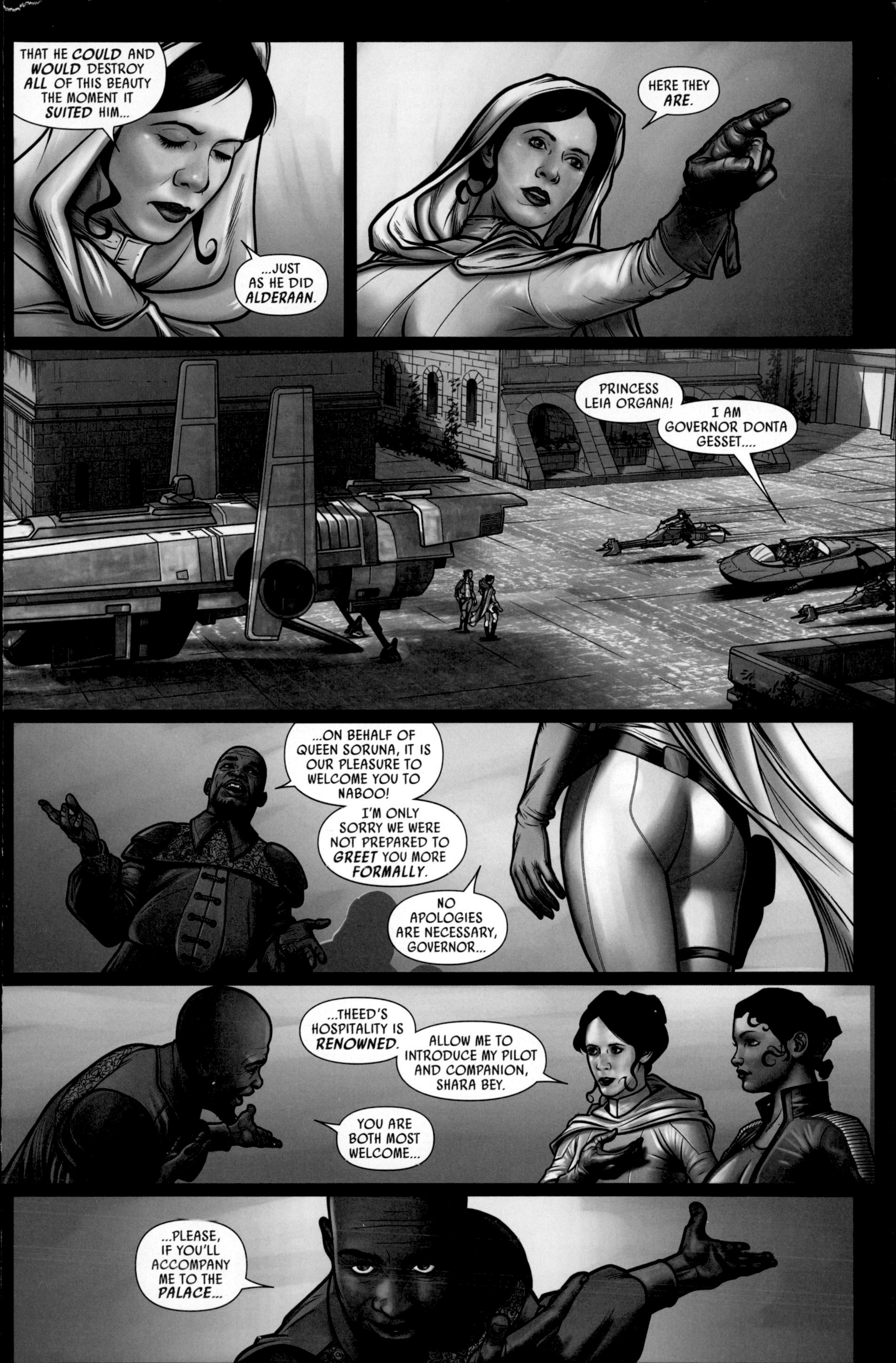
THAT HE COULD AND WOULD DESTROY ALL OF THIS BEAUTY THE MOMENT IT SUITED HIM...
...JUST AS HE DID ALDERAAN.
HERE THEY ARE.
PRINCESS LEIA ORGANA!
I AM GOVERNOR DONTA GESSET....
...ON BEHALF OF QUEEN SORUNA, IT IS OUR PLEASURE TO WELCOME YOU TO NABOO!
I'M ONLY SORRY WE WERE NOT PREPARED TO GREET YOU MORE FORMALLY.
NO APOLOGIES ARE NECESSARY, GOVERNOR...
...THEED'S HOSPITALITY IS RENOWNED.
ALLOW ME TO INTRODUCE MY PILOT AND COMPANION, SHARA BEY.
YOU ARE BOTH MOST WELCOME...
...PLEASE, IF YOU'LL ACCOMPANY ME TO THE PALACE...

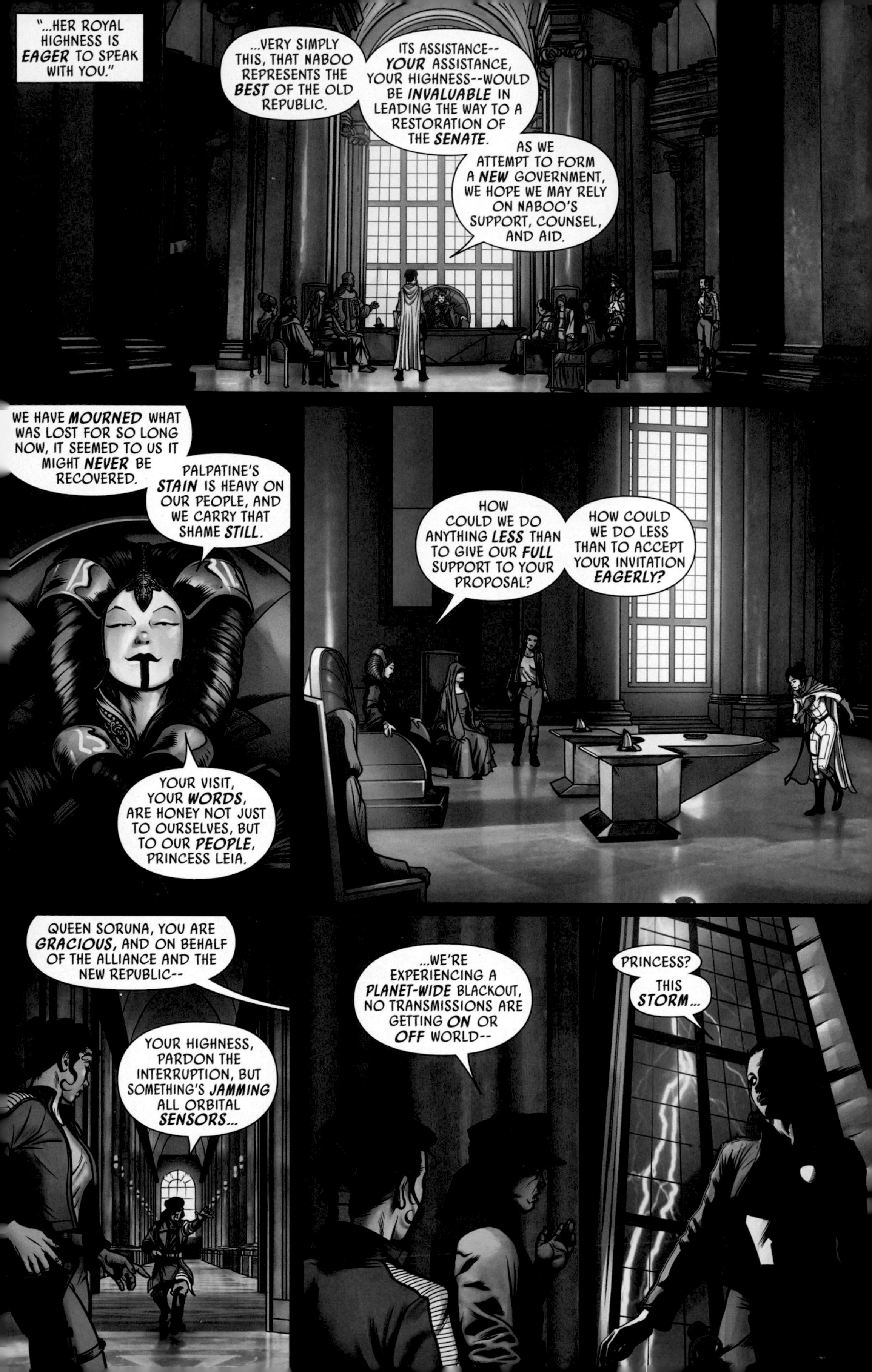
"...HER ROYAL HIGHNESS IS EAGER TO SPEAK WITH YOU."
...VERY SIMPLY THIS, THAT NABOO REPRESENTS THE BEST OF THE OLD REPUBLIC.
ITS ASSISTANCE--YOUR ASSISTANCE, YOUR HIGHNESS--WOULD BE INVALUABLE IN LEADING THE WAY TO A RESTORATION OF THE SENATE.
AS WE ATTEMPT TO FORM A NEW GOVERNMENT, WE HOPE WE MAY RELY ON NABOO'S SUPPORT, COUNSEL, AND AID.
WE HAVE MOURNED WHAT WAS LOST FOR SO LONG NOW, IT SEEMED TO US IT MIGHT NEVER BE RECOVERED.
PALPATINE'S STAIN IS HEAVY ON OUR PEOPLE, AND WE CARRY THAT SHAME STILL.
YOUR VISIT, YOUR WORDS, ARE HONEY NOT JUST TO OURSELVES, BUT TO OUR PEOPLE, PRINCESS LEIA.
HOW COULD WE DO ANYTHING LESS THAN TO GIVE OUR FULL SUPPORT TO YOUR PROPOSAL?
HOW COULD WE DO LESS THAN TO ACCEPT YOUR INVITATION EAGERLY?
QUEEN SORUNA, YOU ARE GRACIOUS, AND ON BEHALF OF THE ALLIANCE AND THE NEW REPUBLIC--
YOUR HIGHNESS, PARDON THE INTERRUPTION, BUT SOMETHING'S JAMMING ALL ORBITAL SENSORS...
...WE'RE EXPERIENCING A PLANET-WIDE BLACKOUT, NO TRANSMISSIONS ARE GETTING ON OR OFF WORLD--
PRINCESS?
THIS STORM...

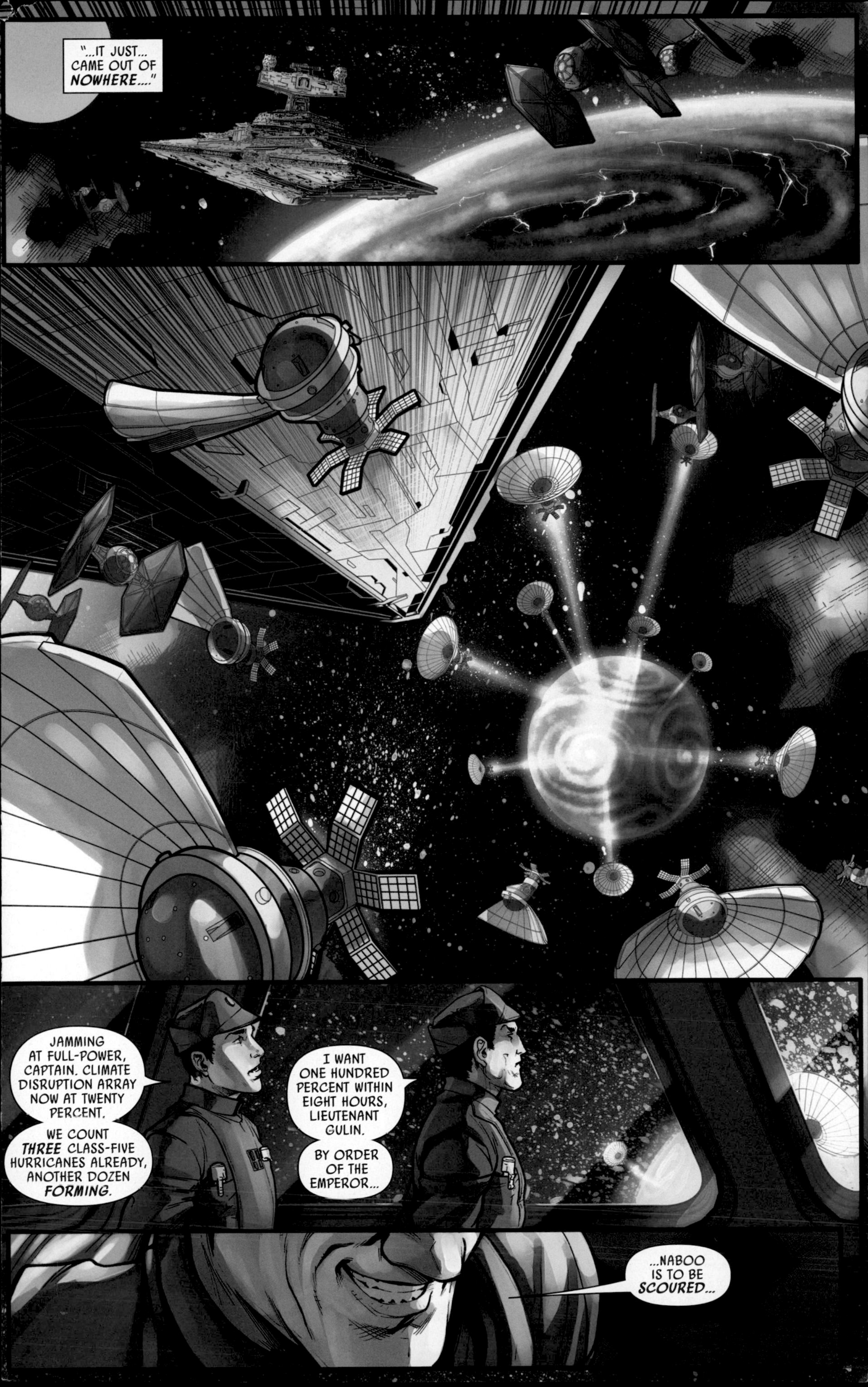
"...IT JUST... CAME OUT OF NOWHERE..."
JAMMING AT FULL-POWER, CAPTAIN. CLIMATE DISRUPTION ARRAY NOW AT TWENTY PERCENT.
WE COUNT THREE CLASS-FIVE HURRICANES ALREADY, ANOTHER DOZEN FORMING.
I WANT ONE HUNDRED PERCENT WITHIN EIGHT HOURS, LIEUTENANT GULIN.
BY ORDER OF THE EMPEROR...
...NABOO IS TO BE SCOURED...

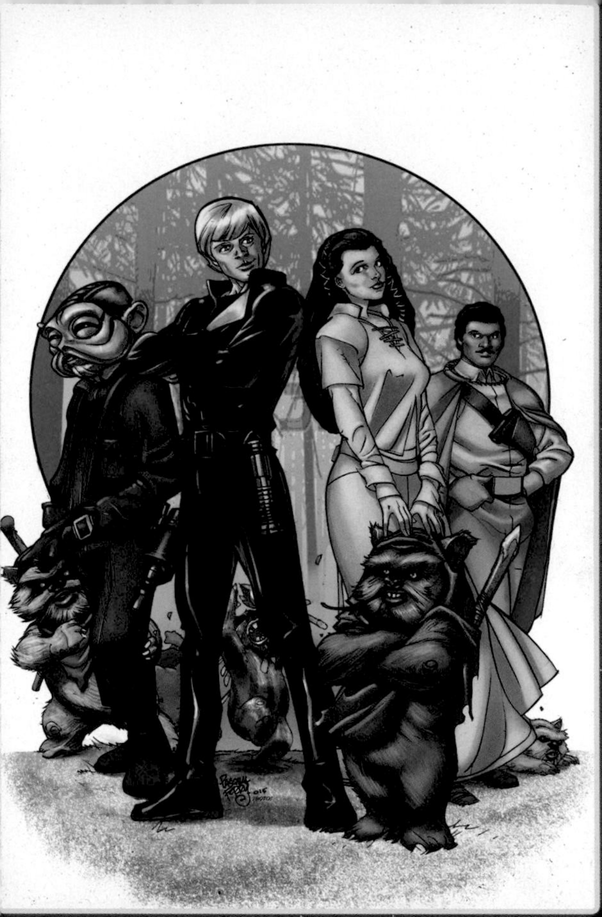

STAR WARS: SHATTERED EMPIRE #1 Variant by PASQUAL FERRY & CHRIS SOTOMAYOR

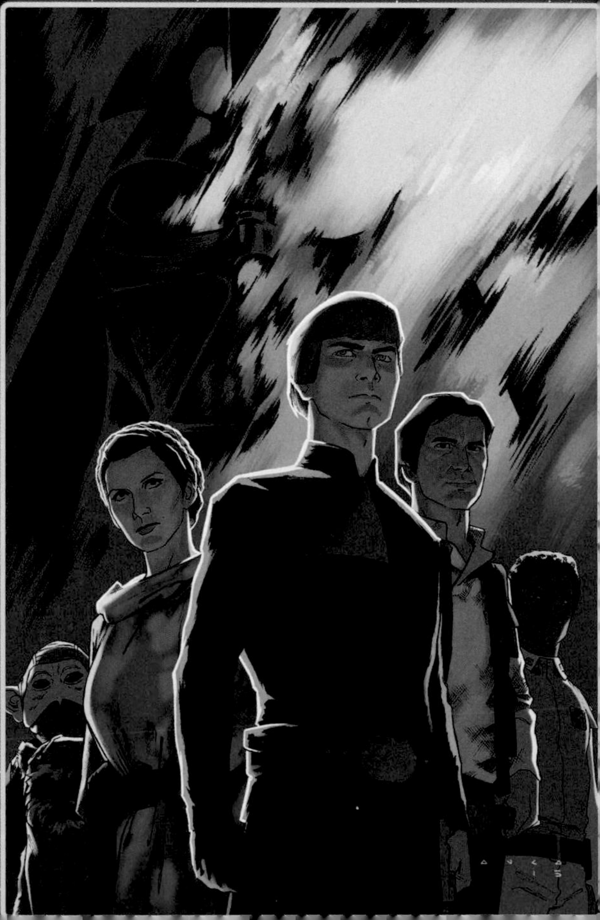

STAR WARS: SHATTERED EMPIRE #2 Variant by KRIS ANKA

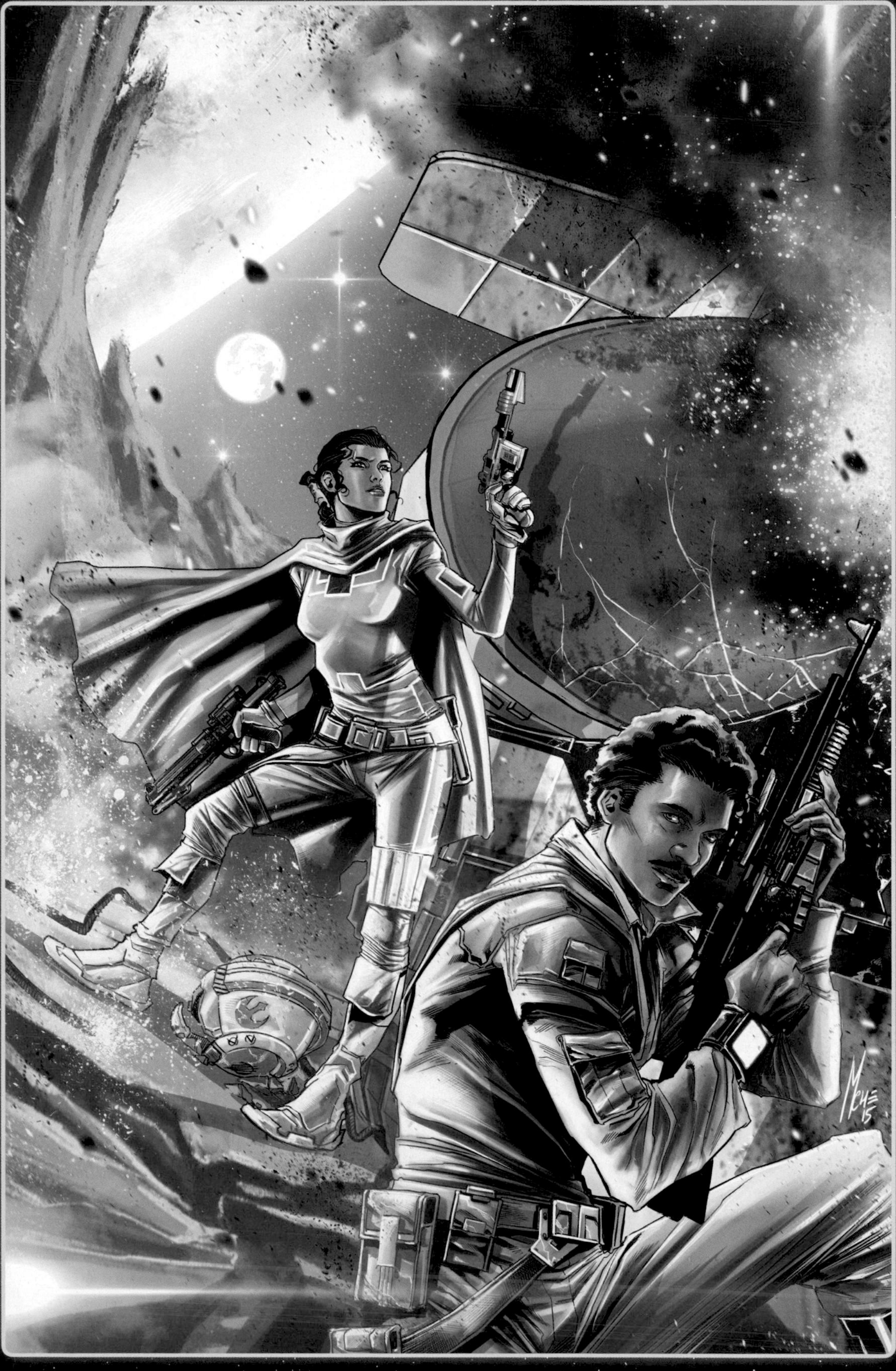

3

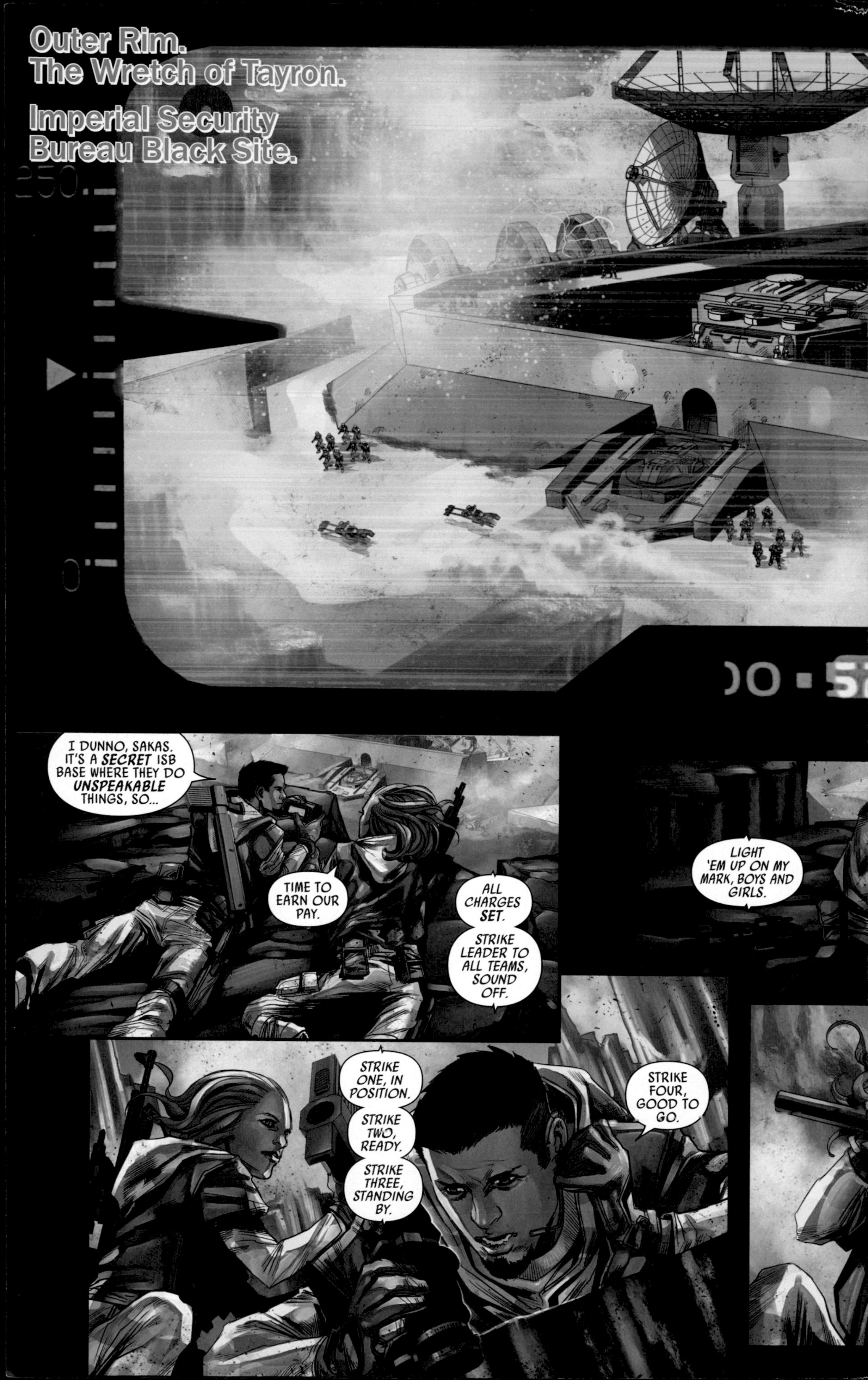
Outer Rim.
The Wretch of Tayron.
Imperial Security Bureau Black Site.
I DUNNO, SAKAS. IT'S A SECRET ISB BASE WHERE THEY DO UNSPEAKABLE THINGS, SO...
TIME TO EARN OUR PAY.
ALL CHARGES SET.
STRIKE LEADER TO ALL TEAMS, SOUND OFF.
LIGHT 'EM UP ON MY MARK, BOYS AND GIRLS.
STRIKE ONE, IN POSITION.
STRIKE TWO, READY.
STRIKE THREE, STANDING BY.
STRIKE FOUR, GOOD TO GO.

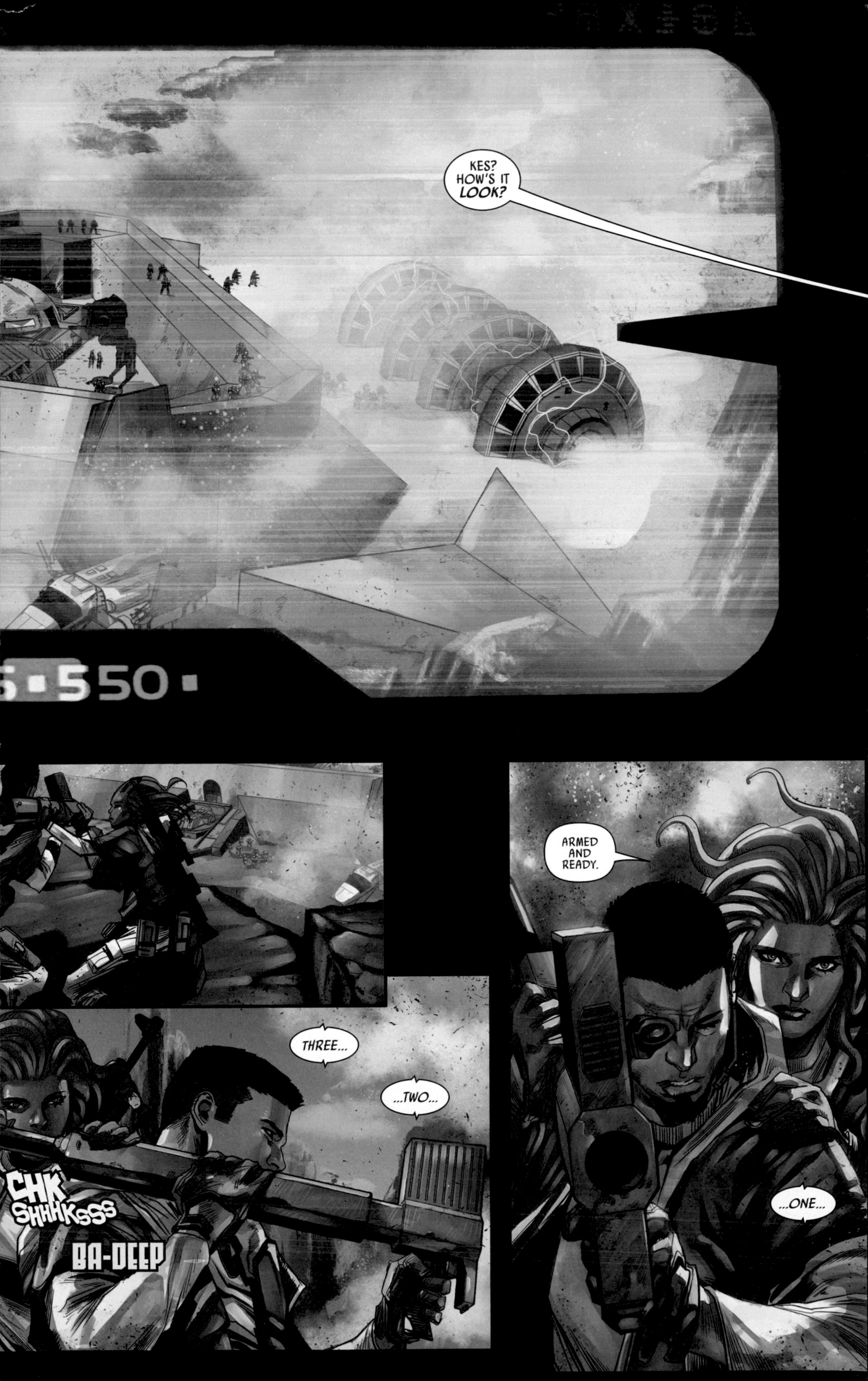

KES? HOW'S IT LOOK?
5 • 550 •
ARMED AND READY.
THREE...
...TWO...
CHK
SHHHKSSS
BA-DEEP
...ONE...

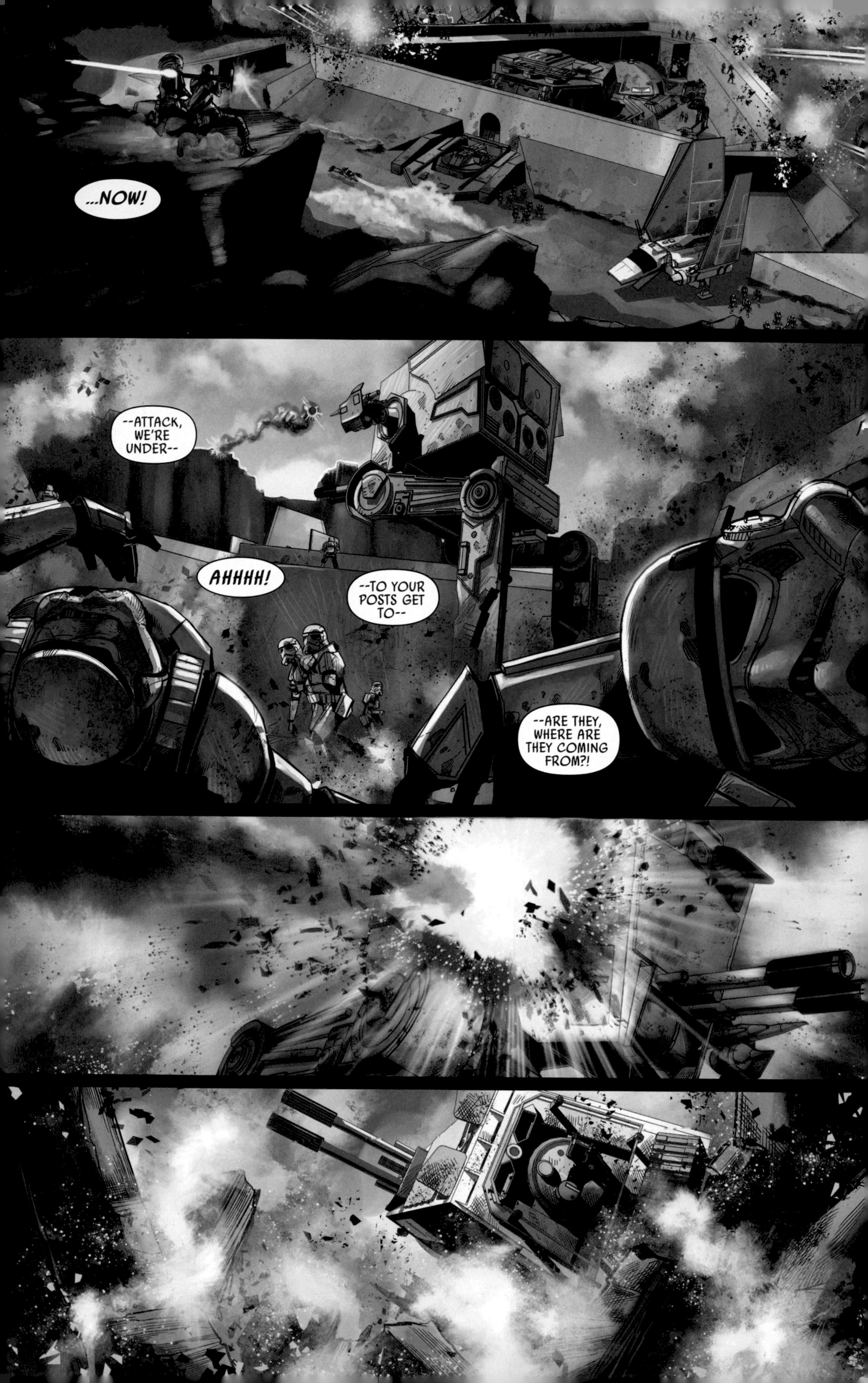
...NOW!
--ATTACK, WE'RE UNDER--
AHHHH!
--TO YOUR POSTS GET TO--
--ARE THEY, WHERE ARE THEY COMING FROM?!

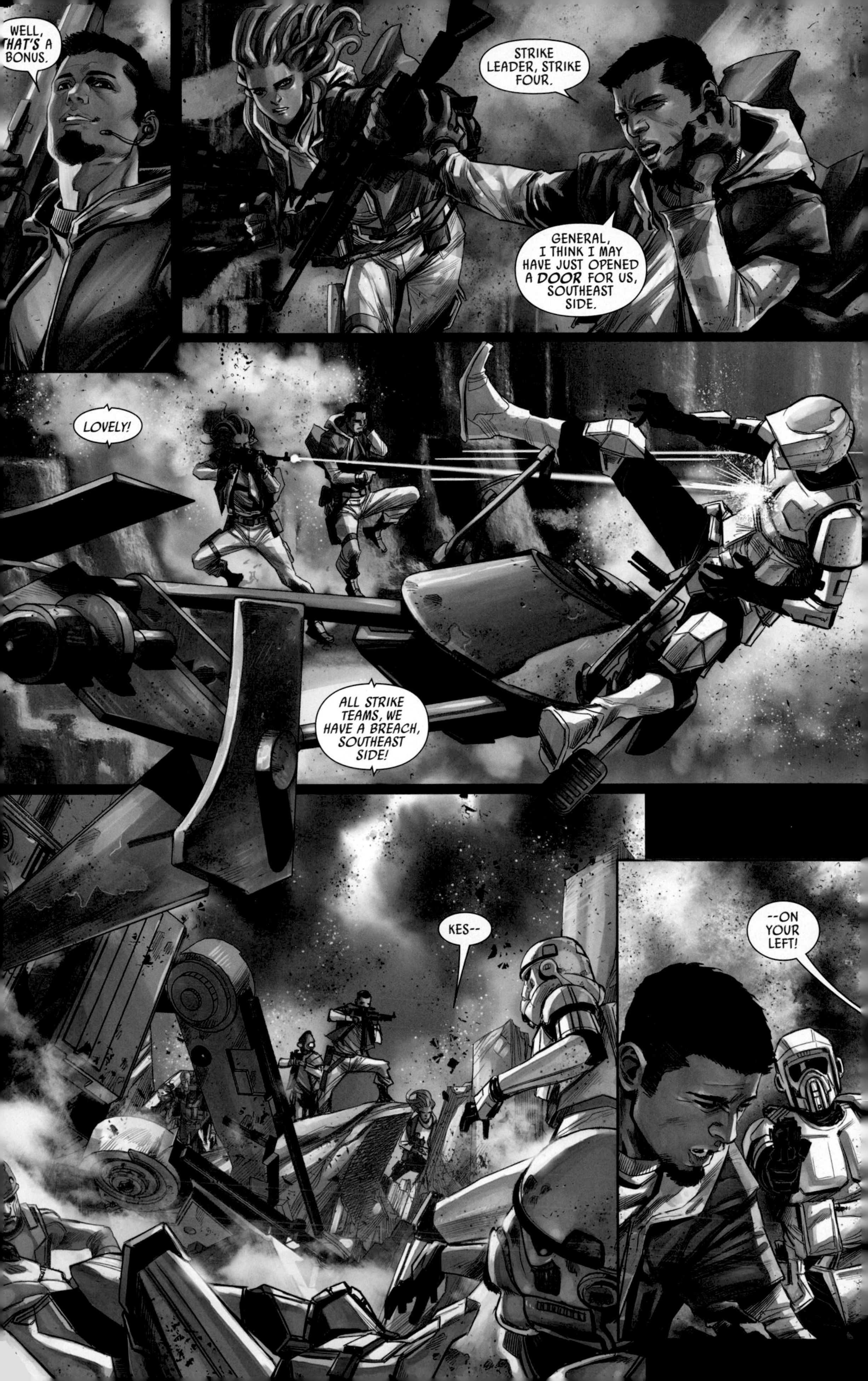
WELL, THAT'S A BONUS.
STRIKE LEADER, STRIKE FOUR.
GENERAL, I THINK I MAY HAVE JUST OPENED A DOOR FOR US, SOUTHEAST SIDE.
LOVELY!
ALL STRIKE TEAMS, WE HAVE A BREACH, SOUTHEAST SIDE!
KES--
--ON YOUR LEFT!

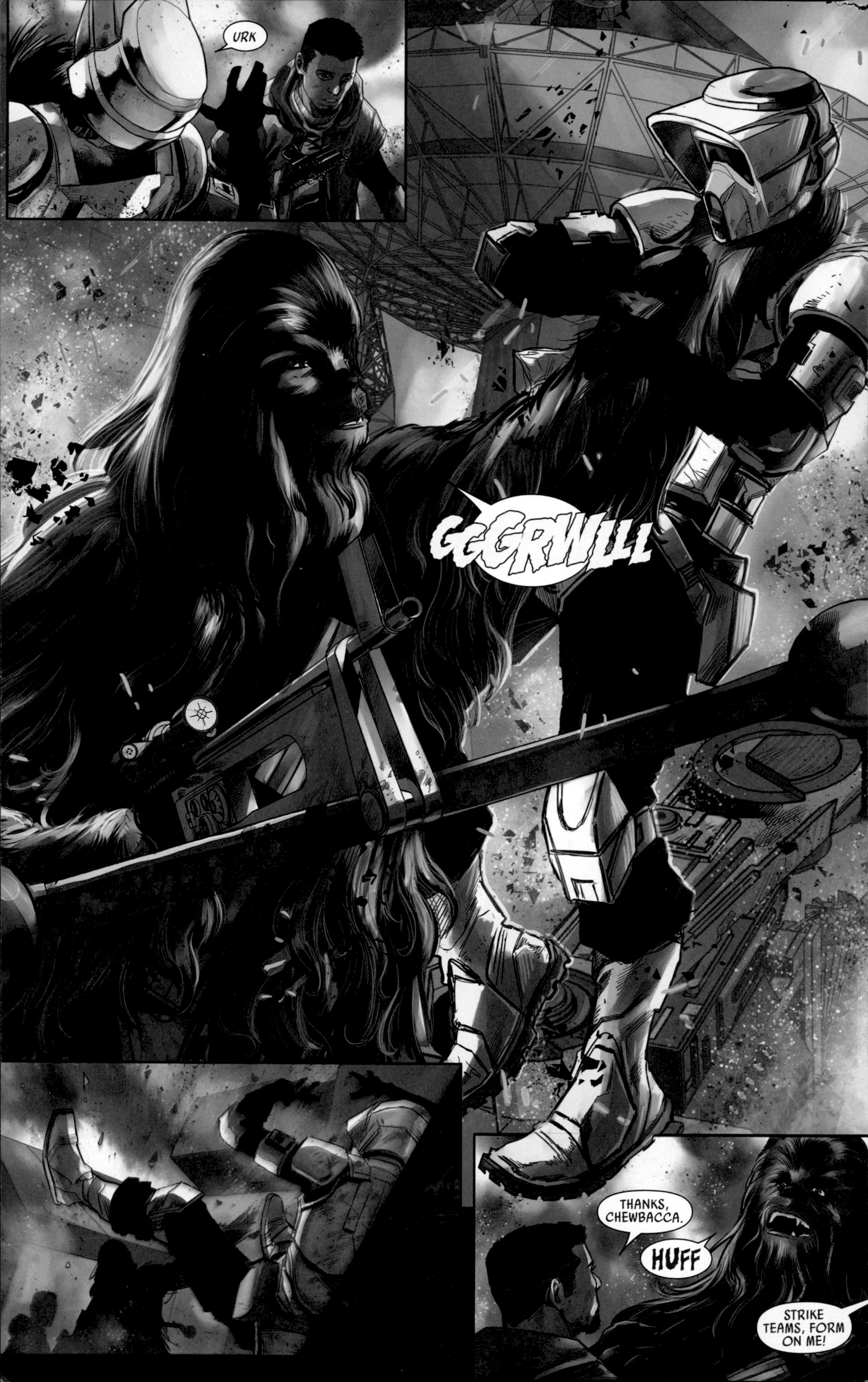
URK
GGGRWLLL
THANKS, CHEWBACCA.
HUFF
STRIKE TEAMS, FORM ON ME!

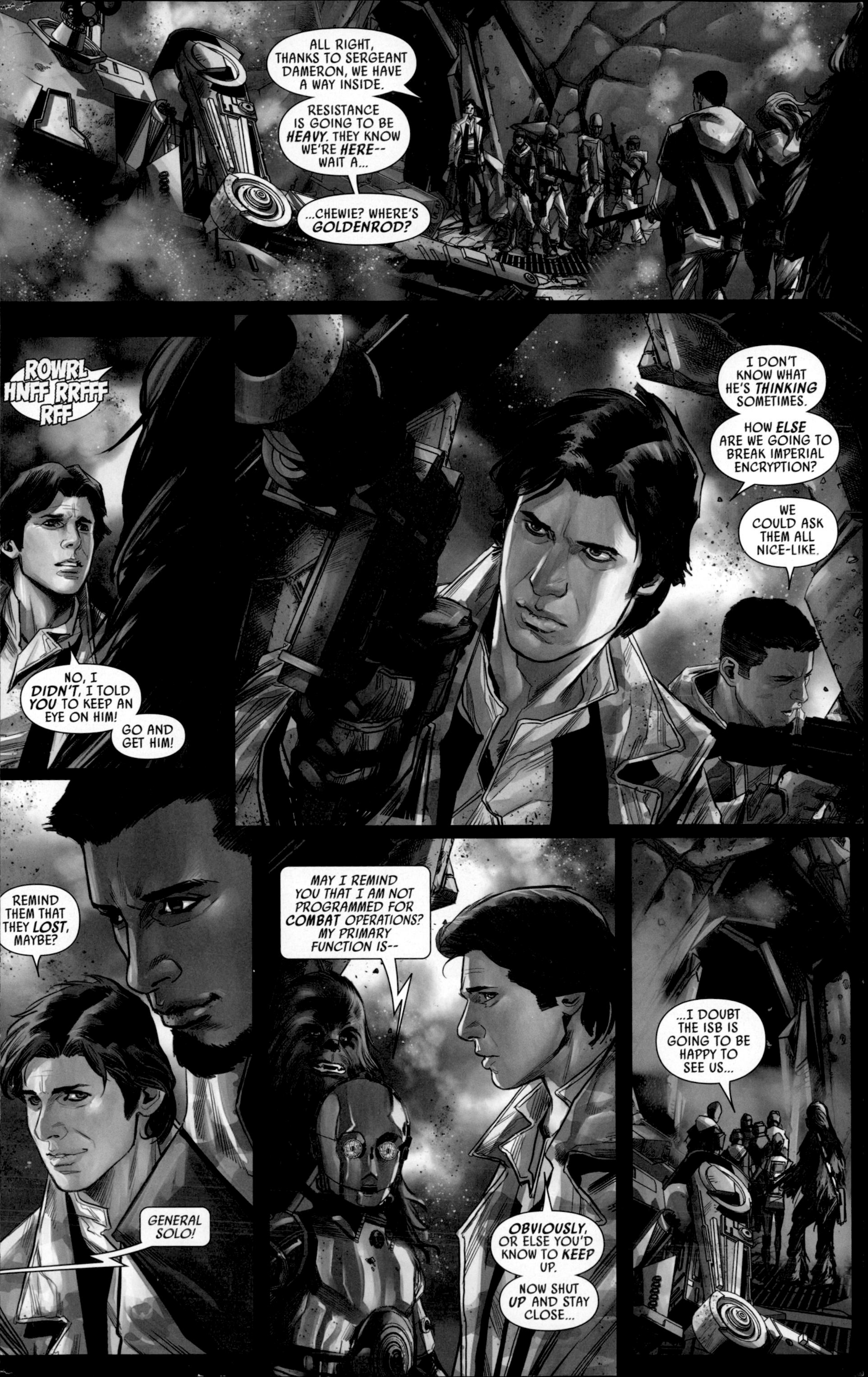
ALL RIGHT, THANKS TO SERGEANT DAMERON, WE HAVE A WAY INSIDE.
RESISTANCE IS GOING TO BE HEAVY. THEY KNOW WE'RE HERE-- WAIT A...
...CHEWIE? WHERE'S GOLDENROD?
ROWRL HNFF RRFFF RFF
NO, I DIDN'T, I TOLD YOU TO KEEP AN EYE ON HIM!
GO AND GET HIM!
I DON'T KNOW WHAT HE'S THINKING SOMETIMES.
HOW ELSE ARE WE GOING TO BREAK IMPERIAL ENCRYPTION?
WE COULD ASK THEM ALL NICE-LIKE.
REMIND THEM THAT THEY LOST, MAYBE?
GENERAL SOLO!
MAY I REMIND YOU THAT I AM NOT PROGRAMMED FOR COMBAT OPERATIONS? MY PRIMARY FUNCTION IS--
OBVIOUSLY, OR ELSE YOU'D KNOW TO KEEP UP.
NOW SHUT UP AND STAY CLOSE...
...I DOUBT THE ISB IS GOING TO BE HAPPY TO SEE US...

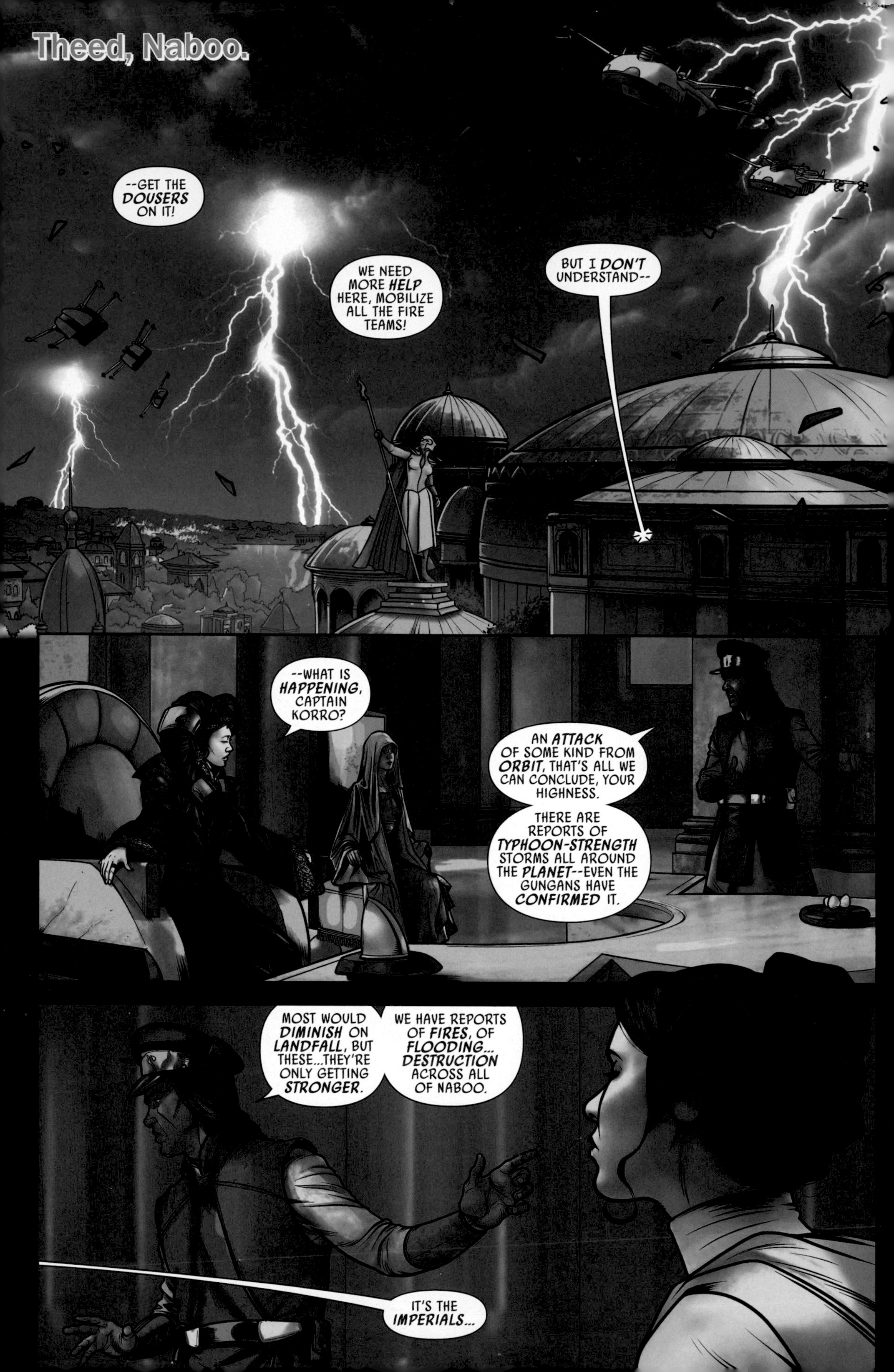
Theed, Naboo.
--GET THE DOUSERS ON IT!
WE NEED MORE HELP HERE, MOBILIZE ALL THE FIRE TEAMS!
BUT I DON'T UNDERSTAND--
--WHAT IS HAPPENING, CAPTAIN KORRO?
AN ATTACK OF SOME KIND FROM ORBIT, THAT'S ALL WE CAN CONCLUDE, YOUR HIGHNESS.
THERE ARE REPORTS OF TYPHOON-STRENGTH STORMS ALL AROUND THE PLANET--EVEN THE GUNGANS HAVE CONFIRMED IT.
MOST WOULD DIMINISH ON LANDFALL, BUT THESE...THEY'RE ONLY GETTING STRONGER.
WE HAVE REPORTS OF FIRES, OF FLOODING... DESTRUCTION ACROSS ALL OF NABOO.
IT'S THE IMPERIALS...

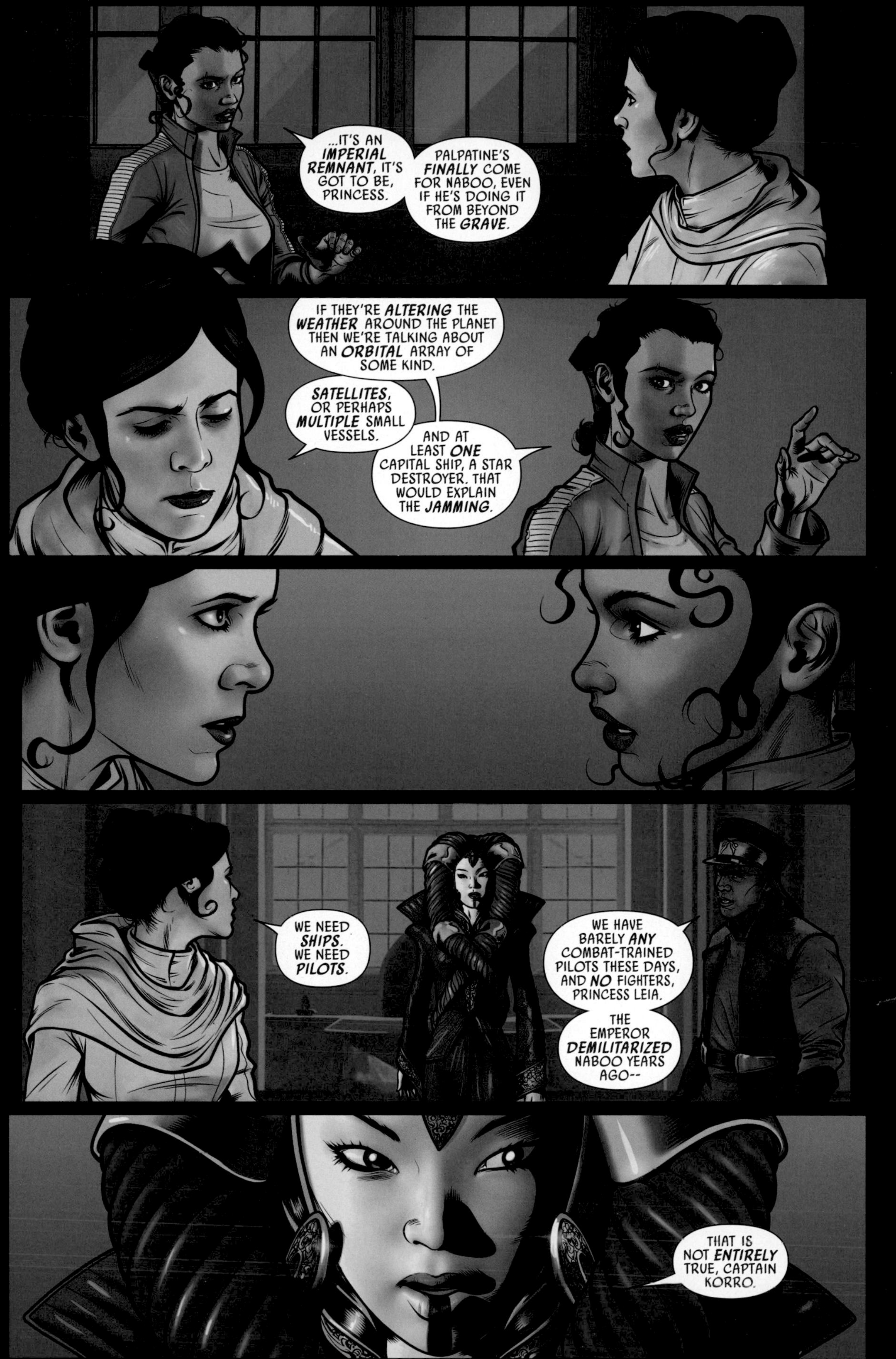
...IT'S AN IMPERIAL REMNANT, IT'S GOT TO BE, PRINCESS.
PALPATINE'S FINALLY COME FOR NABOO, EVEN IF HE'S DOING IT FROM BEYOND THE GRAVE.
IF THEY'RE ALTERING THE WEATHER AROUND THE PLANET THEN WE'RE TALKING ABOUT AN ORBITAL ARRAY OF SOME KIND.
SATELLITES, OR PERHAPS MULTIPLE SMALL VESSELS.
AND AT LEAST ONE CAPITAL SHIP, A STAR DESTROYER. THAT WOULD EXPLAIN THE JAMMING.
WE NEED SHIPS. WE NEED PILOTS.
WE HAVE BARELY ANY COMBAT-TRAINED PILOTS THESE DAYS, AND NO FIGHTERS, PRINCESS LEIA.
THE EMPEROR DEMILITARIZED NABOO YEARS AGO--
THAT IS NOT ENTIRELY TRUE, CAPTAIN KORRO.

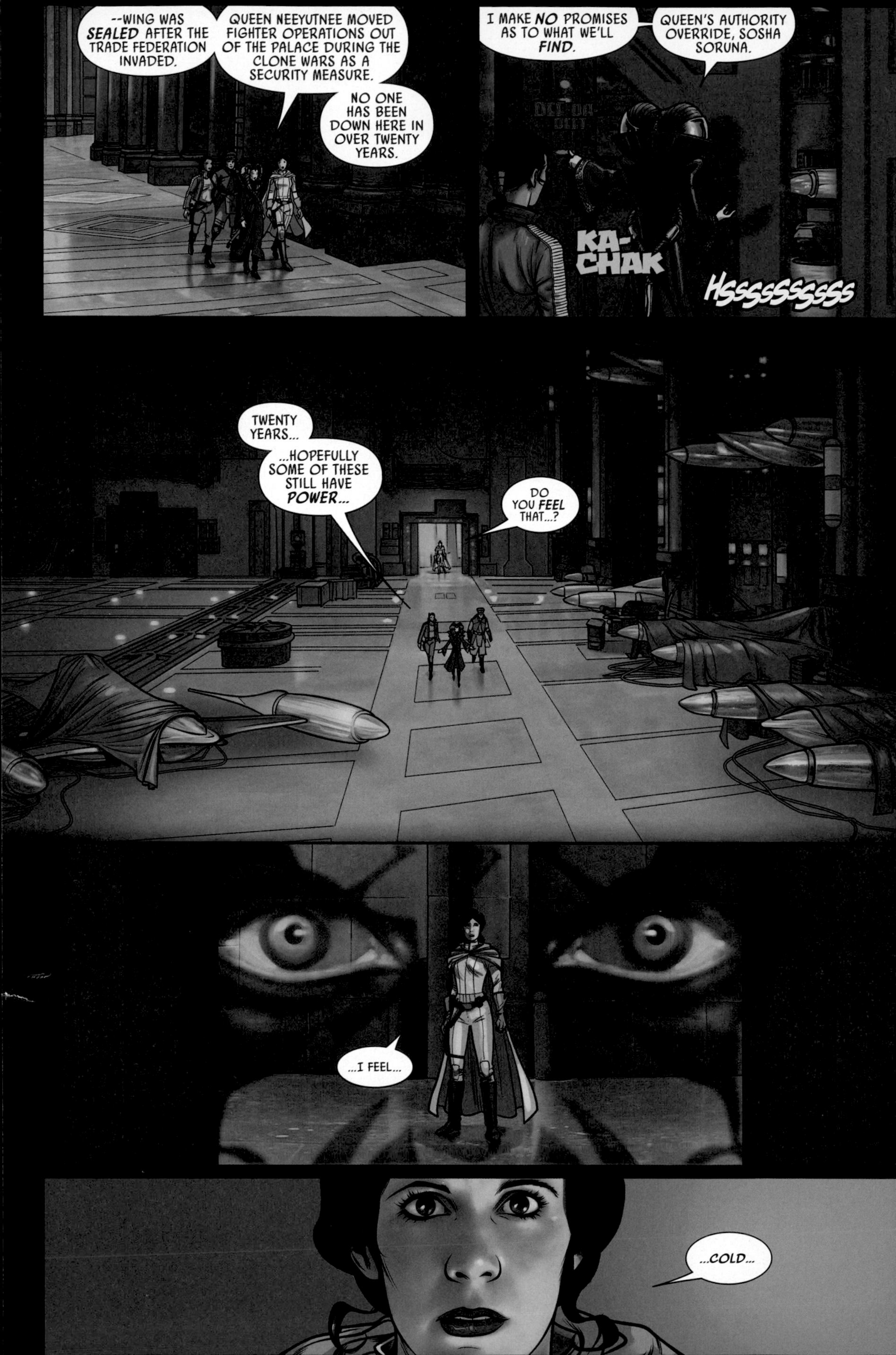

--WING WAS SEALED AFTER THE TRADE FEDERATION INVADED.
QUEEN NEEYUTNEE MOVED FIGHTER OPERATIONS OUT OF THE PALACE DURING THE CLONE WARS AS A SECURITY MEASURE.
NO ONE HAS BEEN DOWN HERE IN OVER TWENTY YEARS.
I MAKE NO PROMISES AS TO WHAT WE'LL FIND.
QUEEN'S AUTHORITY OVERRIDE, SOSHA SORUNA.
KA-CHAK
HSSSSSSSSSS
TWENTY YEARS...
...HOPEFULLY SOME OF THESE STILL HAVE POWER...
DO YOU FEEL THAT...?
...I FEEL...
...COLD...

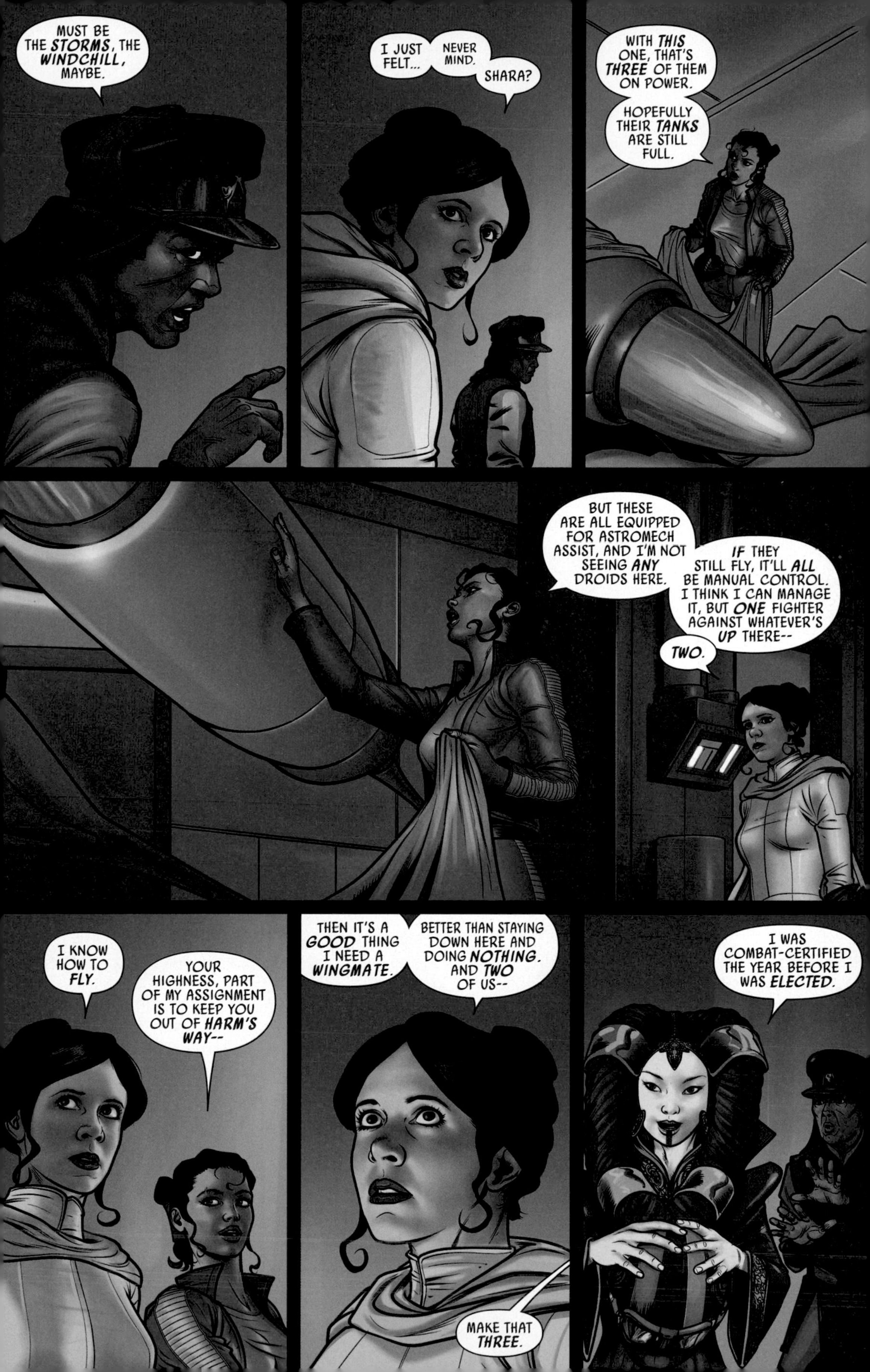
MUST BE THE STORMS, THE WINDCHILL, MAYBE.
I JUST FELT...
NEVER MIND.
SHARA?
WITH THIS ONE, THAT'S THREE OF THEM ON POWER.
HOPEFULLY THEIR TANKS ARE STILL FULL.
BUT THESE ARE ALL EQUIPPED FOR ASTROMECH ASSIST, AND I'M NOT SEEING ANY DROIDS HERE.
IF THEY STILL FLY, IT'LL ALL BE MANUAL CONTROL. I THINK I CAN MANAGE IT, BUT ONE FIGHTER AGAINST WHATEVER'S UP THERE--
TWO.
I KNOW HOW TO FLY.
YOUR HIGHNESS, PART OF MY ASSIGNMENT IS TO KEEP YOU OUT OF HARM'S WAY--
THEN IT'S A GOOD THING I NEED A WINGMATE.
BETTER THAN STAYING DOWN HERE AND DOING NOTHING. AND TWO OF US--
MAKE THAT THREE.
I WAS COMBAT-CERTIFIED THE YEAR BEFORE I WAS ELECTED.

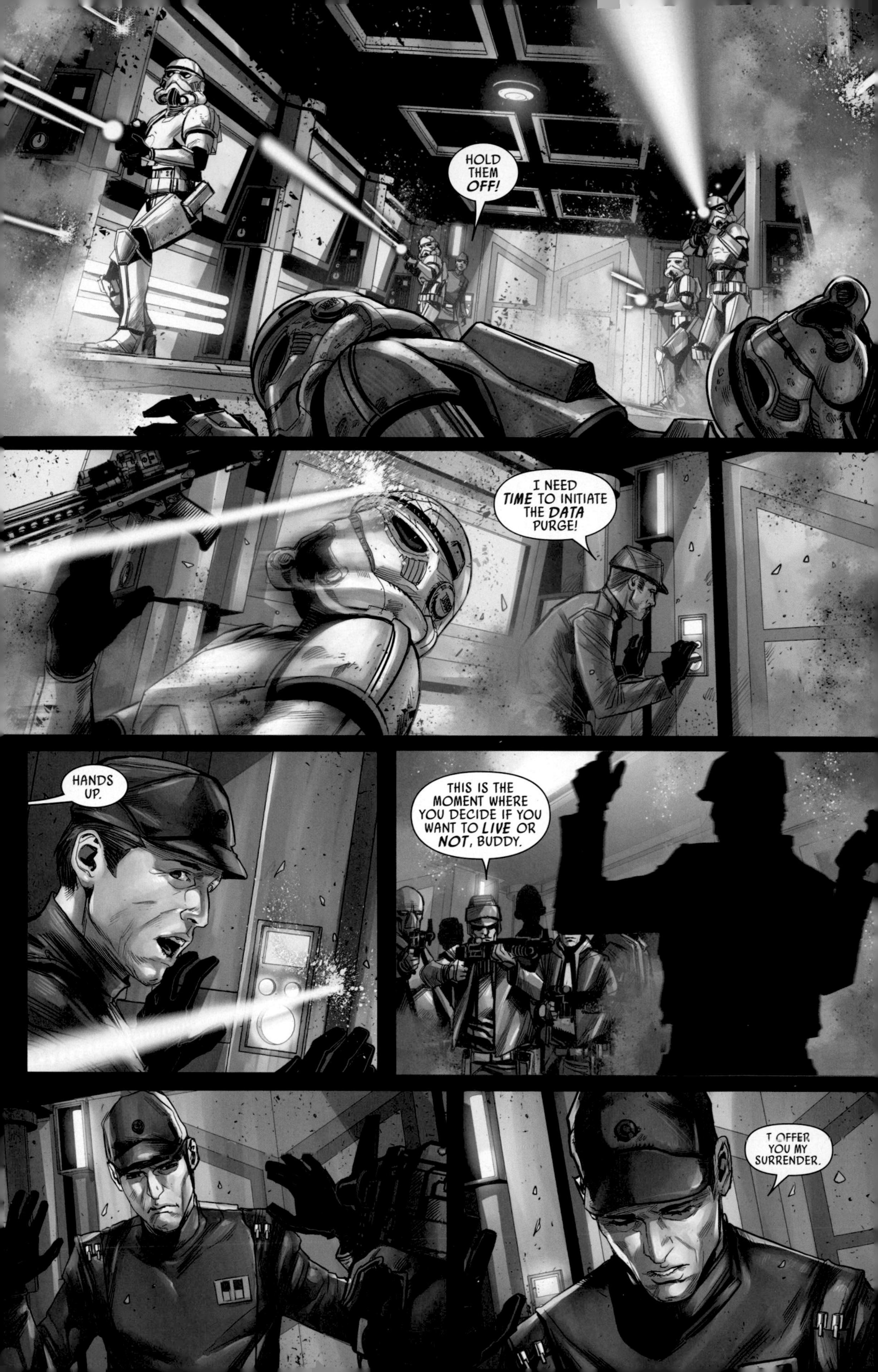
HOLD THEM OFF!
I NEED TIME TO INITIATE THE DATA PURGE!
HANDS UP.
THIS IS THE MOMENT WHERE YOU DECIDE IF YOU WANT TO LIVE OR NOT, BUDDY.
I OFFER YOU MY SURRENDER.

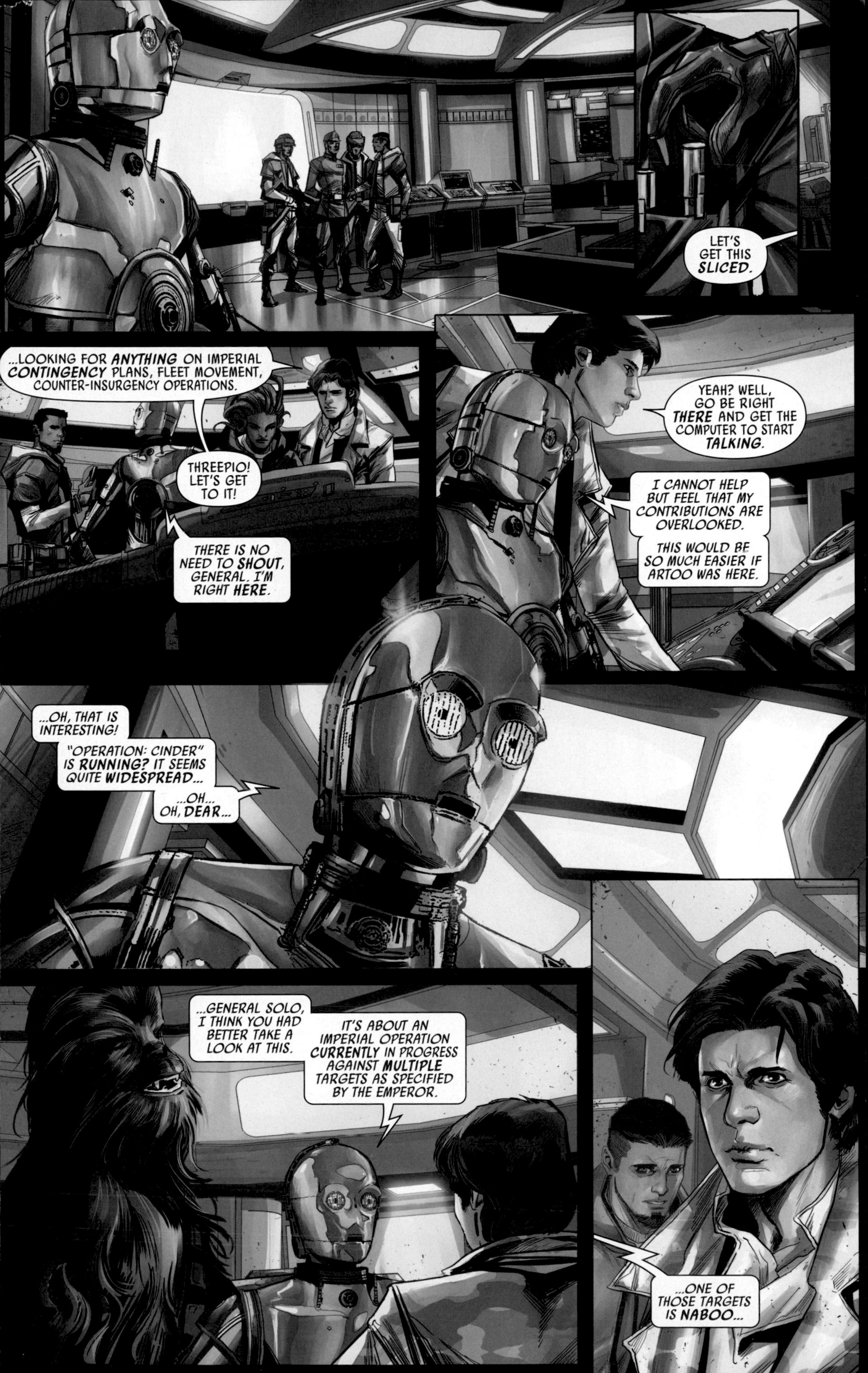

LET'S GET THIS SLICED.
...LOOKING FOR ANYTHING ON IMPERIAL CONTINGENCY PLANS, FLEET MOVEMENT, COUNTER-INSURGENCY OPERATIONS.
THREEPIO! LET'S GET TO IT!
THERE IS NO NEED TO SHOUT, GENERAL. I'M RIGHT HERE.
YEAH? WELL, GO BE RIGHT THERE AND GET THE COMPUTER TO START TALKING.
I CANNOT HELP BUT FEEL THAT MY CONTRIBUTIONS ARE OVERLOOKED.
THIS WOULD BE SO MUCH EASIER IF ARTOO WAS HERE.
...OH, THAT IS INTERESTING!
"OPERATION: CINDER" IS RUNNING? IT SEEMS QUITE WIDESPREAD...
...OH... OH, DEAR...
...GENERAL SOLO, I THINK YOU HAD BETTER TAKE A LOOK AT THIS.
IT'S ABOUT AN IMPERIAL OPERATION CURRENTLY IN PROGRESS AGAINST MULTIPLE TARGETS AS SPECIFIED BY THE EMPEROR.
...ONE OF THOSE TARGETS IS NABOO...

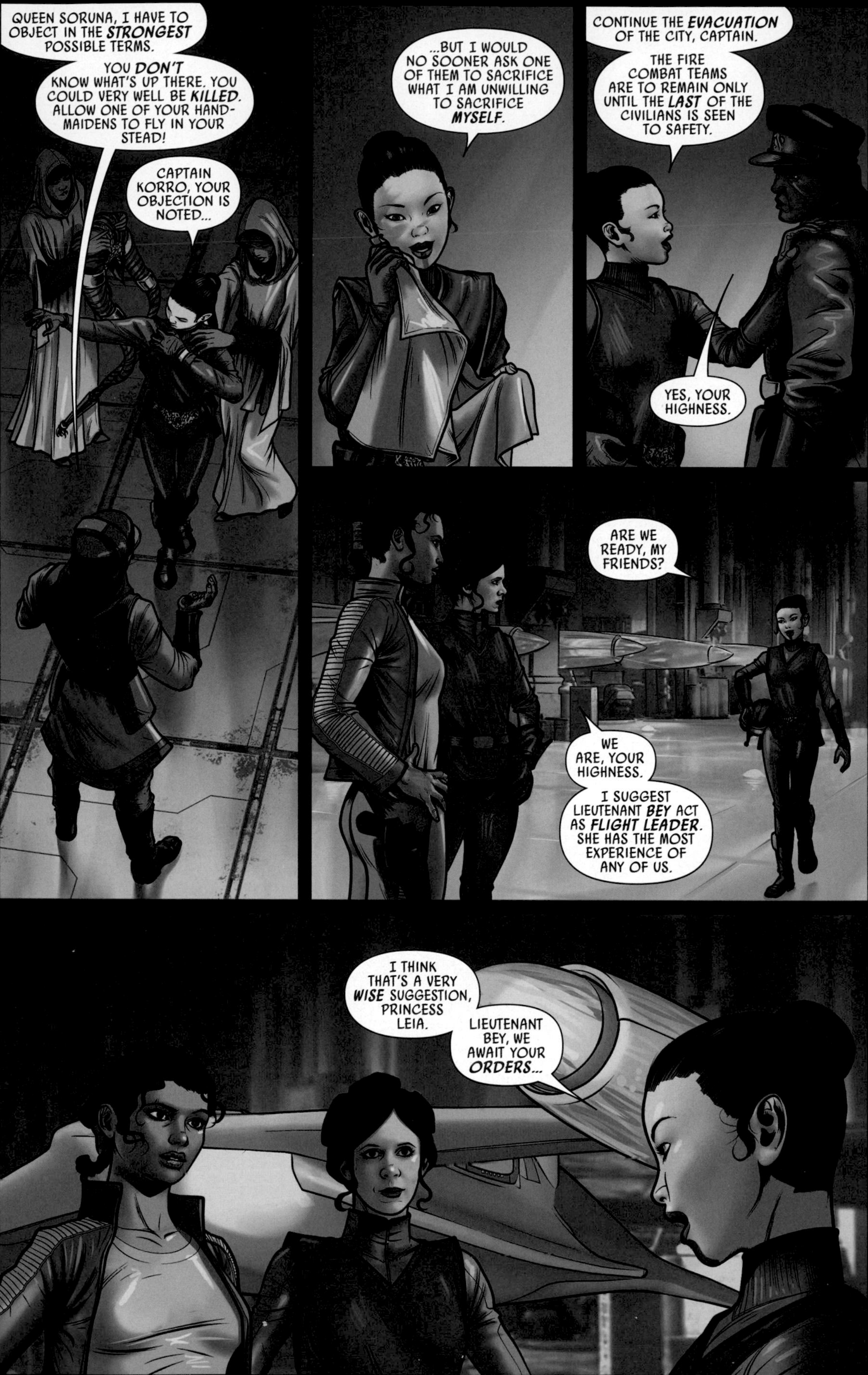
QUEEN SORUNA, I HAVE TO OBJECT IN THE STRONGEST POSSIBLE TERMS.
YOU DON'T KNOW WHAT'S UP THERE. YOU COULD VERY WELL BE KILLED. ALLOW ONE OF YOUR HAND-MAIDENS TO FLY IN YOUR STEAD!
CAPTAIN KORRO, YOUR OBJECTION IS NOTED...
...BUT I WOULD NO SOONER ASK ONE OF THEM TO SACRIFICE WHAT I AM UNWILLING TO SACRIFICE MYSELF.
CONTINUE THE EVACUATION OF THE CITY, CAPTAIN.
THE FIRE COMBAT TEAMS ARE TO REMAIN ONLY UNTIL THE LAST OF THE CIVILIANS IS SEEN TO SAFETY.
YES, YOUR HIGHNESS.
ARE WE READY, MY FRIENDS?
WE ARE, YOUR HIGHNESS.
I SUGGEST LIEUTENANT BEY ACT AS FLIGHT LEADER. SHE HAS THE MOST EXPERIENCE OF ANY OF US.
I THINK THAT'S A VERY WISE SUGGESTION, PRINCESS LEIA.
LIEUTENANT BEY, WE AWAIT YOUR ORDERS...

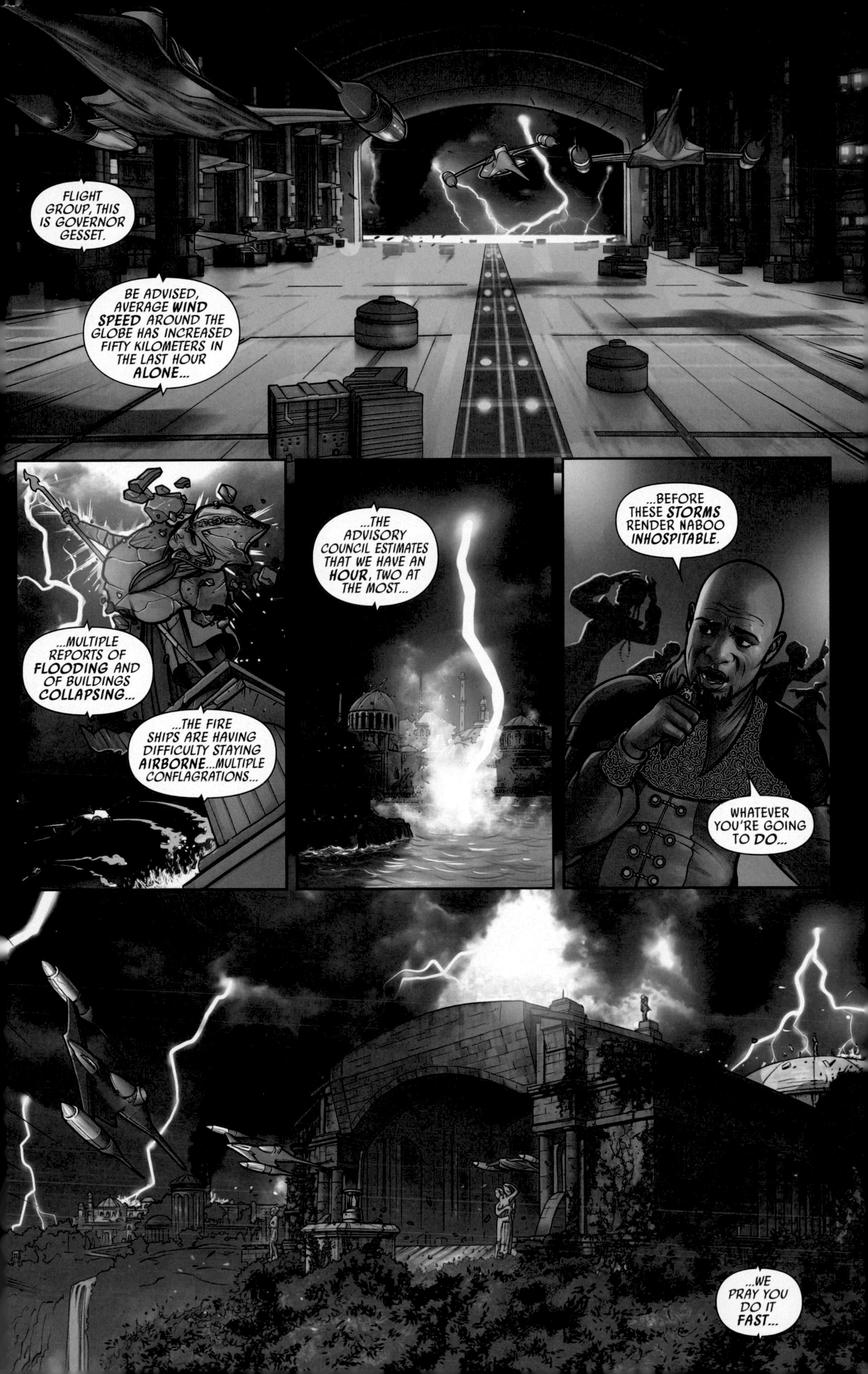

FLIGHT GROUP, THIS IS GOVERNOR GESSET.
BE ADVISED, AVERAGE **WIND SPEED** AROUND THE GLOBE HAS INCREASED FIFTY KILOMETERS IN THE LAST HOUR **ALONE**...
...MULTIPLE REPORTS OF **FLOODING** AND OF BUILDINGS **COLLAPSING**...
...THE FIRE SHIPS ARE HAVING DIFFICULTY STAYING **AIRBORNE**...MULTIPLE CONFLAGRATIONS...
...THE ADVISORY COUNCIL ESTIMATES THAT WE HAVE AN **HOUR**, TWO AT THE MOST...
...BEFORE THESE **STORMS** RENDER NABOO **INHOSPITABLE**.
WHATEVER YOU'RE GOING TO **DO**...
...WE PRAY YOU DO IT **FAST**...

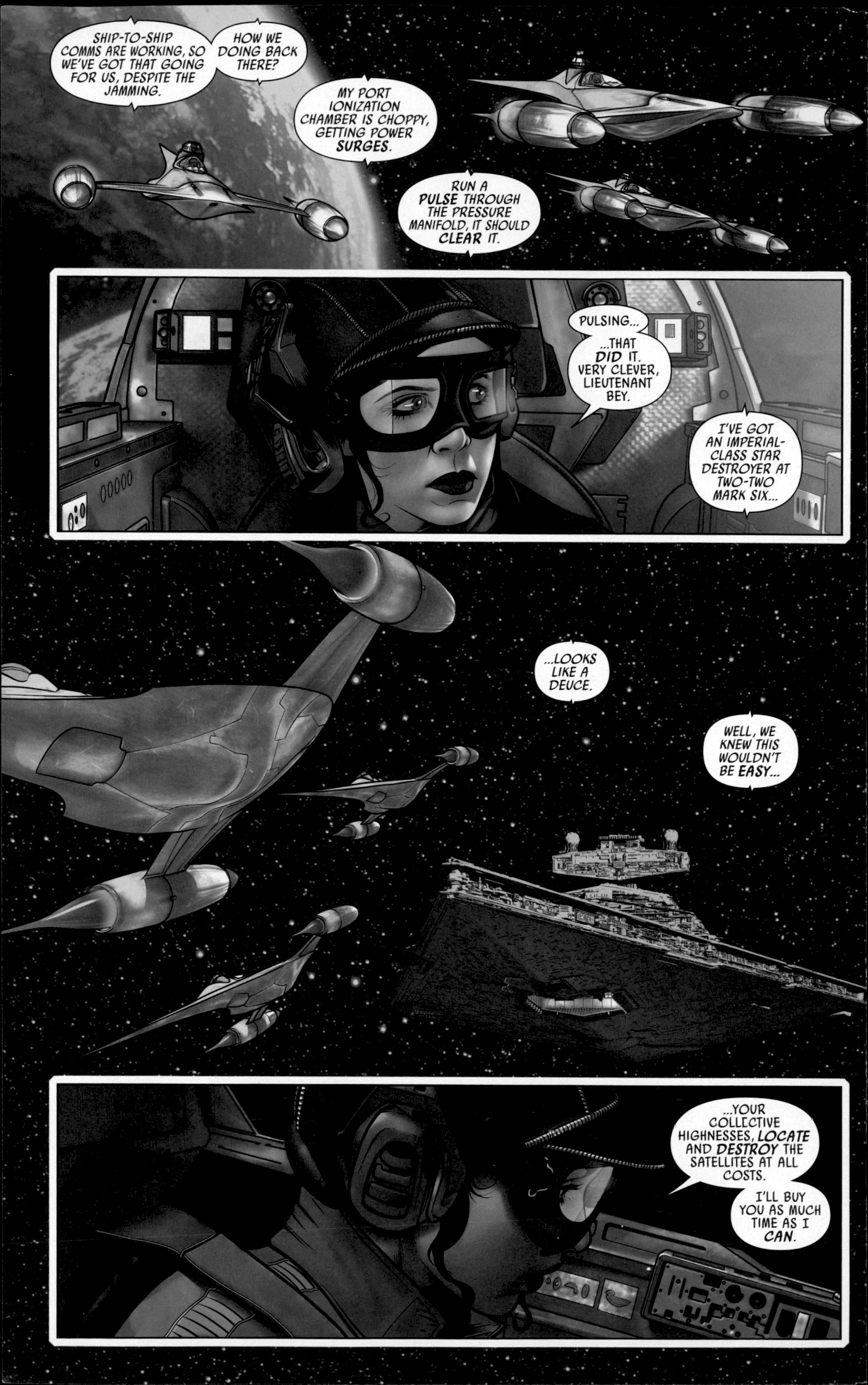
SHIP-TO-SHIP COMMS ARE WORKING, SO WE'VE GOT THAT GOING FOR US, DESPITE THE JAMMING.
HOW WE DOING BACK THERE?
MY PORT IONIZATION CHAMBER IS CHOPPY, GETTING POWER SURGES.
RUN A PULSE THROUGH THE PRESSURE MANIFOLD, IT SHOULD CLEAR IT.
PULSING...
...THAT DID IT. VERY CLEVER, LIEUTENANT BEY.
I'VE GOT AN IMPERIAL-CLASS STAR DESTROYER AT TWO-TWO MARK SIX...
...LOOKS LIKE A DEUCE.
WELL, WE KNEW THIS WOULDN'T BE EASY...
...YOUR COLLECTIVE HIGHNESSES, LOCATE AND DESTROY THE SATELLITES AT ALL COSTS.
I'LL BUY YOU AS MUCH TIME AS I CAN.

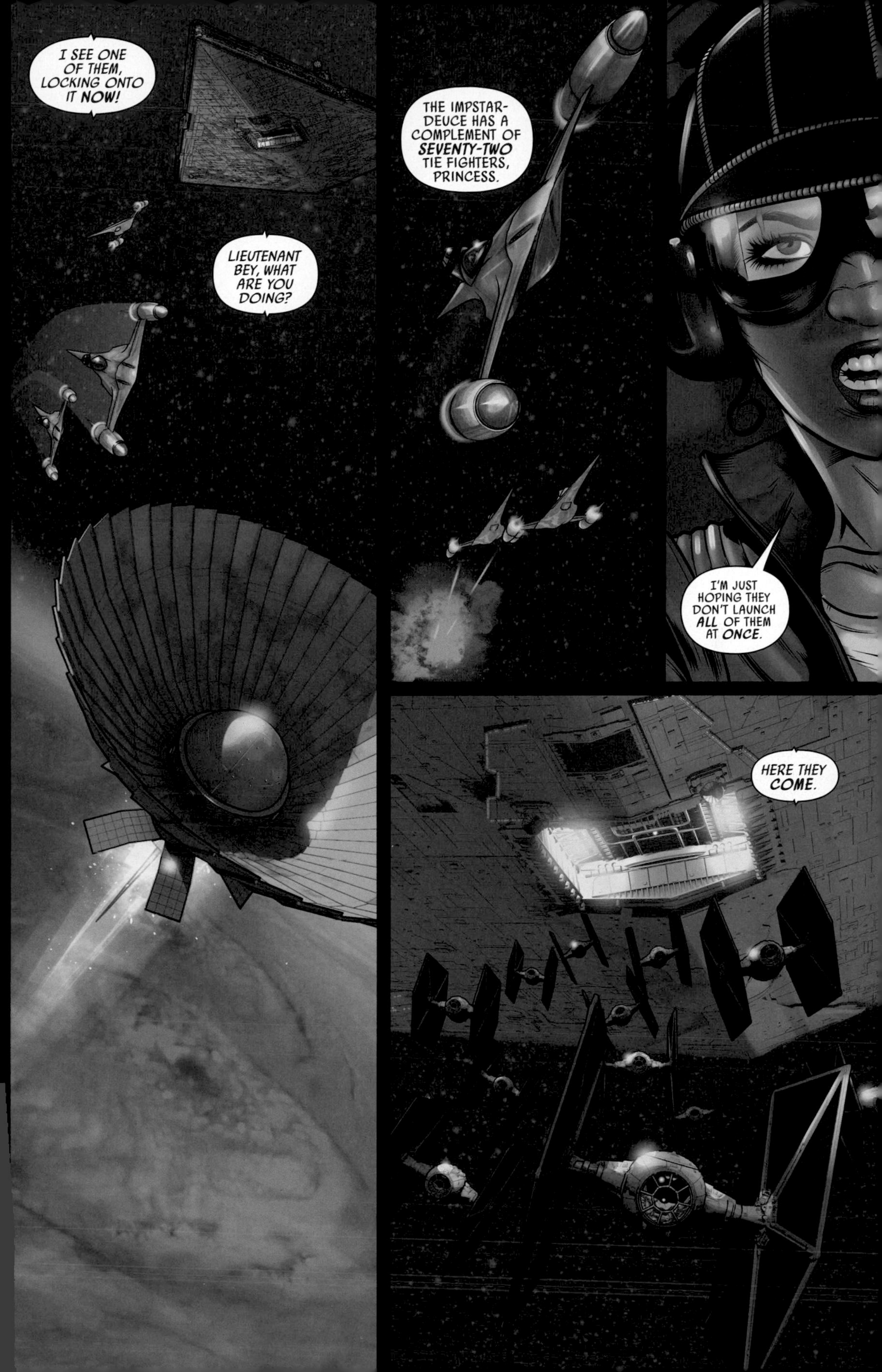
I SEE ONE OF THEM, LOCKING ONTO IT NOW!
LIEUTENANT BEY, WHAT ARE YOU DOING?
THE IMPSTAR-DEUCE HAS A COMPLEMENT OF SEVENTY-TWO TIE FIGHTERS, PRINCESS.
I'M JUST HOPING THEY DON'T LAUNCH ALL OF THEM AT ONCE.
HERE THEY COME.

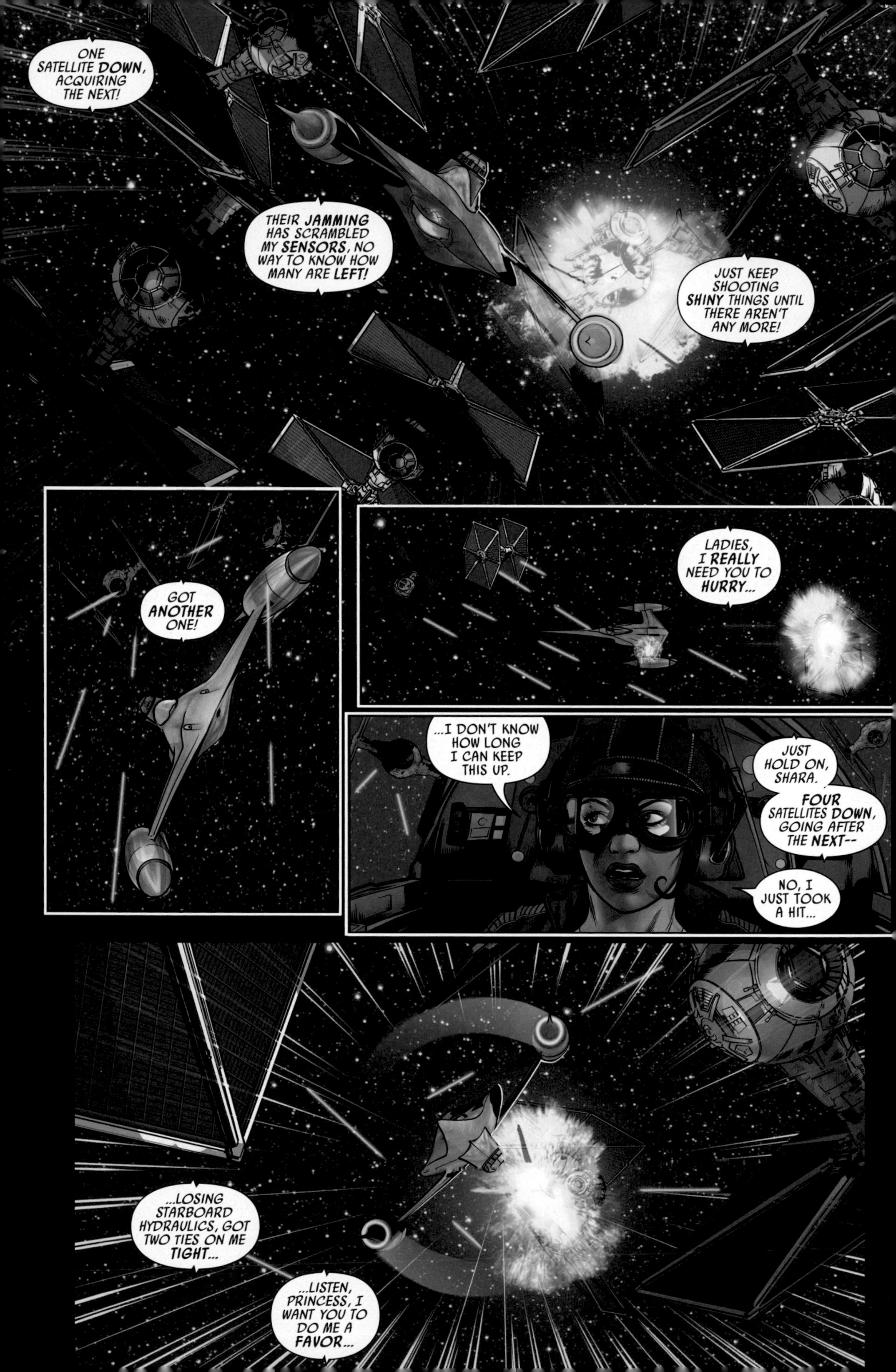
ONE SATELLITE DOWN, ACQUIRING THE NEXT!
THEIR JAMMING HAS SCRAMBLED MY SENSORS, NO WAY TO KNOW HOW MANY ARE LEFT!
JUST KEEP SHOOTING SHINY THINGS UNTIL THERE AREN'T ANY MORE!
GOT ANOTHER ONE!
LADIES, I REALLY NEED YOU TO HURRY...
...I DON'T KNOW HOW LONG I CAN KEEP THIS UP.
JUST HOLD ON, SHARA.
FOUR SATELLITES DOWN, GOING AFTER THE NEXT--
NO, I JUST TOOK A HIT...
...LOSING STARBOARD HYDRAULICS, GOT TWO TIES ON ME TIGHT...
...LISTEN, PRINCESS, I WANT YOU TO DO ME A FAVOR...

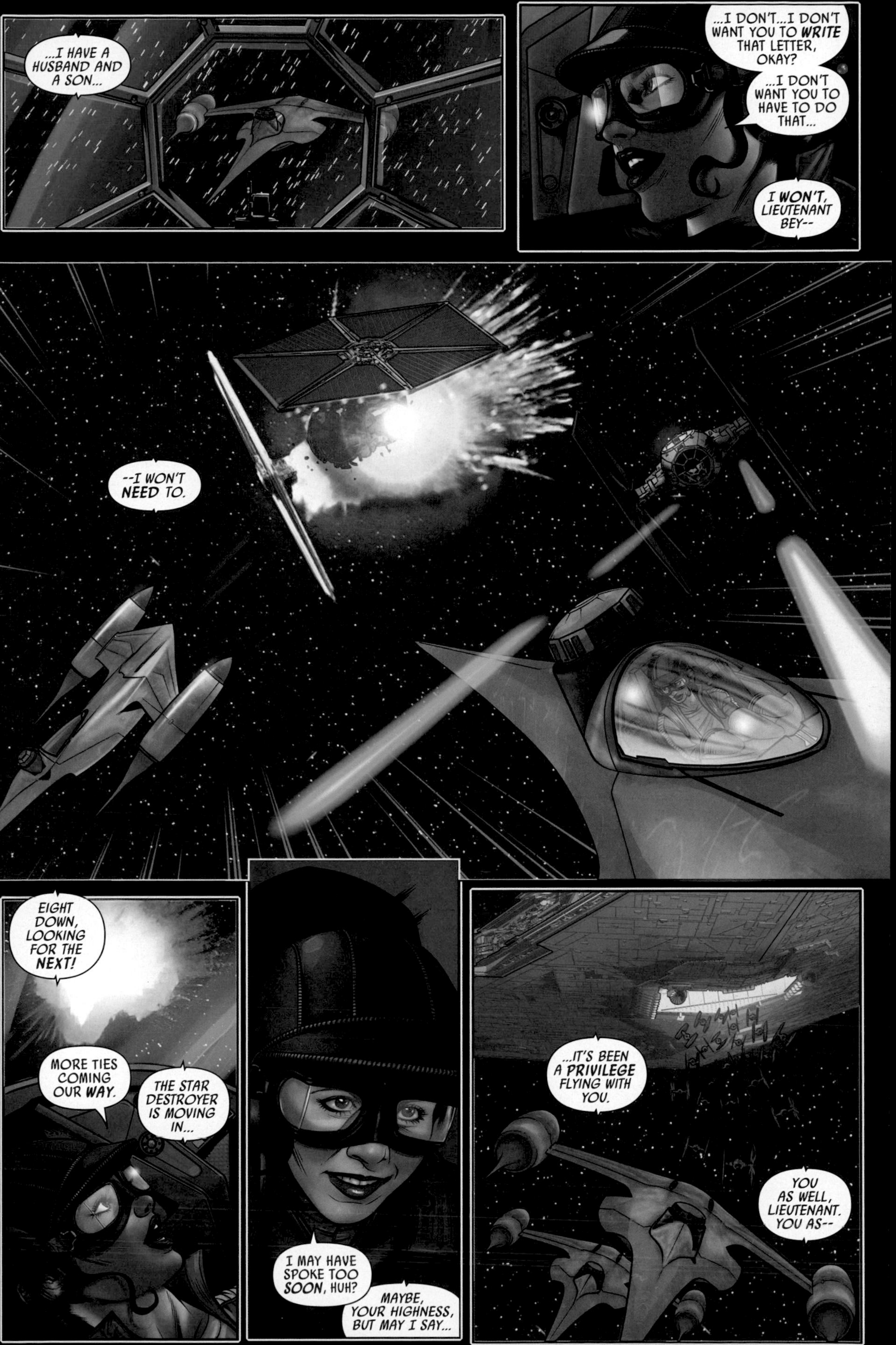
...I HAVE A HUSBAND AND A SON...
...I DON'T...I DON'T WANT YOU TO WRITE THAT LETTER, OKAY?
...I DON'T WANT YOU TO HAVE TO DO THAT...
I WON'T, LIEUTENANT BEY--
--I WON'T NEED TO.
EIGHT DOWN, LOOKING FOR THE NEXT!
MORE TIES COMING OUR WAY.
THE STAR DESTROYER IS MOVING IN...
I MAY HAVE SPOKE TOO SOON, HUH?
MAYBE, YOUR HIGHNESS, BUT MAY I SAY...
...IT'S BEEN A PRIVILEGE FLYING WITH YOU.
YOU AS WELL, LIEUTENANT. YOU AS--

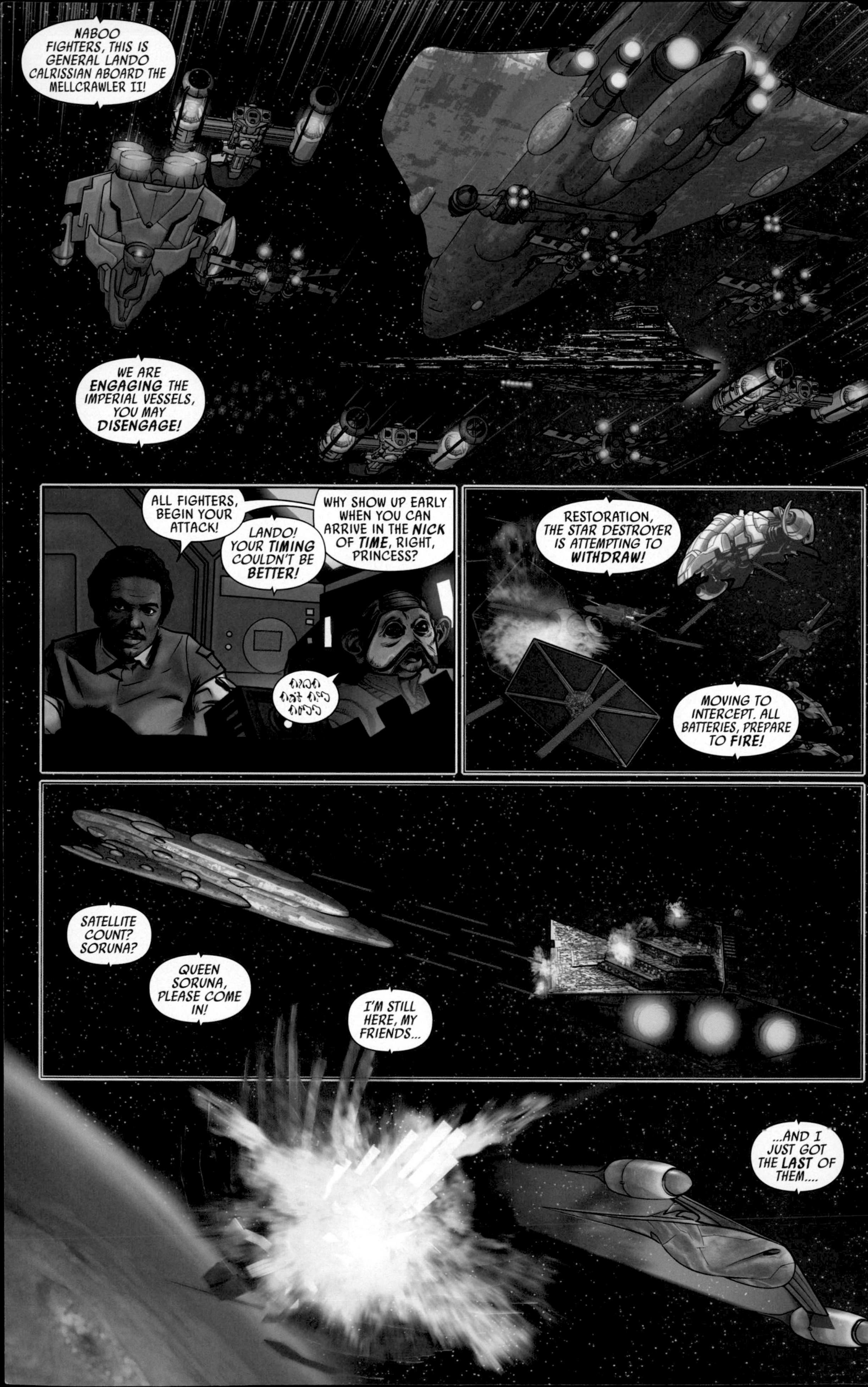
NABOO FIGHTERS, THIS IS GENERAL LANDO CALRISSIAN ABOARD THE MELLCRAWLER II!
WE ARE ENGAGING THE IMPERIAL VESSELS, YOU MAY DISENGAGE!
ALL FIGHTERS, BEGIN YOUR ATTACK!
LANDO! YOUR TIMING COULDN'T BE BETTER!
WHY SHOW UP EARLY WHEN YOU CAN ARRIVE IN THE NICK OF TIME, RIGHT, PRINCESS?
RESTORATION, THE STAR DESTROYER IS ATTEMPTING TO WITHDRAW!
MOVING TO INTERCEPT. ALL BATTERIES, PREPARE TO FIRE!
SATELLITE COUNT? SORUNA?
QUEEN SORUNA, PLEASE COME IN!
I'M STILL HERE, MY FRIENDS...
...AND I JUST GOT THE LAST OF THEM....

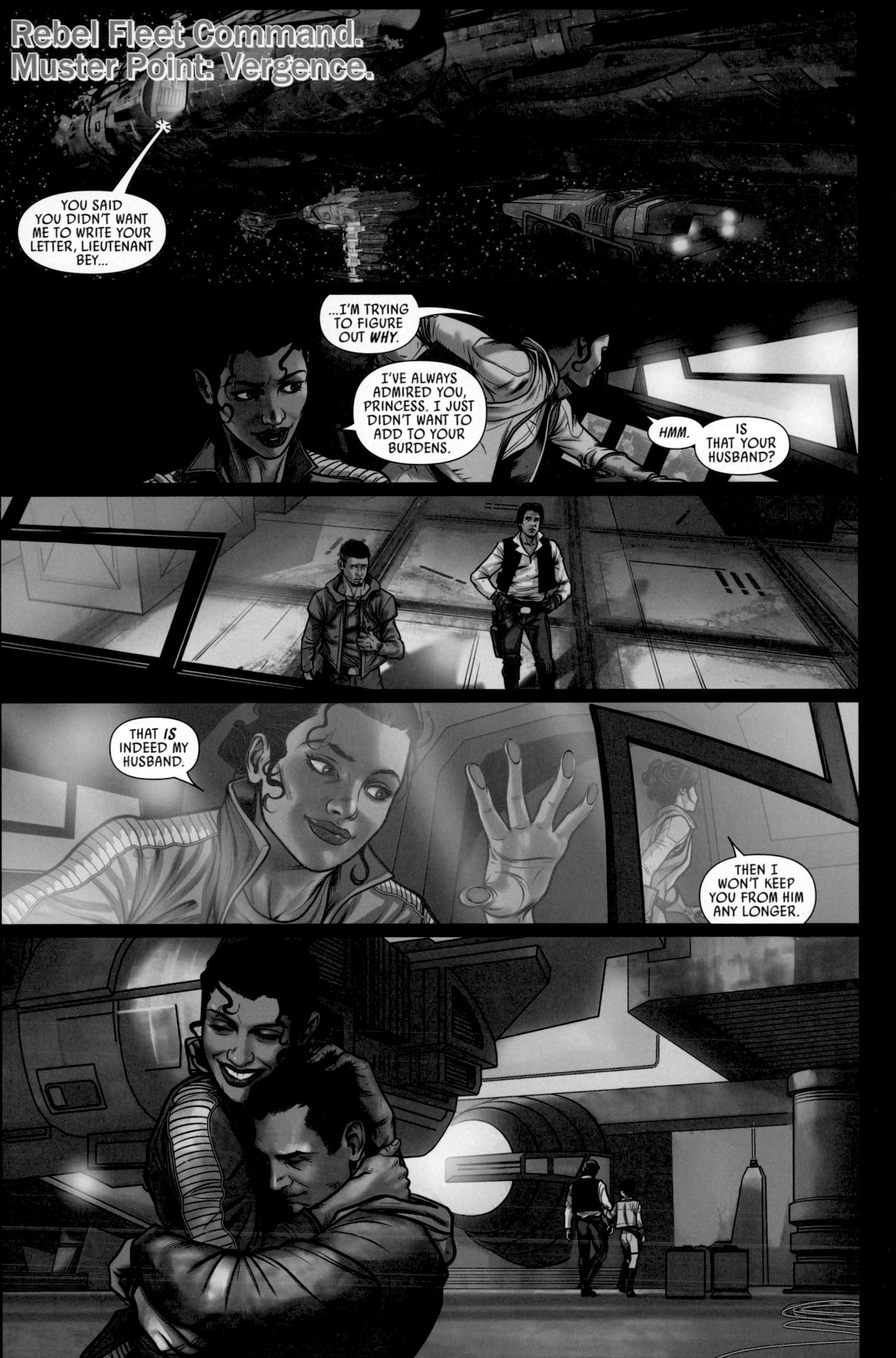
Rebel Fleet Command.
Muster Point: Vergence.
YOU SAID YOU DIDN'T WANT ME TO WRITE YOUR LETTER, LIEUTENANT BEY...
...I'M TRYING TO FIGURE OUT WHY.
I'VE ALWAYS ADMIRED YOU, PRINCESS. I JUST DIDN'T WANT TO ADD TO YOUR BURDENS.
HMM.
IS THAT YOUR HUSBAND?
THAT IS INDEED MY HUSBAND.
THEN I WON'T KEEP YOU FROM HIM ANY LONGER.

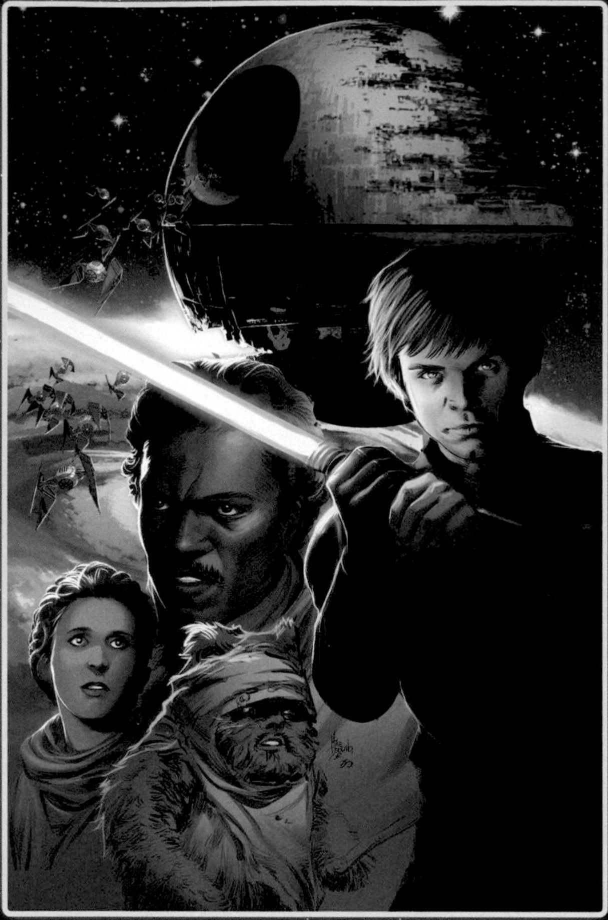

STAR WARS:SHATTERED EMPIRE **#3 Variant**
by MIKE DEODATO

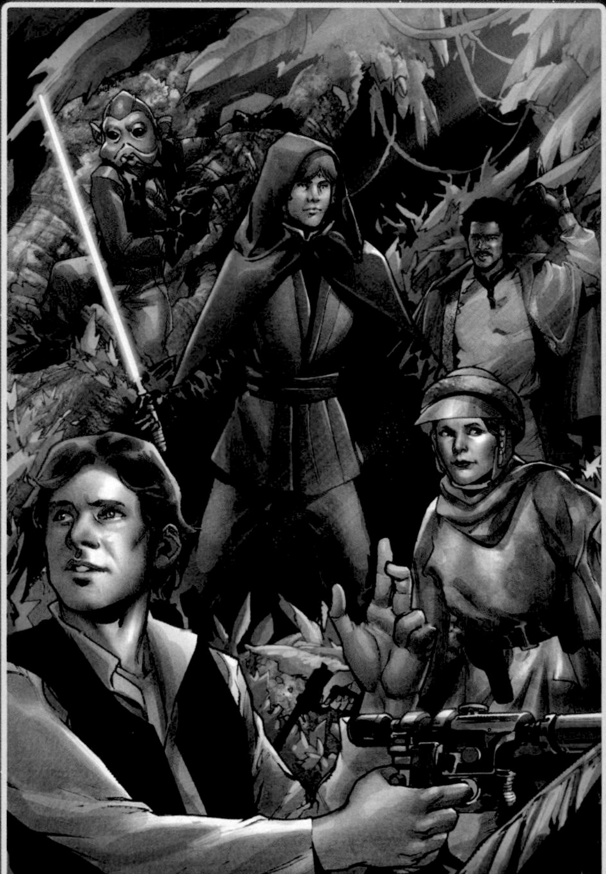

STAR WARS: SHATTERED EMPIRE **#4 Variant**
by SARAH PICHELLI & PAUL MOUNTS

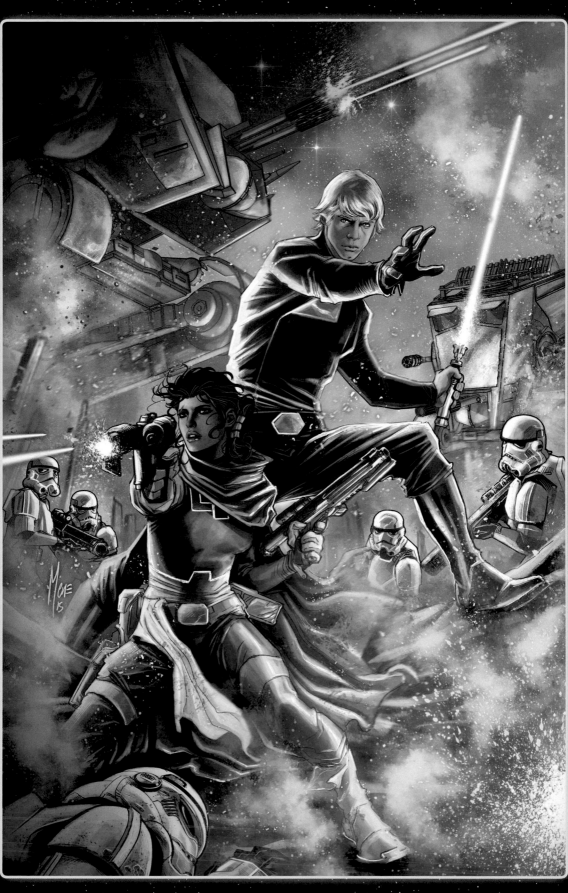

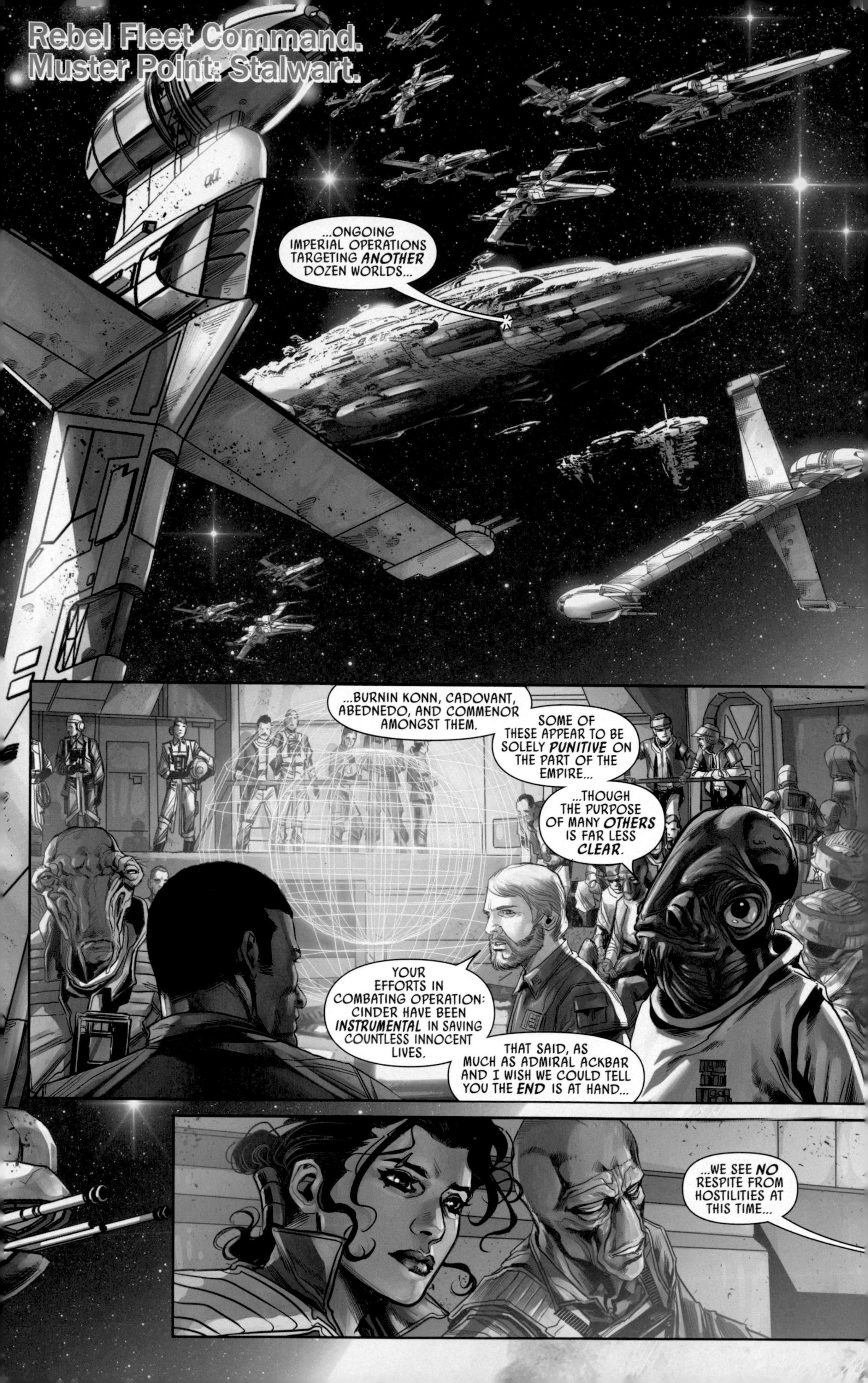
Rebel Fleet Command.
Muster Point: Stalwart.
...ONGOING IMPERIAL OPERATIONS TARGETING ANOTHER DOZEN WORLDS...
...BURNIN KONN, CADOVANT, ABEDNEDO, AND COMMENOR AMONGST THEM.
SOME OF THESE APPEAR TO BE SOLELY PUNITIVE ON THE PART OF THE EMPIRE...
...THOUGH THE PURPOSE OF MANY OTHERS IS FAR LESS CLEAR.
YOUR EFFORTS IN COMBATING OPERATION: CINDER HAVE BEEN INSTRUMENTAL IN SAVING COUNTLESS INNOCENT LIVES.
THAT SAID, AS MUCH AS ADMIRAL ACKBAR AND I WISH WE COULD TELL YOU THE END IS AT HAND...
...WE SEE NO RESPITE FROM HOSTILITIES AT THIS TIME...

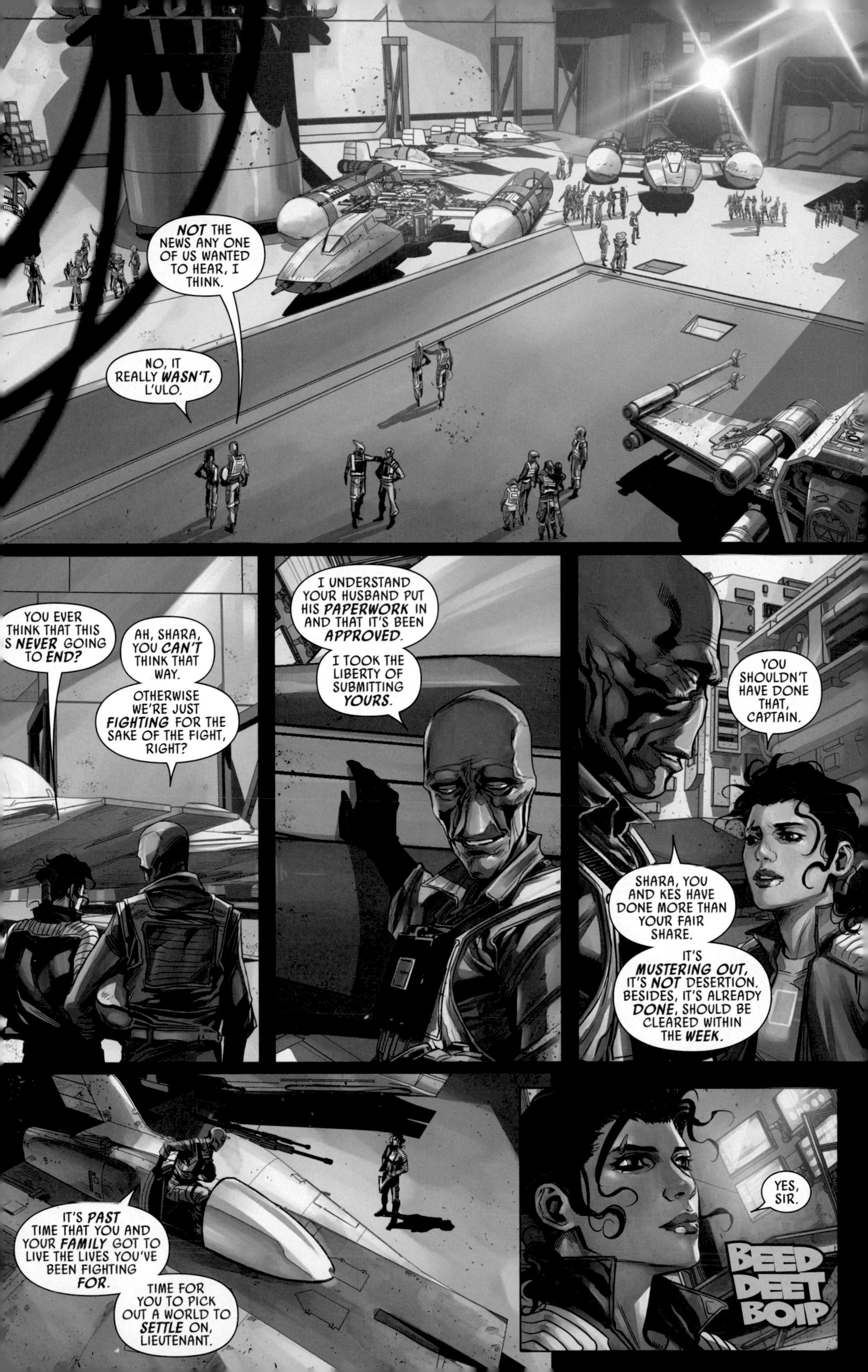
NOT THE NEWS ANY ONE OF US WANTED TO HEAR, I THINK.
NO, IT REALLY WASN'T, L'ULO.
YOU EVER THINK THAT THIS S NEVER GOING TO END?
AH, SHARA, YOU CAN'T THINK THAT WAY.
OTHERWISE WE'RE JUST FIGHTING FOR THE SAKE OF THE FIGHT, RIGHT?
I UNDERSTAND YOUR HUSBAND PUT HIS PAPERWORK IN AND THAT IT'S BEEN APPROVED.
I TOOK THE LIBERTY OF SUBMITTING YOURS.
YOU SHOULDN'T HAVE DONE THAT, CAPTAIN.
SHARA, YOU AND KES HAVE DONE MORE THAN YOUR FAIR SHARE.
IT'S MUSTERING OUT, IT'S NOT DESERTION. BESIDES, IT'S ALREADY DONE, SHOULD BE CLEARED WITHIN THE WEEK.
IT'S PAST TIME THAT YOU AND YOUR FAMILY GOT TO LIVE THE LIVES YOU'VE BEEN FIGHTING FOR.
TIME FOR YOU TO PICK OUT A WORLD TO SETTLE ON, LIEUTENANT.
YES, SIR.
BEED DEET BOIP

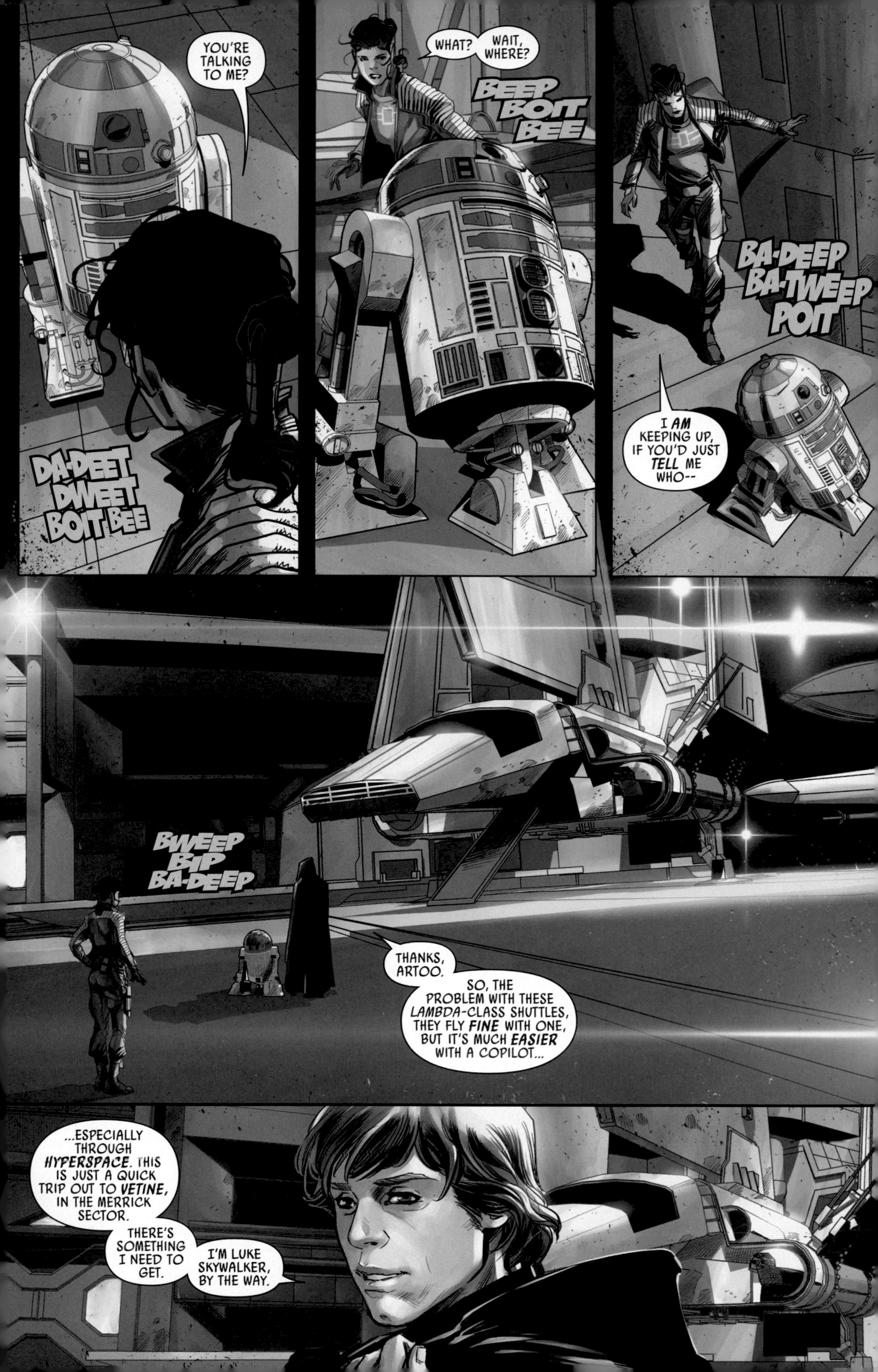
YOU'RE TALKING TO ME?
DA-DEET DWEET BOIT BEE
WHAT?
WAIT, WHERE?
BEEP BOIT BEE
BA-DEEP BA-TWEEP POIT
I AM KEEPING UP, IF YOU'D JUST TELL ME WHO--
BWEEP BIP BA-DEEP
THANKS, ARTOO.
SO, THE PROBLEM WITH THESE LAMBDA-CLASS SHUTTLES, THEY FLY FINE WITH ONE, BUT IT'S MUCH EASIER WITH A COPILOT...
...ESPECIALLY THROUGH HYPERSPACE. THIS IS JUST A QUICK TRIP OUT TO VETINE, IN THE MERRICK SECTOR.
THERE'S SOMETHING I NEED TO GET.
I'M LUKE SKYWALKER, BY THE WAY.

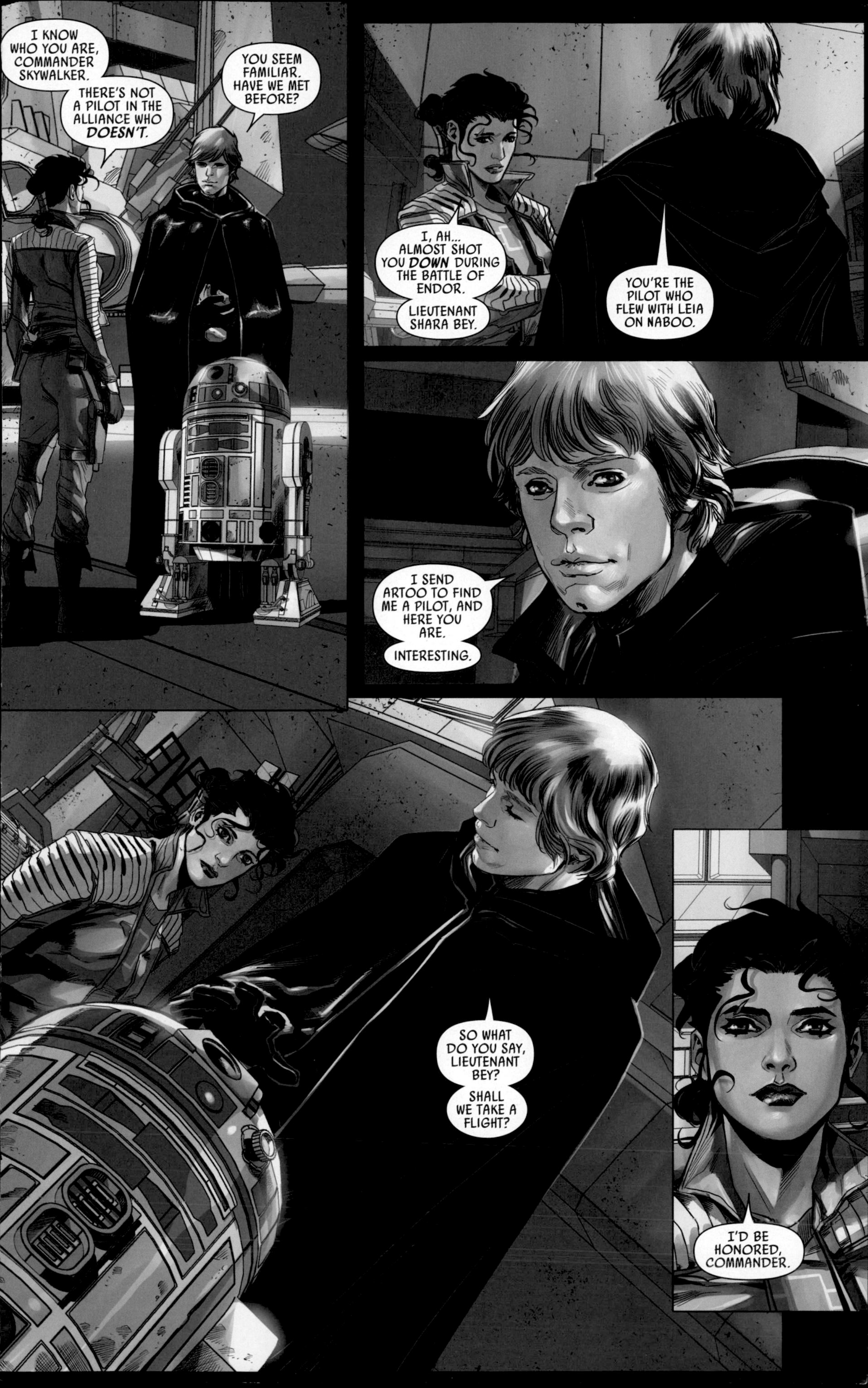
I KNOW WHO YOU ARE, COMMANDER SKYWALKER.
THERE'S NOT A PILOT IN THE ALLIANCE WHO *DOESN'T*.
YOU SEEM FAMILIAR. HAVE WE MET BEFORE?
I, AH... ALMOST SHOT YOU **DOWN** DURING THE BATTLE OF ENDOR.
LIEUTENANT SHARA BEY.
YOU'RE THE PILOT WHO FLEW WITH LEIA ON NABOO.
I SEND ARTOO TO FIND ME A PILOT, AND HERE YOU ARE.
INTERESTING.
SO WHAT DO YOU SAY, LIEUTENANT BEY?
SHALL WE TAKE A FLIGHT?
I'D BE HONORED, COMMANDER.

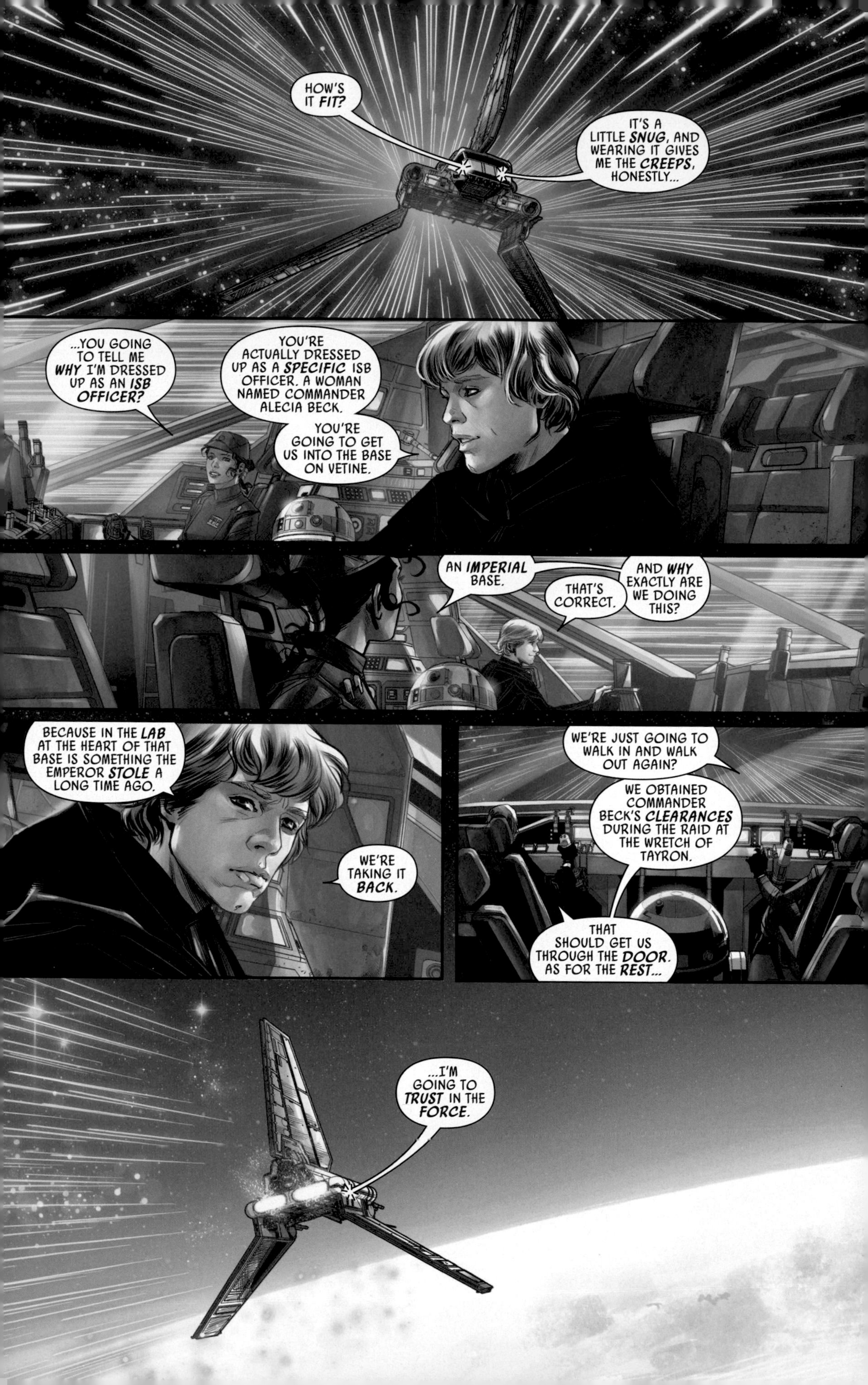
HOW'S IT FIT?
IT'S A LITTLE SNUG, AND WEARING IT GIVES ME THE CREEPS, HONESTLY...
...YOU GOING TO TELL ME WHY I'M DRESSED UP AS AN ISB OFFICER?
YOU'RE ACTUALLY DRESSED UP AS A SPECIFIC ISB OFFICER. A WOMAN NAMED COMMANDER ALECIA BECK.
YOU'RE GOING TO GET US INTO THE BASE ON VETINE.
AN IMPERIAL BASE.
THAT'S CORRECT.
AND WHY EXACTLY ARE WE DOING THIS?
BECAUSE IN THE LAB AT THE HEART OF THAT BASE IS SOMETHING THE EMPEROR STOLE A LONG TIME AGO.
WE'RE TAKING IT BACK.
WE'RE JUST GOING TO WALK IN AND WALK OUT AGAIN?
WE OBTAINED COMMANDER BECK'S CLEARANCES DURING THE RAID AT THE WRETCH OF TAYRON.
THAT SHOULD GET US THROUGH THE DOOR. AS FOR THE REST...
...I'M GOING TO TRUST IN THE FORCE.

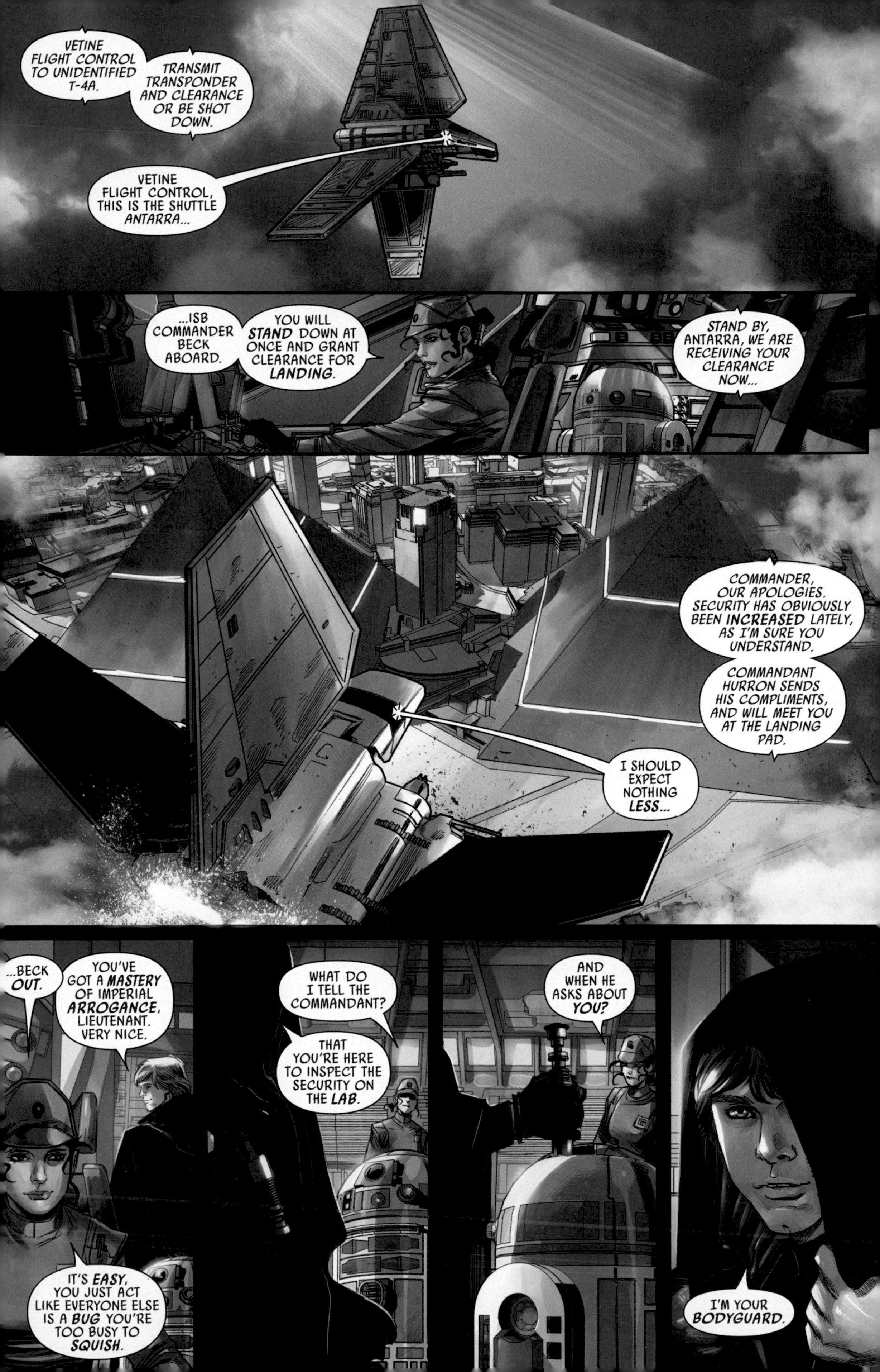
VETINE FLIGHT CONTROL TO UNIDENTIFIED T-4A.
TRANSMIT TRANSPONDER AND CLEARANCE OR BE SHOT DOWN.
VETINE FLIGHT CONTROL, THIS IS THE SHUTTLE ANTARRA...
...ISB COMMANDER BECK ABOARD.
YOU WILL STAND DOWN AT ONCE AND GRANT CLEARANCE FOR LANDING.
STAND BY, ANTARRA, WE ARE RECEIVING YOUR CLEARANCE NOW...
COMMANDER, OUR APOLOGIES. SECURITY HAS OBVIOUSLY BEEN INCREASED LATELY, AS I'M SURE YOU UNDERSTAND.
COMMANDANT HURRON SENDS HIS COMPLIMENTS, AND WILL MEET YOU AT THE LANDING PAD.
I SHOULD EXPECT NOTHING LESS...
...BECK OUT.
YOU'VE GOT A MASTERY OF IMPERIAL ARROGANCE, LIEUTENANT. VERY NICE.
IT'S EASY, YOU JUST ACT LIKE EVERYONE ELSE IS A BUG YOU'RE TOO BUSY TO SQUISH.
WHAT DO I TELL THE COMMANDANT?
THAT YOU'RE HERE TO INSPECT THE SECURITY ON THE LAB.
AND WHEN HE ASKS ABOUT YOU?
I'M YOUR BODYGUARD.

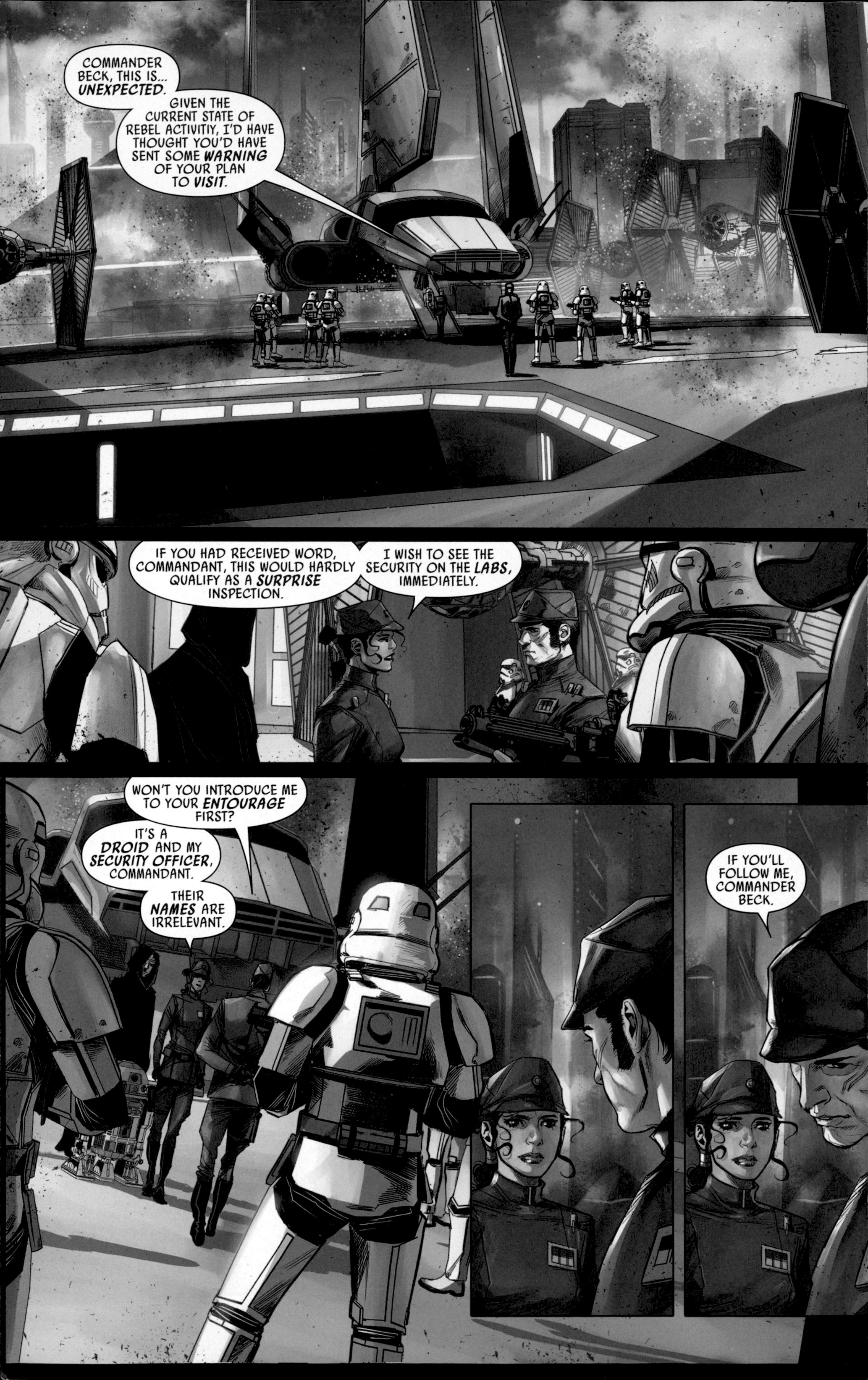
COMMANDER BECK, THIS IS... UNEXPECTED.
GIVEN THE CURRENT STATE OF REBEL ACTIVITIY, I'D HAVE THOUGHT YOU'D HAVE SENT SOME WARNING OF YOUR PLAN TO VISIT.
IF YOU HAD RECEIVED WORD, COMMANDANT, THIS WOULD HARDLY QUALIFY AS A SURPRISE INSPECTION.
I WISH TO SEE THE SECURITY ON THE LABS, IMMEDIATELY.
WON'T YOU INTRODUCE ME TO YOUR ENTOURAGE FIRST?
IT'S A DROID AND MY SECURITY OFFICER, COMMANDANT.
THEIR NAMES ARE IRRELEVANT.
IF YOU'LL FOLLOW ME, COMMANDER BECK.

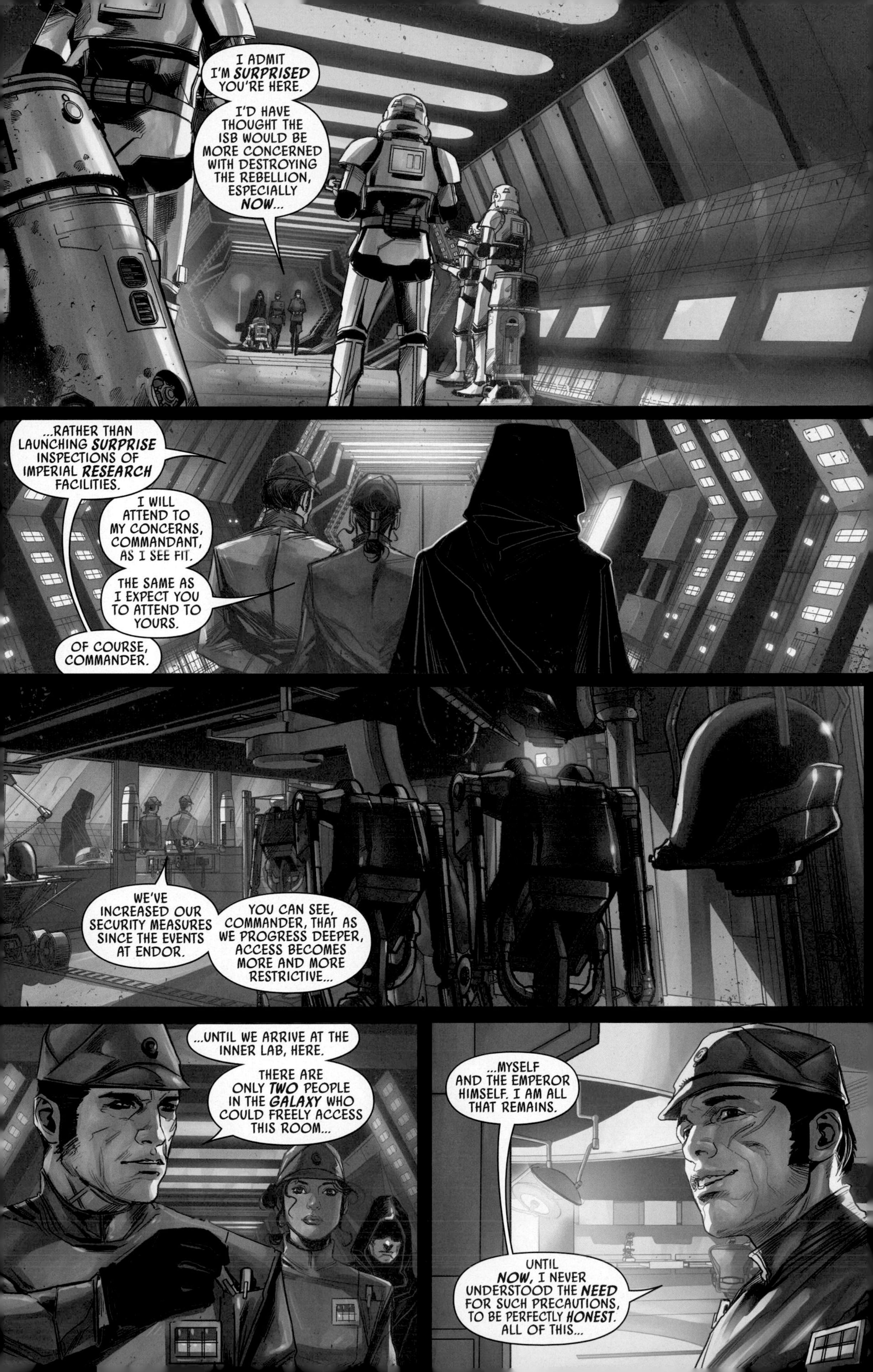
I ADMIT I'M SURPRISED YOU'RE HERE.
I'D HAVE THOUGHT THE ISB WOULD BE MORE CONCERNED WITH DESTROYING THE REBELLION, ESPECIALLY NOW...
...RATHER THAN LAUNCHING SURPRISE INSPECTIONS OF IMPERIAL RESEARCH FACILITIES.
I WILL ATTEND TO MY CONCERNS, COMMANDANT, AS I SEE FIT.
THE SAME AS I EXPECT YOU TO ATTEND TO YOURS.
OF COURSE, COMMANDER.
WE'VE INCREASED OUR SECURITY MEASURES SINCE THE EVENTS AT ENDOR.
YOU CAN SEE, COMMANDER, THAT AS WE PROGRESS DEEPER, ACCESS BECOMES MORE AND MORE RESTRICTIVE...
...UNTIL WE ARRIVE AT THE INNER LAB, HERE.
THERE ARE ONLY TWO PEOPLE IN THE GALAXY WHO COULD FREELY ACCESS THIS ROOM...
...MYSELF AND THE EMPEROR HIMSELF. I AM ALL THAT REMAINS.
UNTIL NOW, I NEVER UNDERSTOOD THE NEED FOR SUCH PRECAUTIONS, TO BE PERFECTLY HONEST. ALL OF THIS...

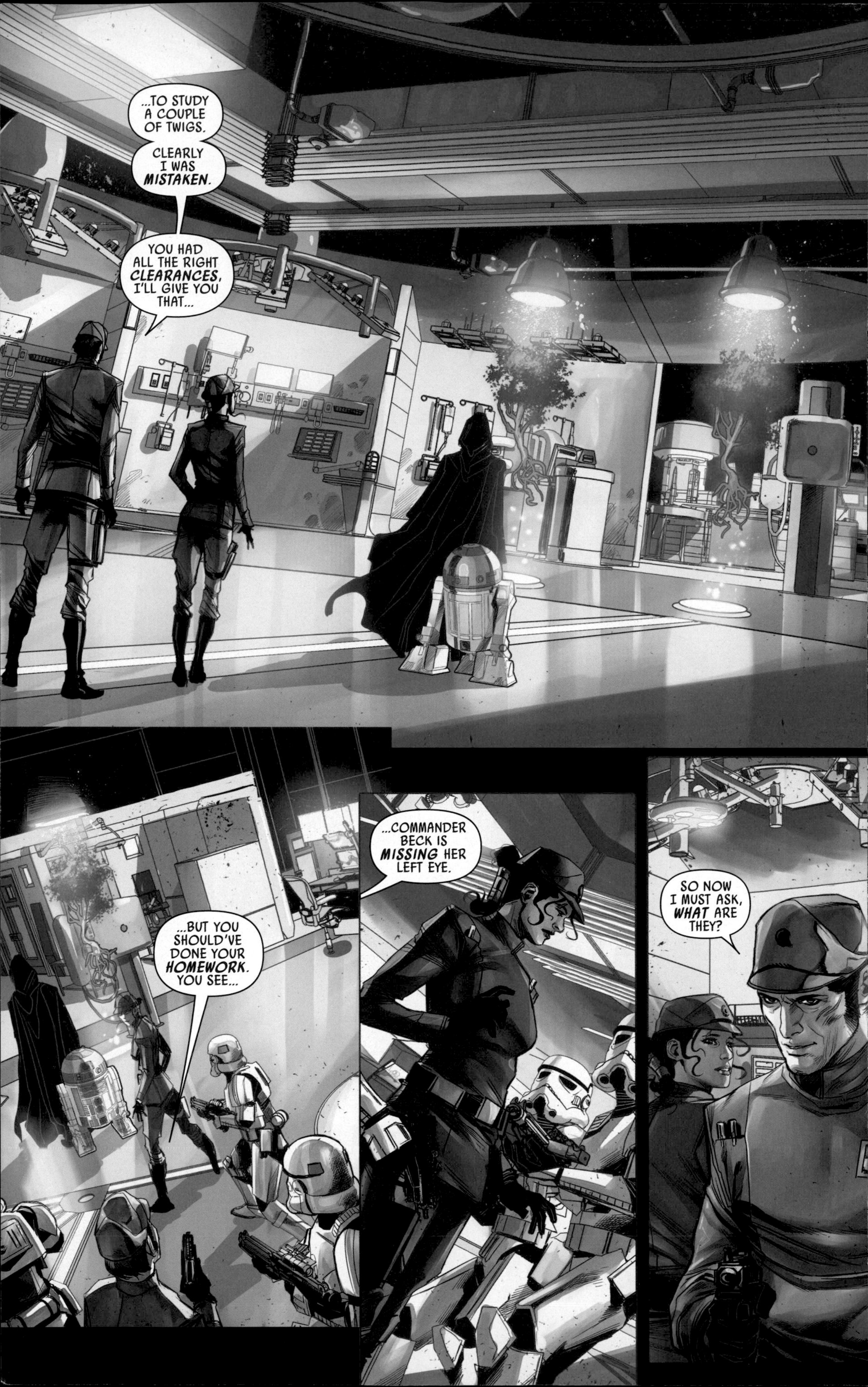
...TO STUDY A COUPLE OF TWIGS.
CLEARLY I WAS MISTAKEN.
YOU HAD ALL THE RIGHT CLEARANCES, I'LL GIVE YOU THAT...
...BUT YOU SHOULD'VE DONE YOUR HOMEWORK. YOU SEE...
...COMMANDER BECK IS MISSING HER LEFT EYE.
SO NOW I MUST ASK, WHAT ARE THEY?

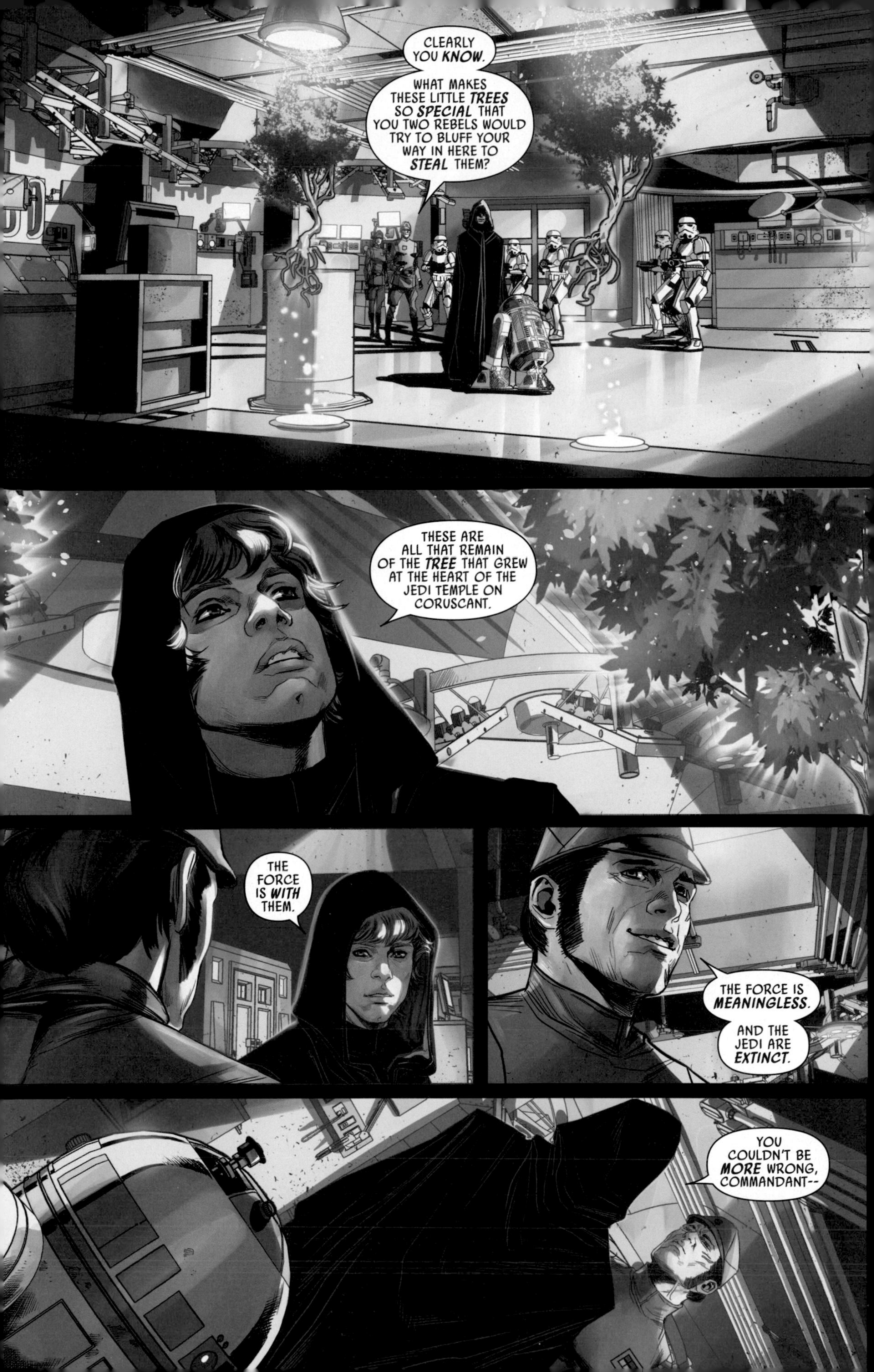

CLEARLY YOU **KNOW**.
WHAT MAKES THESE LITTLE **TREES** SO **SPECIAL** THAT YOU TWO REBELS WOULD TRY TO BLUFF YOUR WAY IN HERE TO **STEAL** THEM?
THESE ARE ALL THAT REMAIN OF THE **TREE** THAT GREW AT THE HEART OF THE JEDI TEMPLE ON CORUSCANT.
THE FORCE IS **WITH** THEM.
THE FORCE IS **MEANINGLESS**.
AND THE JEDI ARE **EXTINCT**.
YOU COULDN'T BE **MORE** WRONG, COMMANDANT--

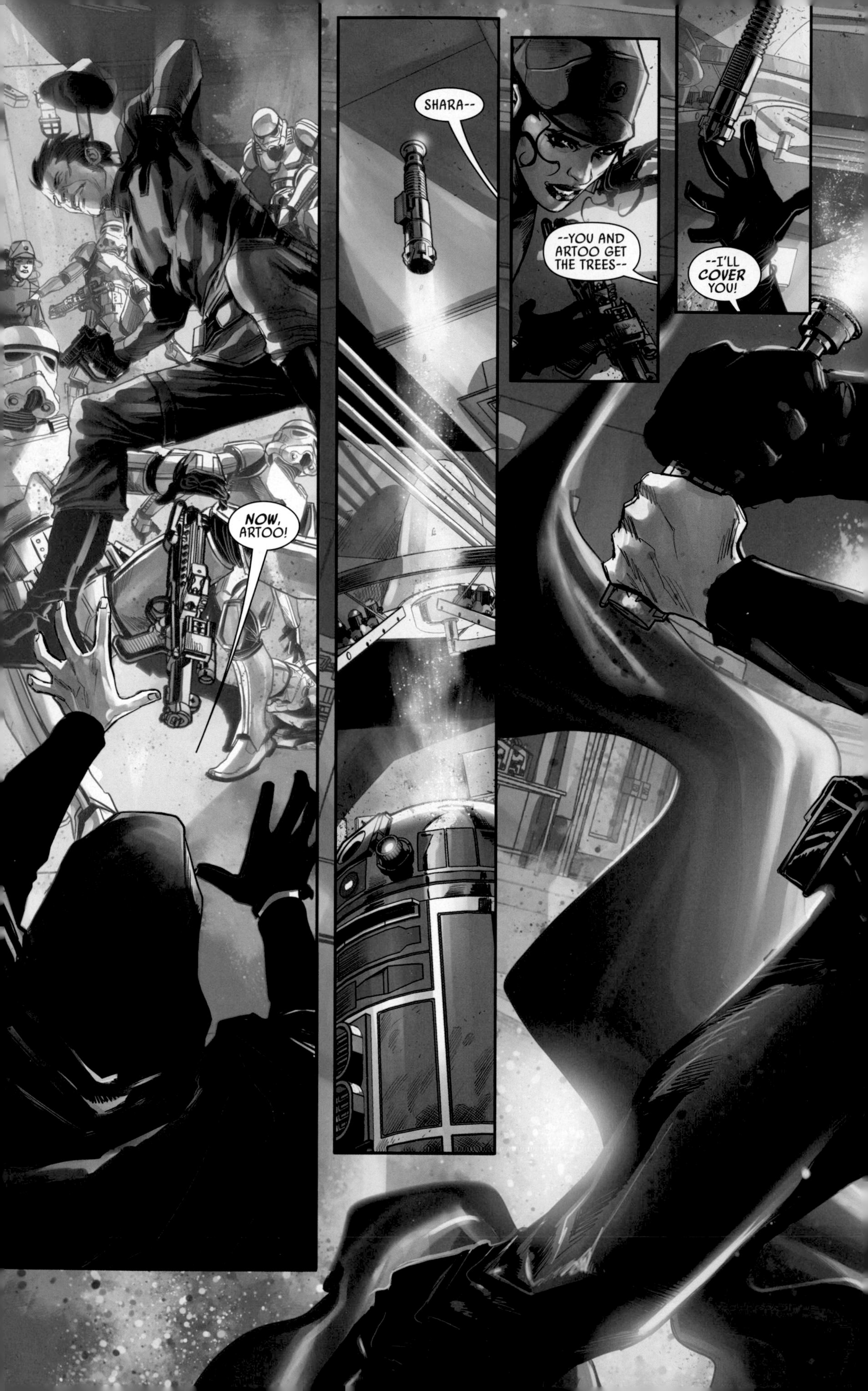
NOW, ARTOO!
SHARA--
--YOU AND ARTOO GET THE TREES--
--I'LL COVER YOU!

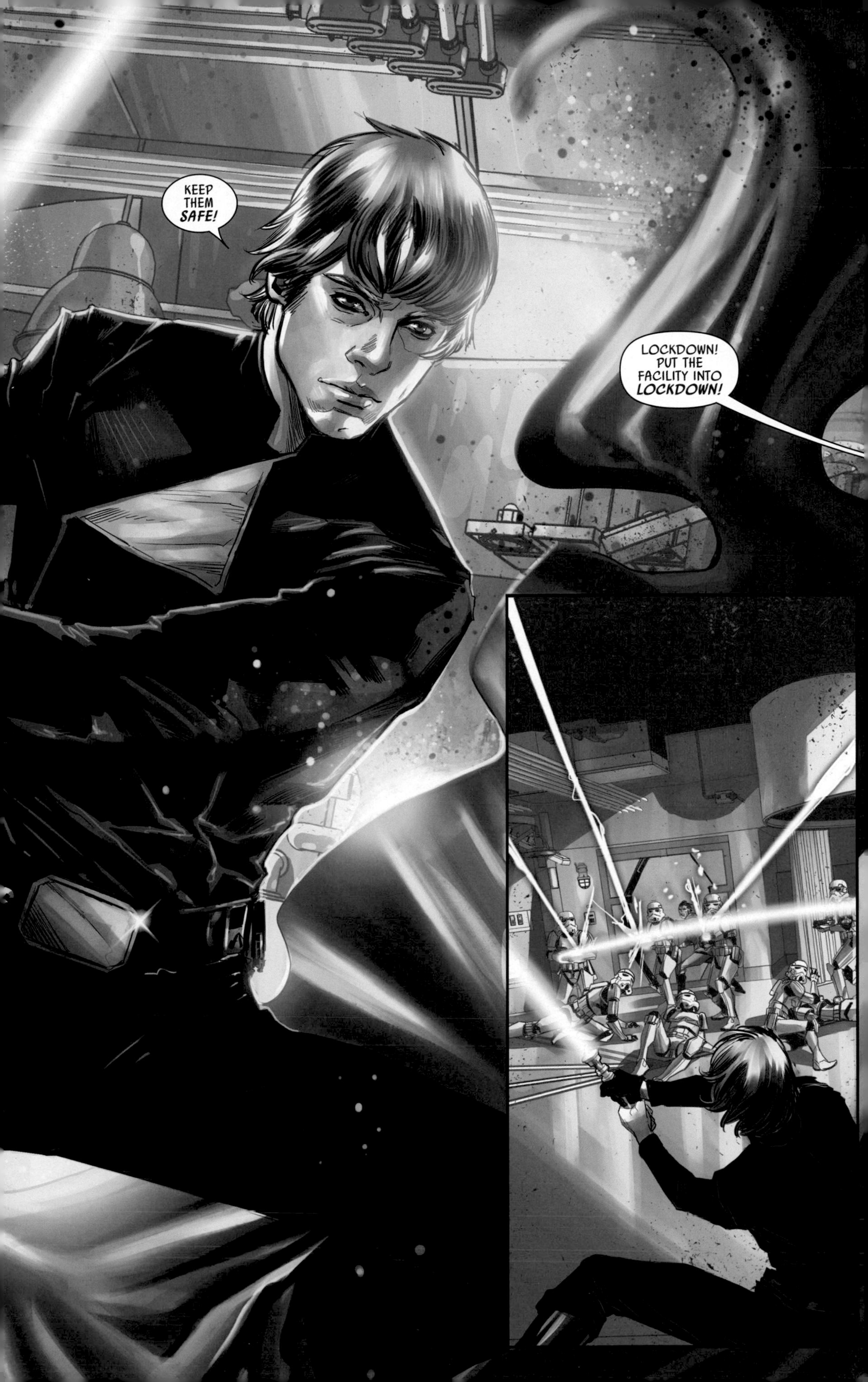
KEEP THEM SAFE!
LOCKDOWN! PUT THE FACILITY INTO LOCKDOWN!

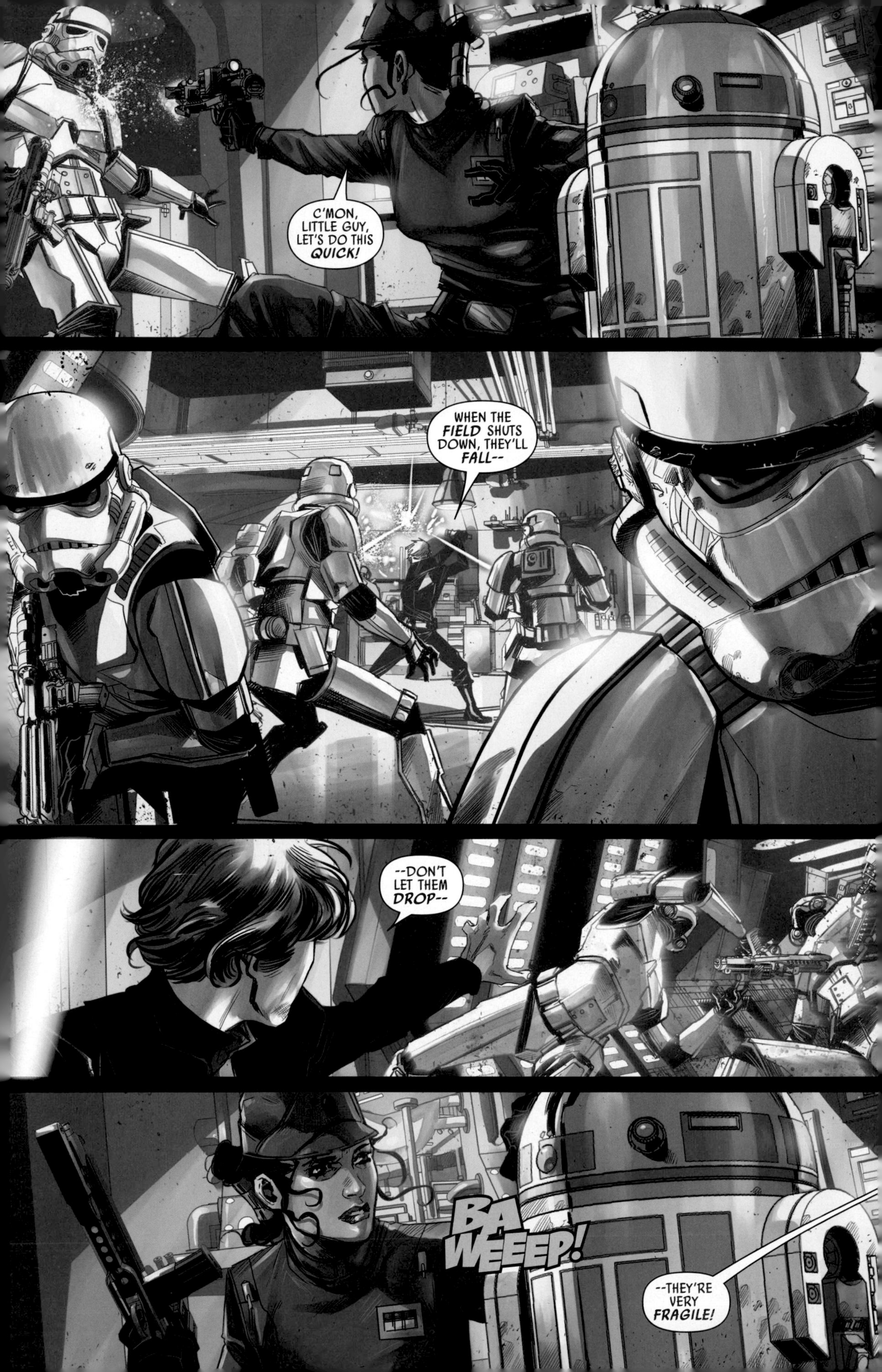
C'MON, LITTLE GUY, LET'S DO THIS QUICK!
WHEN THE FIELD SHUTS DOWN, THEY'LL FALL--
--DON'T LET THEM DROP--
BA WEEEP!
--THEY'RE VERY FRAGILE!

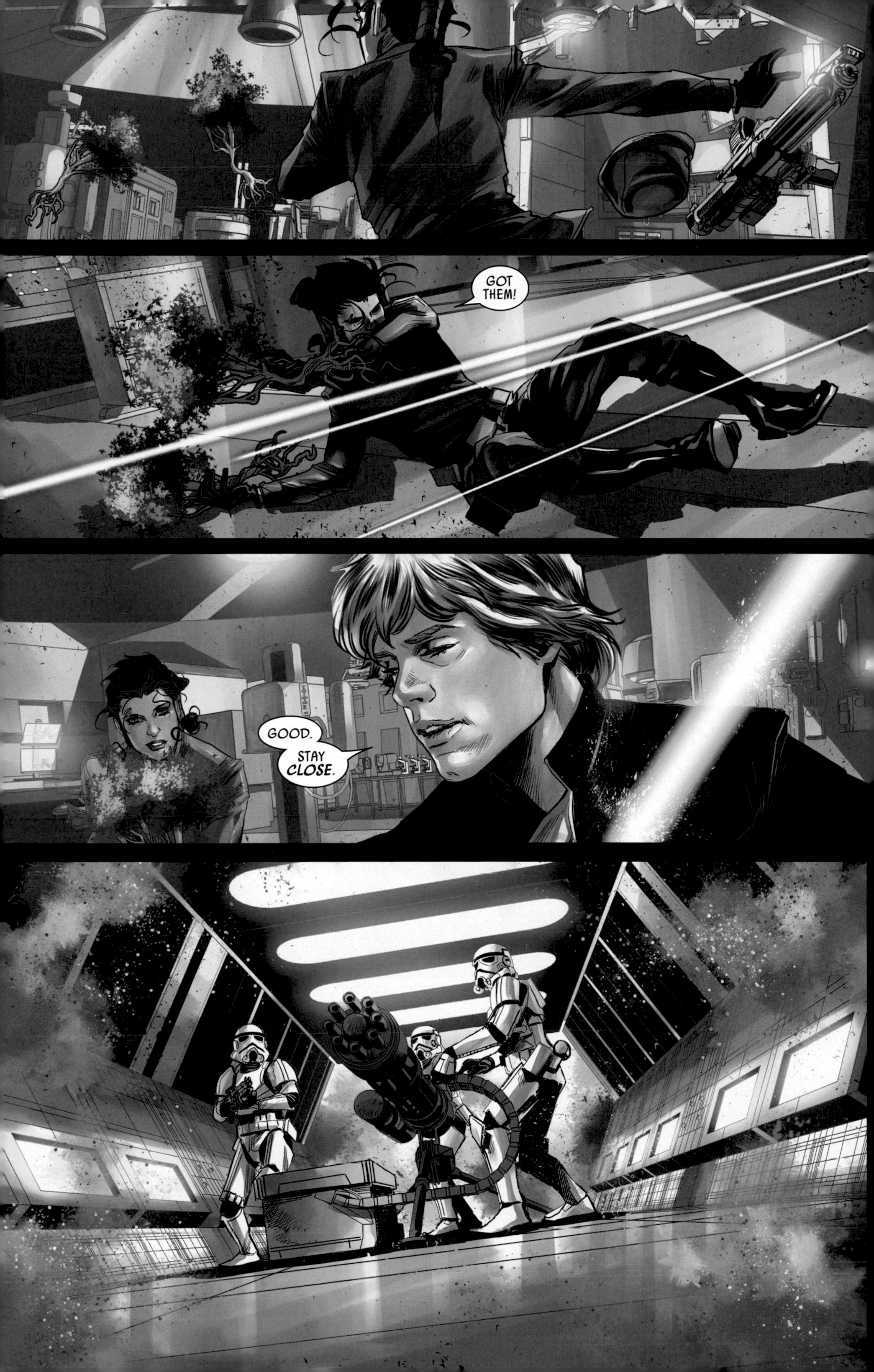

GOT THEM!
GOOD. STAY CLOSE.

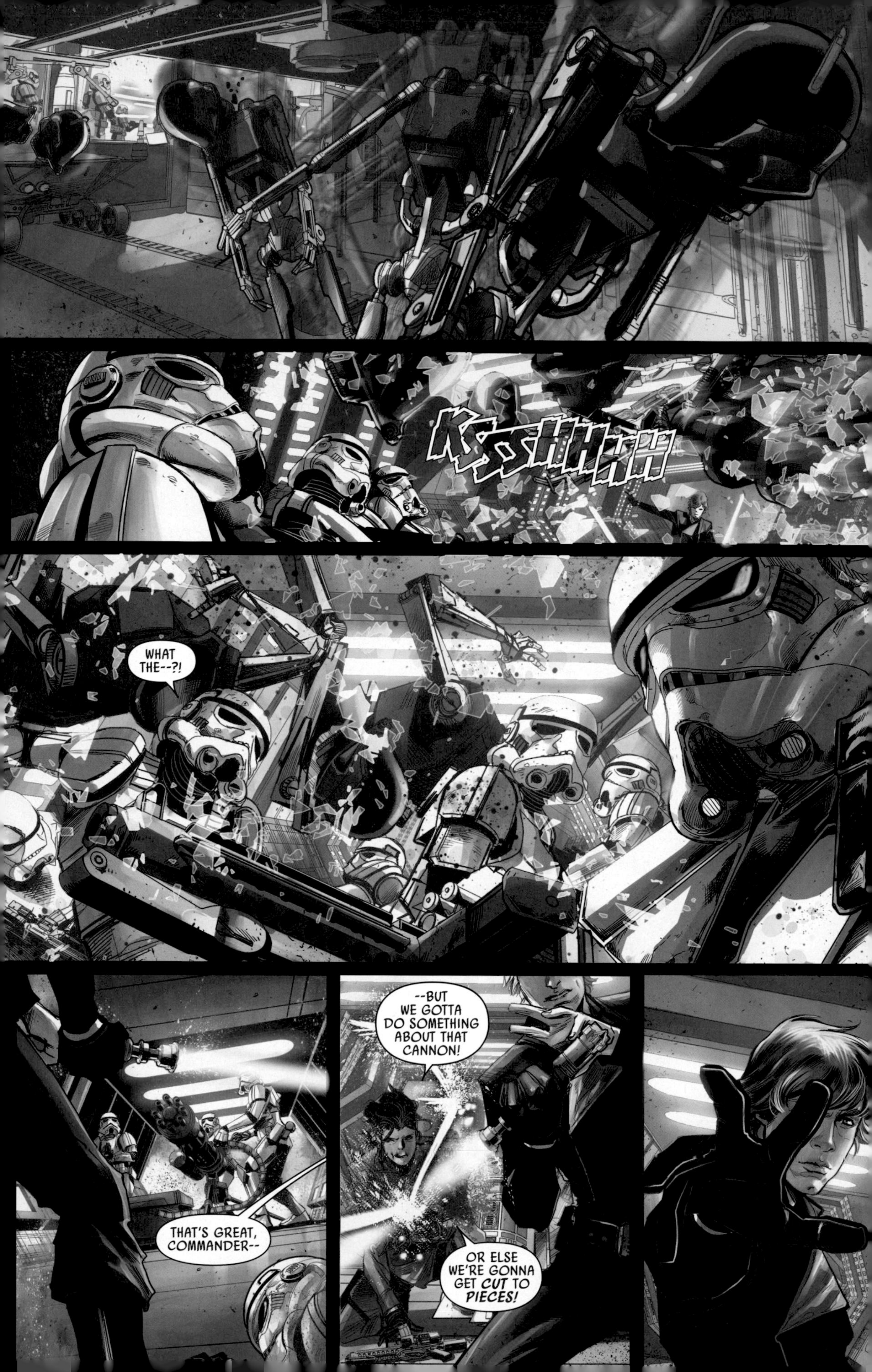
KSSHHHH
WHAT THE--?!
THAT'S GREAT, COMMANDER--
--BUT WE GOTTA DO SOMETHING ABOUT THAT CANNON!
OR ELSE WE'RE GONNA GET CUT TO PIECES!

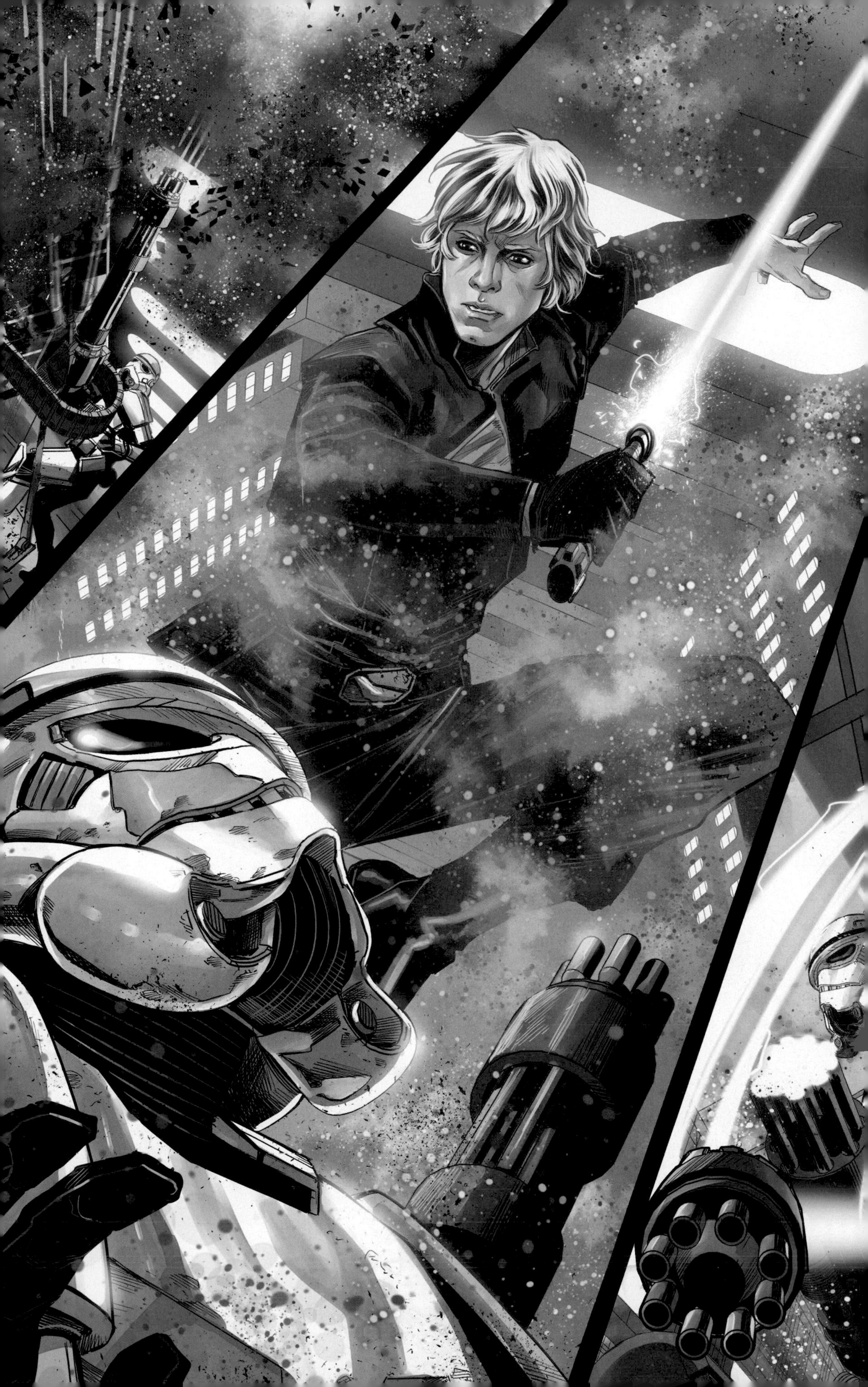

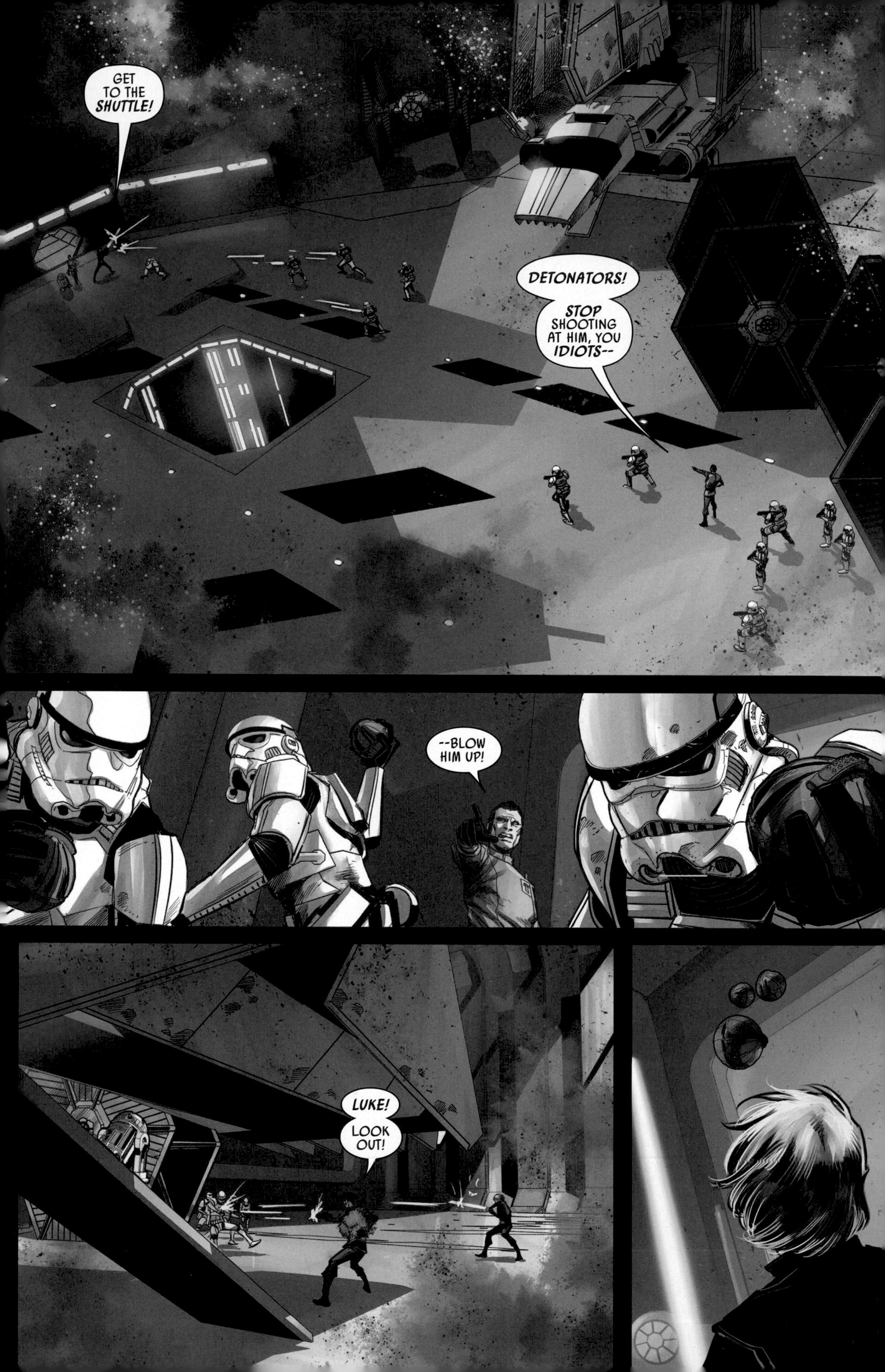
GET TO THE SHUTTLE!
DETONATORS!
STOP SHOOTING AT HIM, YOU IDIOTS--
--BLOW HIM UP!
LUKE!
LOOK OUT!

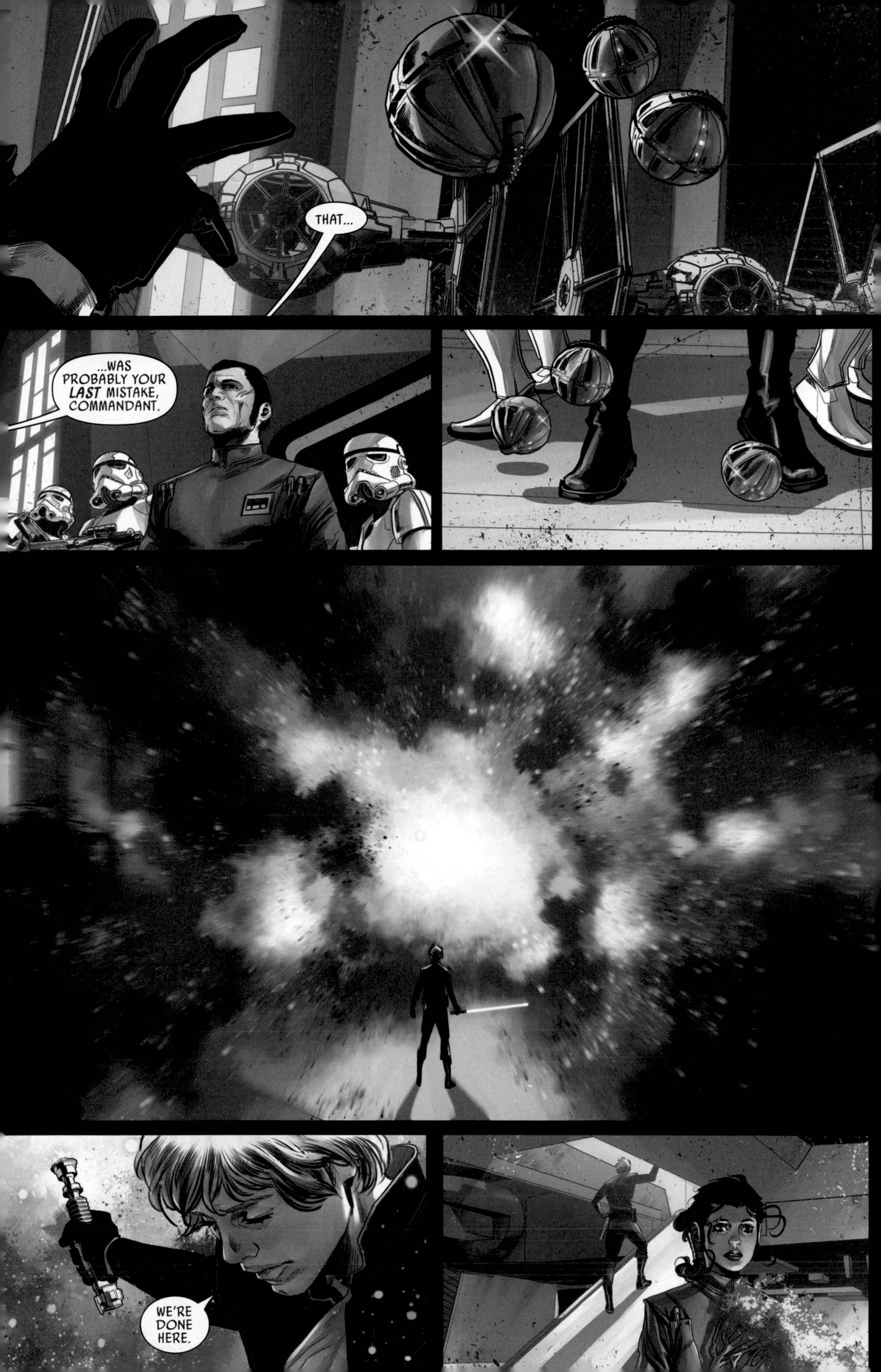
THAT...
...WAS PROBABLY YOUR LAST MISTAKE, COMMANDANT.
WE'RE DONE HERE.

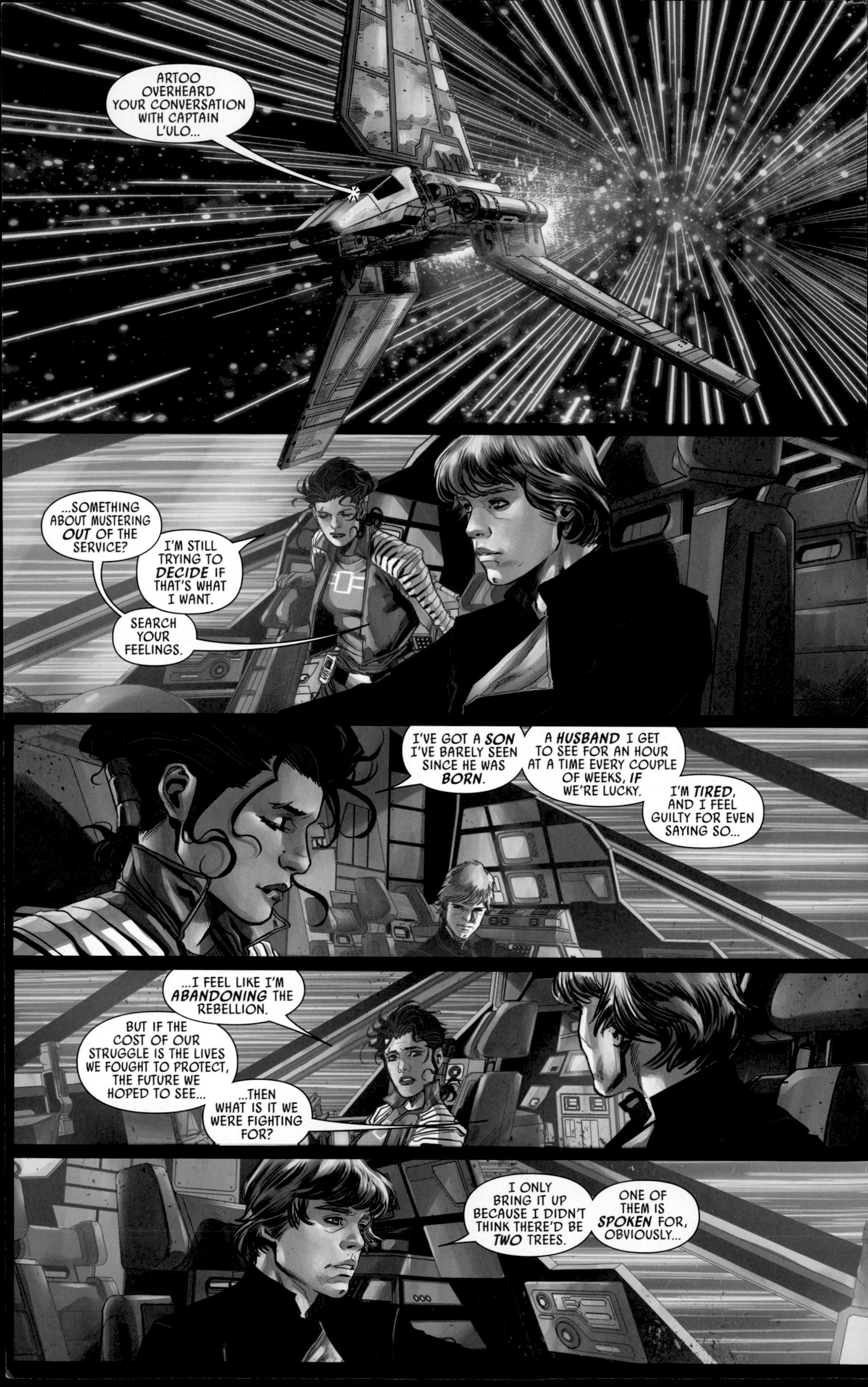
ARTOO OVERHEARD YOUR CONVERSATION WITH CAPTAIN L'ULO...
...SOMETHING ABOUT MUSTERING OUT OF THE SERVICE?
I'M STILL TRYING TO DECIDE IF THAT'S WHAT I WANT.
SEARCH YOUR FEELINGS.
I'VE GOT A SON I'VE BARELY SEEN SINCE HE WAS BORN.
A HUSBAND I GET TO SEE FOR AN HOUR AT A TIME EVERY COUPLE OF WEEKS, IF WE'RE LUCKY.
I'M TIRED, AND I FEEL GUILTY FOR EVEN SAYING SO...
...I FEEL LIKE I'M ABANDONING THE REBELLION.
BUT IF THE COST OF OUR STRUGGLE IS THE LIVES WE FOUGHT TO PROTECT, THE FUTURE WE HOPED TO SEE...
...THEN WHAT IS IT WE WERE FIGHTING FOR?
I ONLY BRING IT UP BECAUSE I DIDN'T THINK THERE'D BE TWO TREES.
ONE OF THEM IS SPOKEN FOR, OBVIOUSLY...

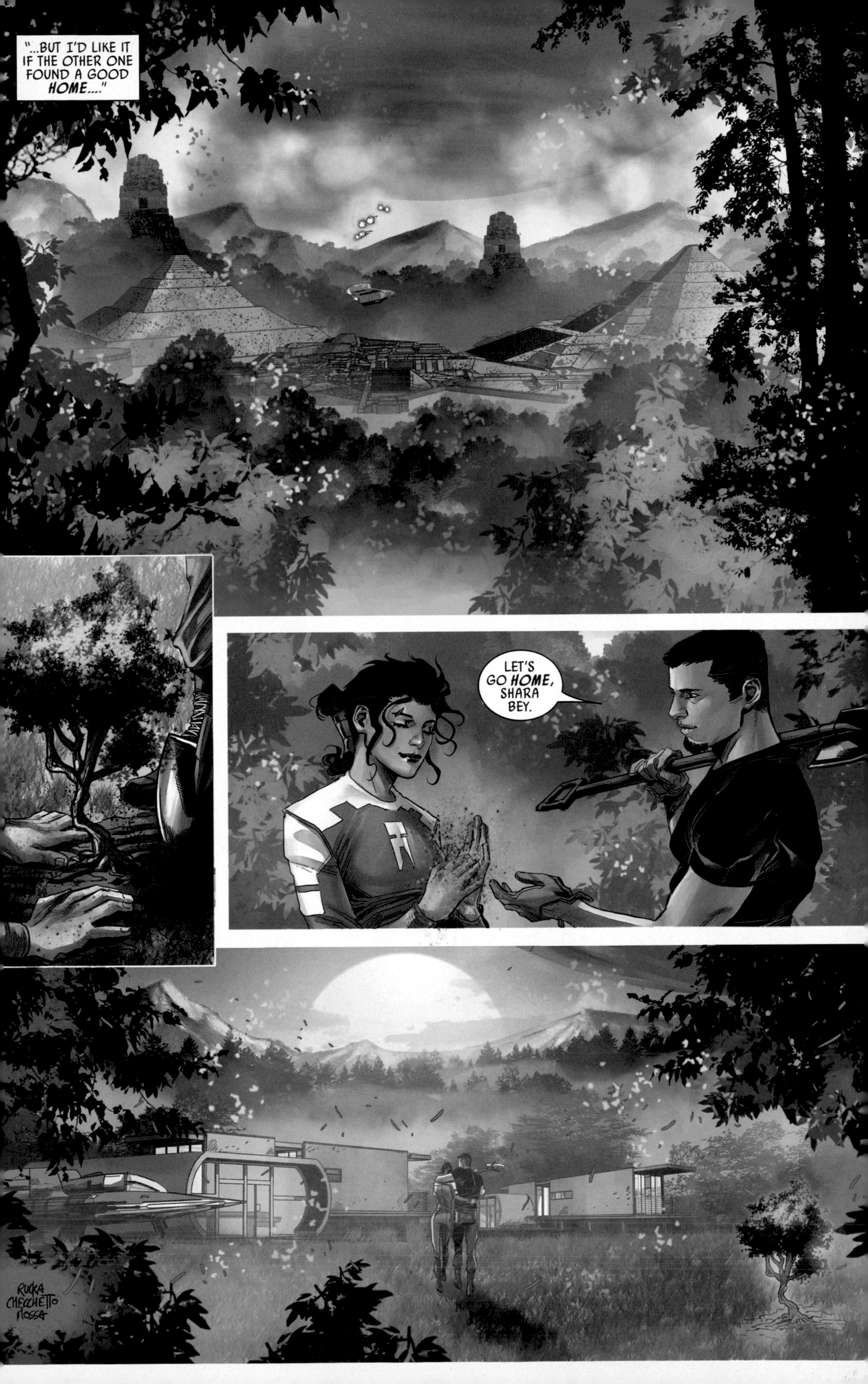
"...BUT I'D LIKE IT IF THE OTHER ONE FOUND A GOOD HOME...."
LET'S GO HOME, SHARA BEY.
RUCKA CHECCHETTO MOSSA

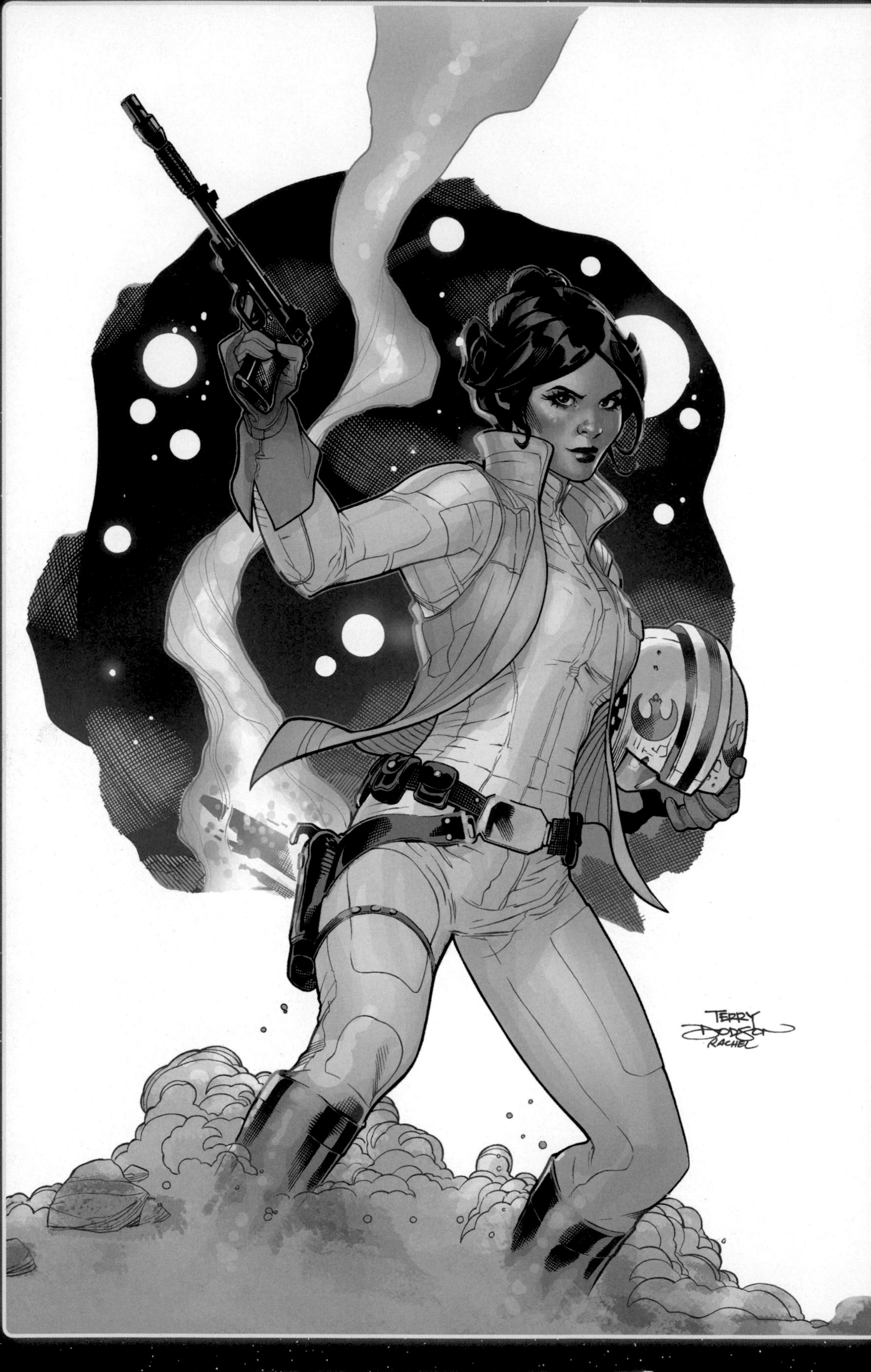
TERRY
DODSON
RACHEL

PRINCES LEIA #1

PRINCESS LEIA
Part I

It is a time of both hope and mourning within the Rebellion. While on a secret mission to deliver stolen plans for the Death Star to the Rebel Alliance, PRINCESS LEIA ORGANA was captured by the Galactic Empire and forced to witness the battle station's power as it destroyed her home planet of Alderaan.

With the help of a farmboy pilot and a fast-talking smuggler, Leia escaped her captors and completed her mission. Using the plans, the Alliance was able to destroy the Empire's ultimate weapon.

Having proven themselves a formidable enemy to the Empire, the rebels are in more danger now than ever, leaving them with little time to celebrate their triumph, or lament their loss....

MARK WAID
Writer

TERRY DODSON
Pencils

RACHEL DODSON
Inks

JORDIE BELLAIRE
Colorist

VC's JOE CARAMAGNA
Letterer

CHARLES BEACHAM
Assistant Editor

JORDAN D. WHITE
Editor

C.B. CEBULSKI & MIKE MARTS
Executive Editors

AXEL ALONSO
Editor In Chief

JOE QUESADA
Chief Creative Officer

DAN BUCKLEY
Publisher

For Lucasfilm:
Creative Director **MICHAEL SIGLAIN**
Senior Editor **JENNIFER HEDDLE**
Lucasfilm Story Group **RAYNE ROBERTS, PABLO HIDALGO, LELAND CHEE**

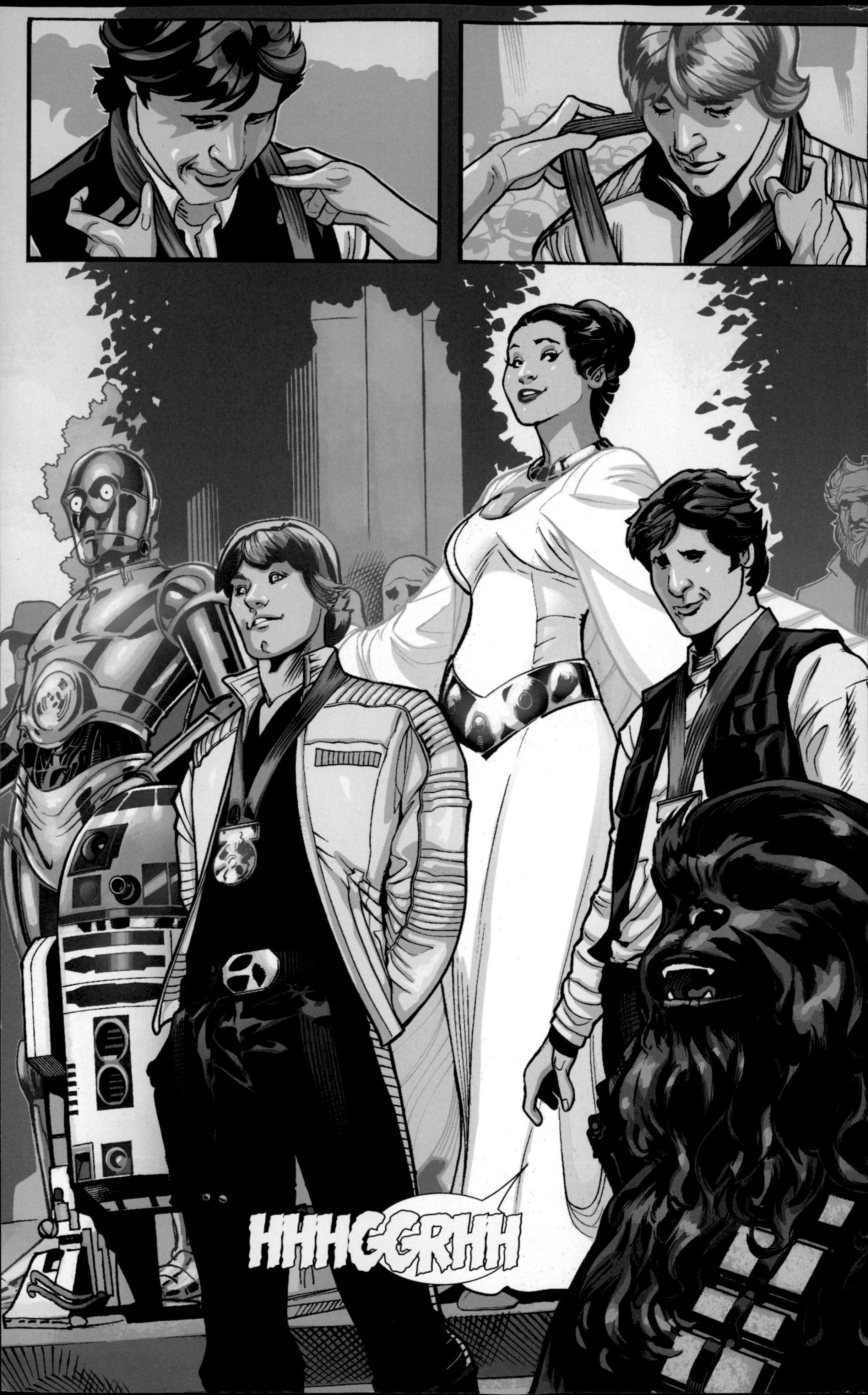
HHHGGRHH

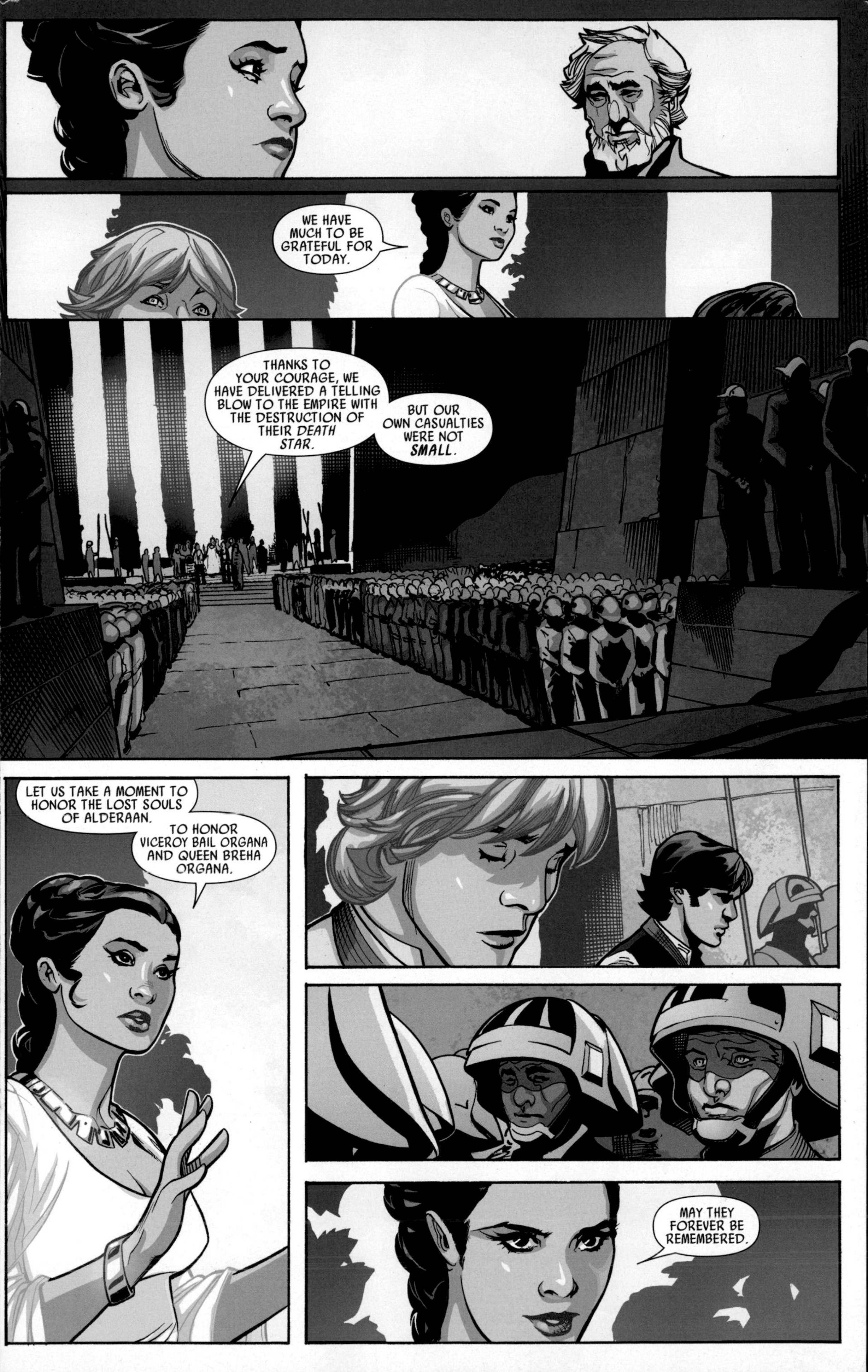
WE HAVE MUCH TO BE GRATEFUL FOR TODAY.
THANKS TO YOUR COURAGE, WE HAVE DELIVERED A TELLING BLOW TO THE EMPIRE WITH THE DESTRUCTION OF THEIR DEATH STAR.
BUT OUR OWN CASUALTIES WERE NOT SMALL.
LET US TAKE A MOMENT TO HONOR THE LOST SOULS OF ALDERAAN.
TO HONOR VICEROY BAIL ORGANA AND QUEEN BREHA ORGANA.
MAY THEY FOREVER BE REMEMBERED.

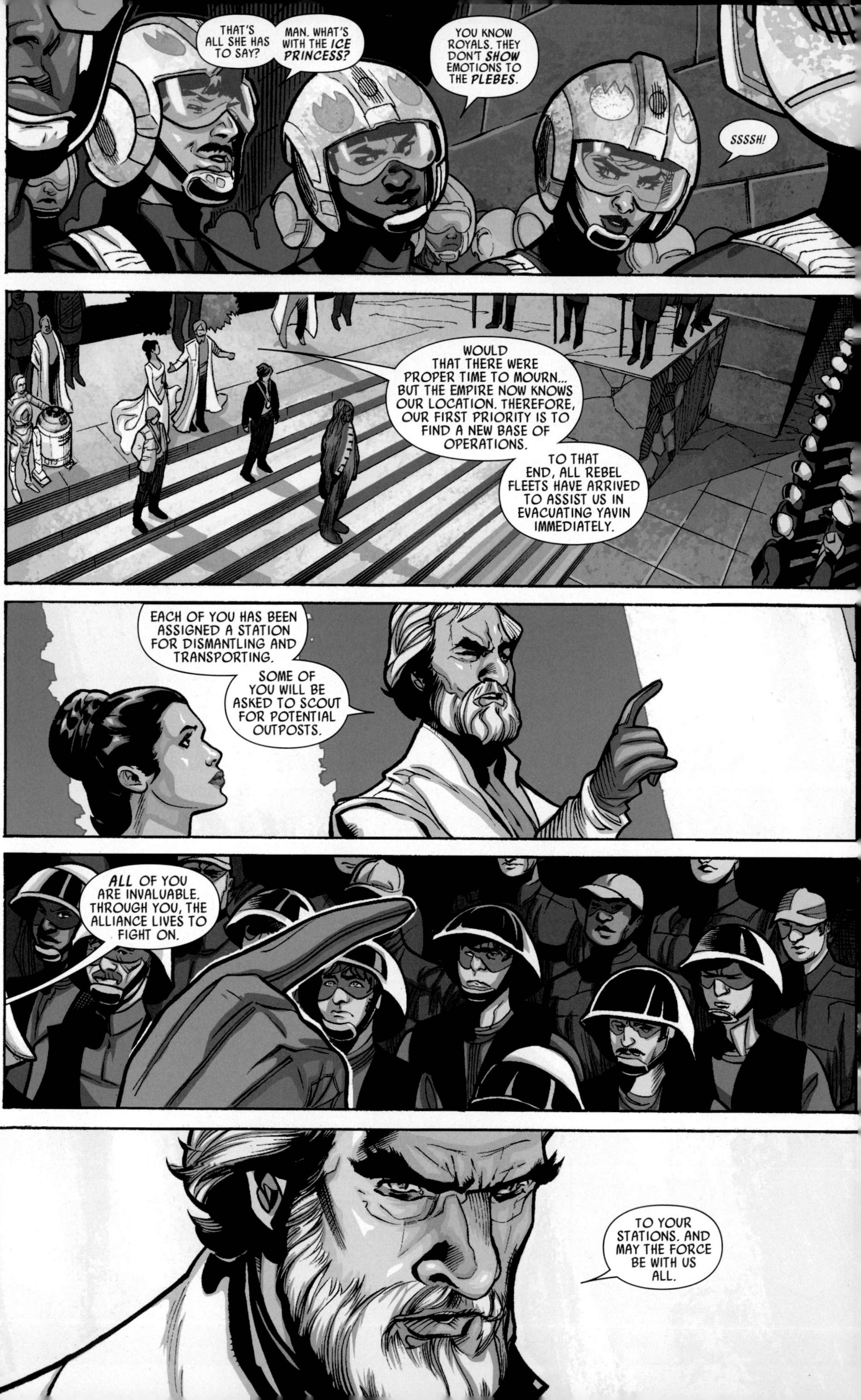
THAT'S ALL SHE HAS TO SAY?
MAN. WHAT'S WITH THE *ICE PRINCESS?*
YOU KNOW ROYALS. THEY DON'T *SHOW* EMOTIONS TO THE *PLEBES*.
SSSSH!
WOULD THAT THERE WERE PROPER TIME TO MOURN... BUT THE EMPIRE NOW KNOWS OUR LOCATION. THEREFORE, OUR FIRST PRIORITY IS TO FIND A NEW BASE OF OPERATIONS.
TO THAT END, ALL REBEL FLEETS HAVE ARRIVED TO ASSIST US IN EVACUATING YAVIN IMMEDIATELY.
EACH OF YOU HAS BEEN ASSIGNED A STATION FOR DISMANTLING AND TRANSPORTING.
SOME OF YOU WILL BE ASKED TO SCOUT FOR POTENTIAL OUTPOSTS.
ALL OF YOU ARE INVALUABLE. THROUGH YOU, THE ALLIANCE LIVES TO FIGHT ON.
TO YOUR STATIONS. AND MAY THE FORCE BE WITH US ALL.

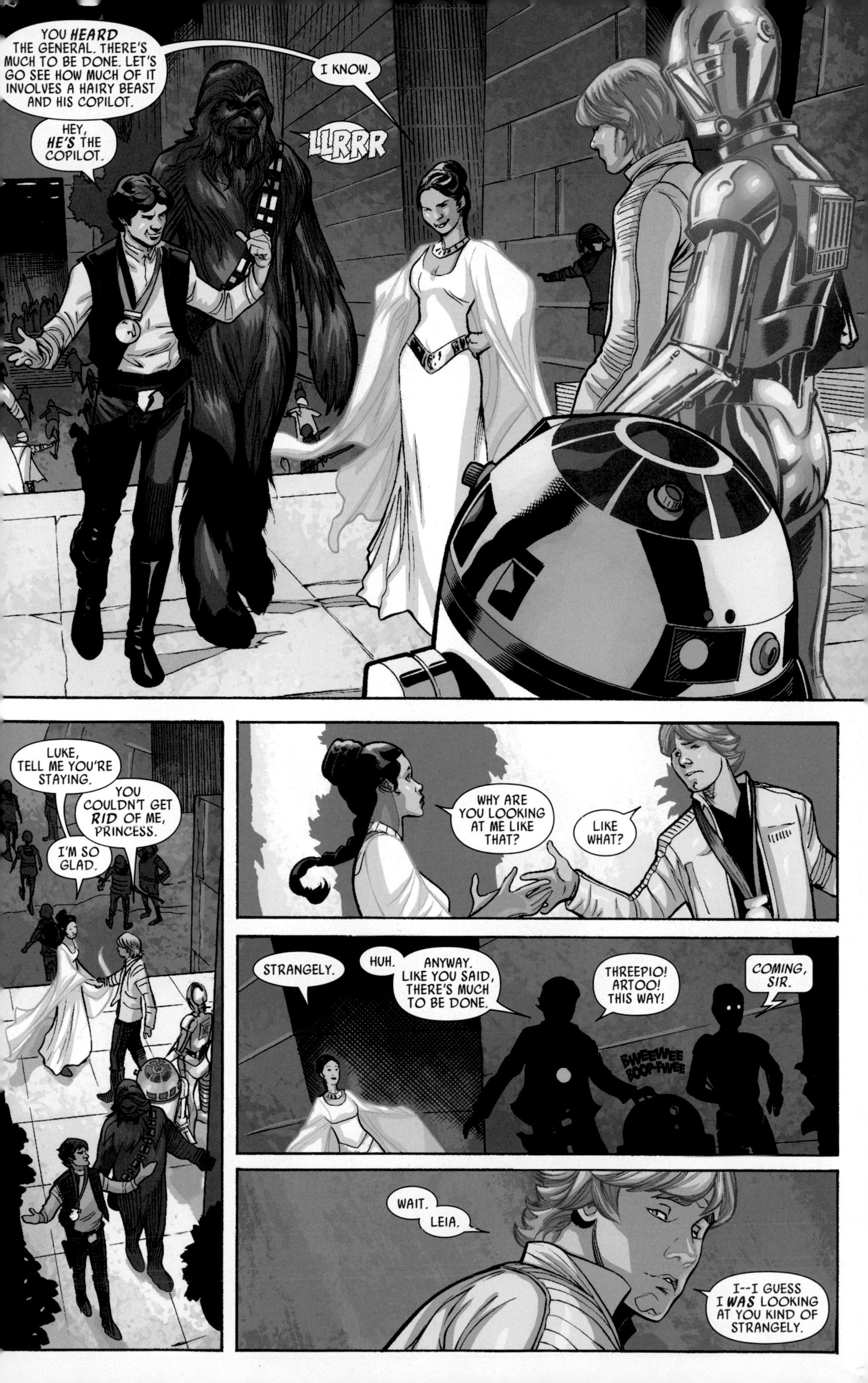
YOU HEARD THE GENERAL. THERE'S MUCH TO BE DONE. LET'S GO SEE HOW MUCH OF IT INVOLVES A HAIRY BEAST AND HIS COPILOT.
I KNOW.
HEY, HE'S THE COPILOT.
LLRRR
LUKE, TELL ME YOU'RE STAYING.
YOU COULDN'T GET RID OF ME, PRINCESS.
I'M SO GLAD.
WHY ARE YOU LOOKING AT ME LIKE THAT?
LIKE WHAT?
STRANGELY.
HUH.
ANYWAY. LIKE YOU SAID, THERE'S MUCH TO BE DONE.
THREEPIO! ARTOO! THIS WAY!
COMING, SIR.
BWEEWEE BOOP-FWEE
WAIT.
LEIA.
I--I GUESS I WAS LOOKING AT YOU KIND OF STRANGELY.

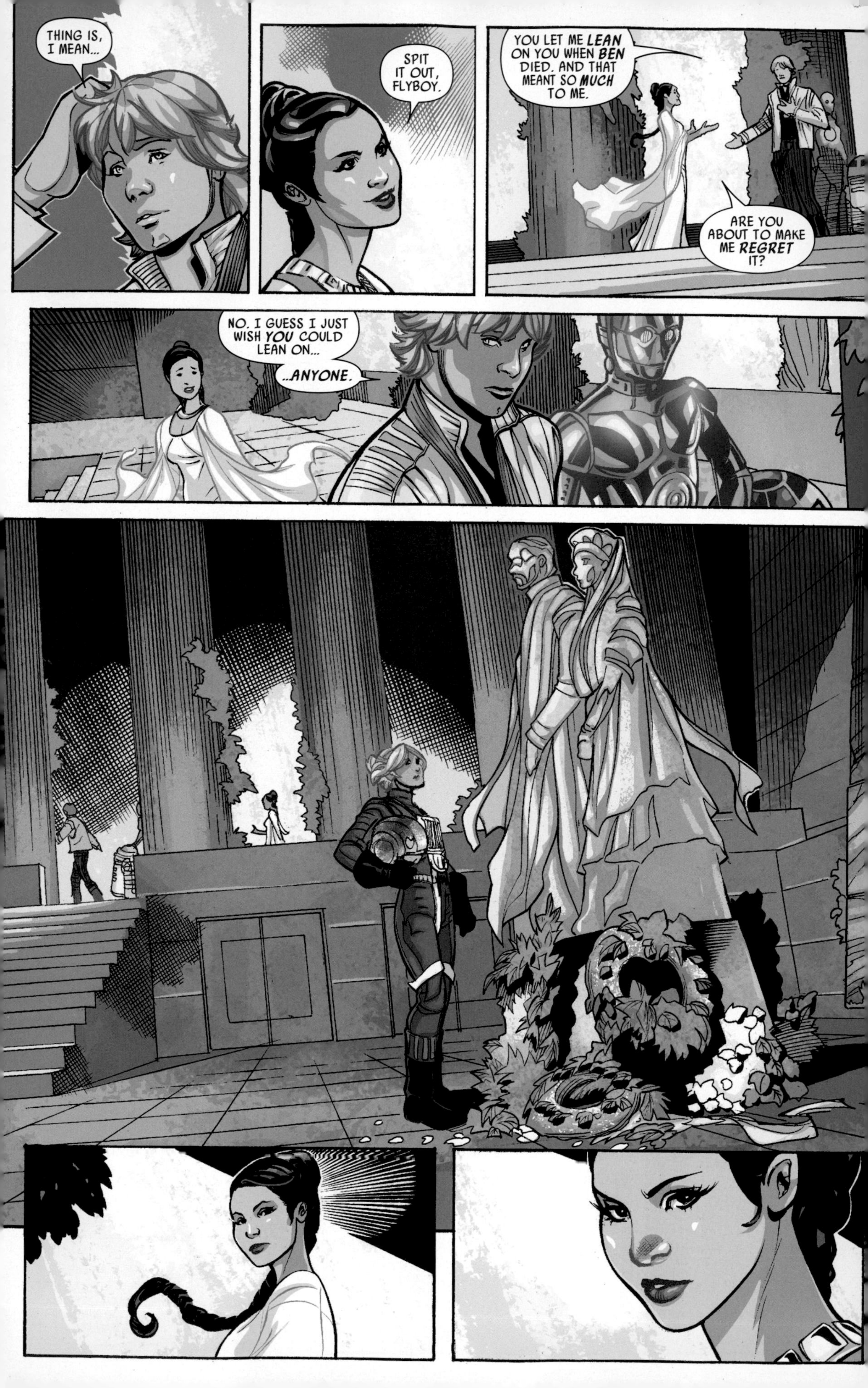
THING IS, I MEAN...
SPIT IT OUT, FLYBOY.
YOU LET ME LEAN ON YOU WHEN BEN DIED. AND THAT MEANT SO MUCH TO ME.
ARE YOU ABOUT TO MAKE ME REGRET IT?
NO. I GUESS I JUST WISH YOU COULD LEAN ON...
...ANYONE.

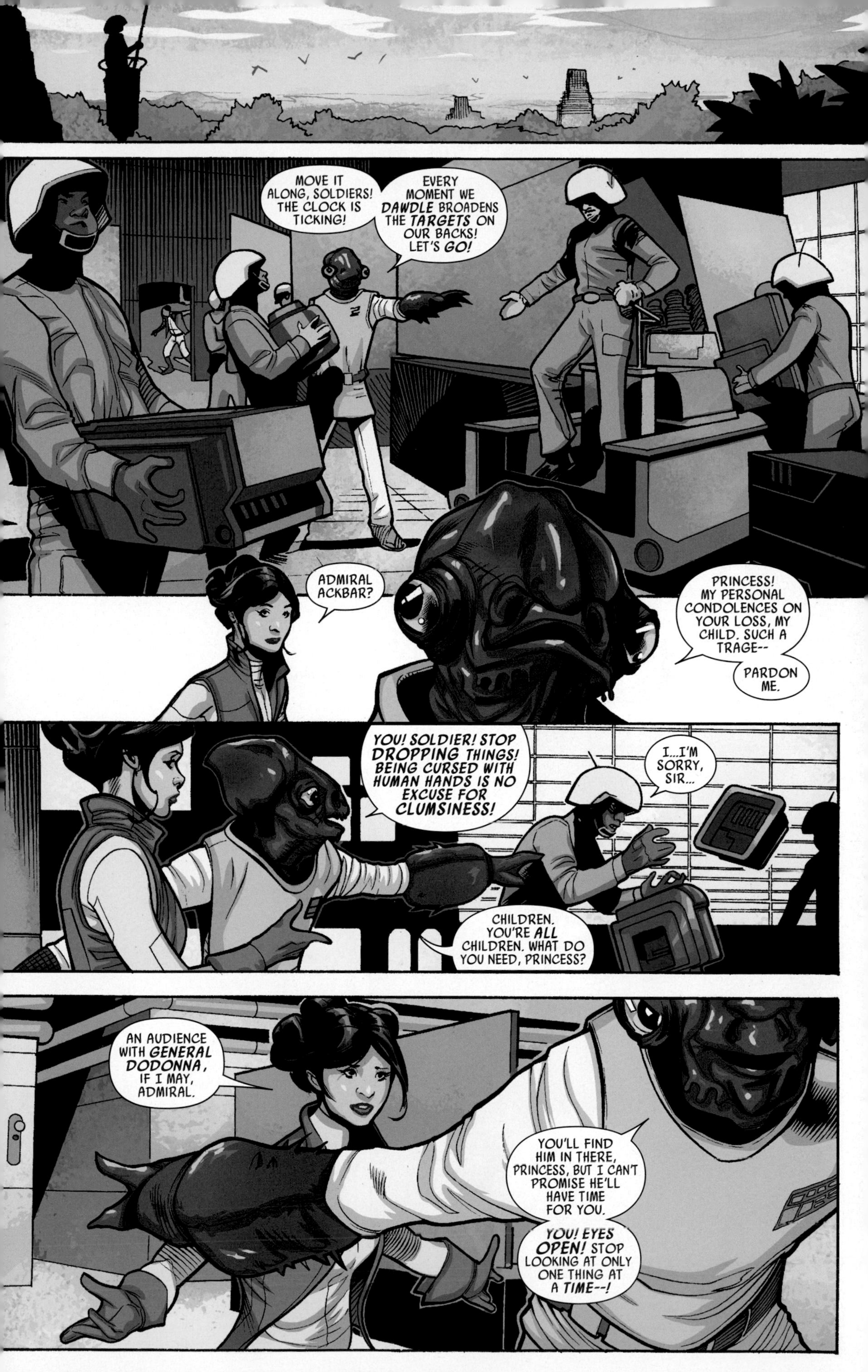

MOVE IT ALONG, SOLDIERS! THE CLOCK IS TICKING!
EVERY MOMENT WE DAWDLE BROADENS THE TARGETS ON OUR BACKS! LET'S GO!
ADMIRAL ACKBAR?
PRINCESS! MY PERSONAL CONDOLENCES ON YOUR LOSS, MY CHILD. SUCH A TRAGE--
PARDON ME.
YOU! SOLDIER! STOP DROPPING THINGS! BEING CURSED WITH HUMAN HANDS IS NO EXCUSE FOR CLUMSINESS!
I...I'M SORRY, SIR...
CHILDREN. YOU'RE ALL CHILDREN. WHAT DO YOU NEED, PRINCESS?
AN AUDIENCE WITH GENERAL DODONNA, IF I MAY, ADMIRAL.
YOU'LL FIND HIM IN THERE, PRINCESS, BUT I CAN'T PROMISE HE'LL HAVE TIME FOR YOU.
YOU! EYES OPEN! STOP LOOKING AT ONLY ONE THING AT A TIME--!

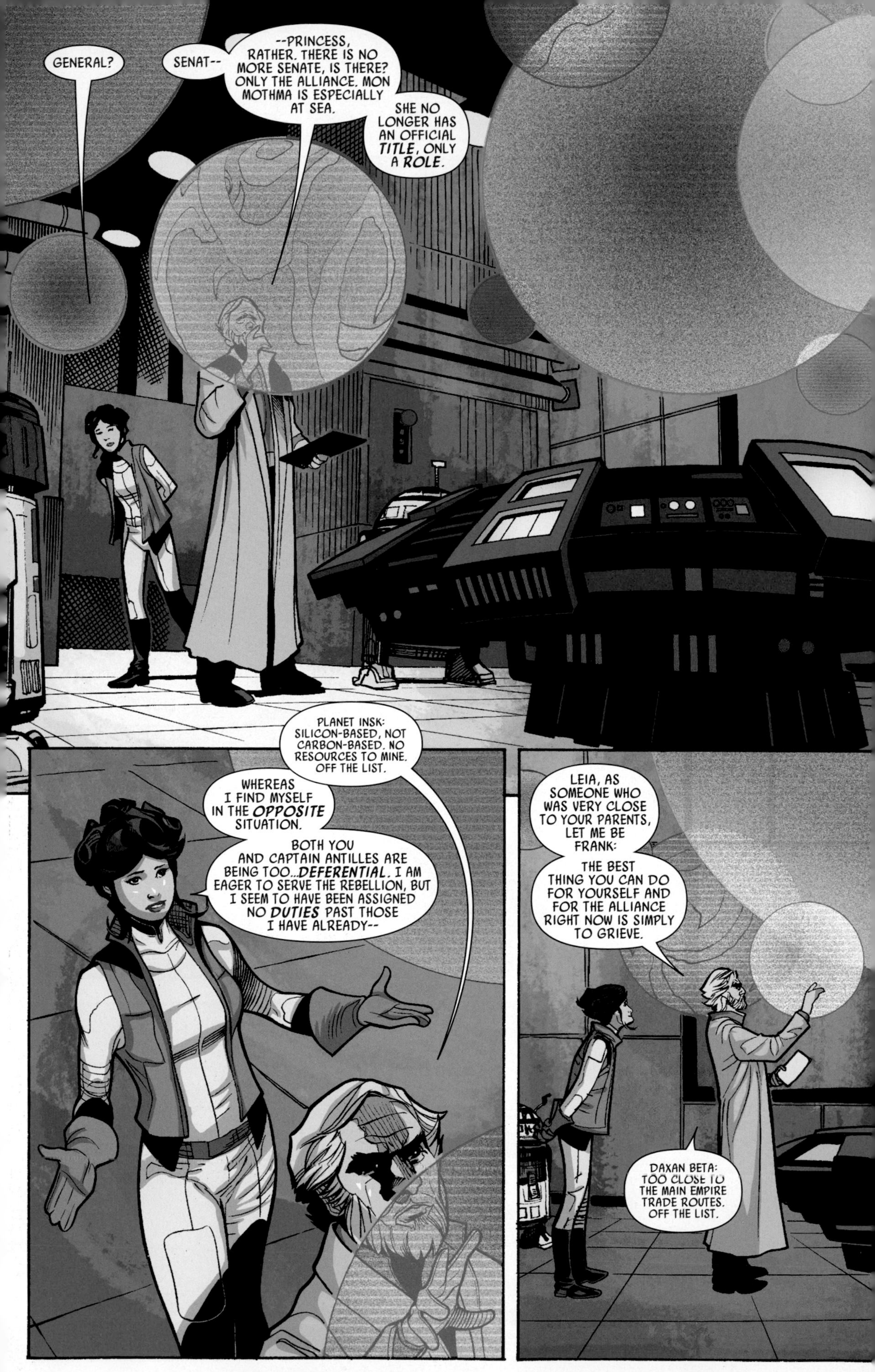
GENERAL?
SENAT--
--PRINCESS, RATHER. THERE IS NO MORE SENATE, IS THERE? ONLY THE ALLIANCE. MON MOTHMA IS ESPECIALLY AT SEA.
SHE NO LONGER HAS AN OFFICIAL TITLE, ONLY A ROLE.
PLANET INSK: SILICON-BASED, NOT CARBON-BASED. NO RESOURCES TO MINE. OFF THE LIST.
WHEREAS I FIND MYSELF IN THE OPPOSITE SITUATION.
BOTH YOU AND CAPTAIN ANTILLES ARE BEING TOO...DEFERENTIAL. I AM EAGER TO SERVE THE REBELLION, BUT I SEEM TO HAVE BEEN ASSIGNED NO DUTIES PAST THOSE I HAVE ALREADY--
LEIA, AS SOMEONE WHO WAS VERY CLOSE TO YOUR PARENTS, LET ME BE FRANK:
THE BEST THING YOU CAN DO FOR YOURSELF AND FOR THE ALLIANCE RIGHT NOW IS SIMPLY TO GRIEVE.
DAXAN BETA: TOO CLOSE TO THE MAIN EMPIRE TRADE ROUTES. OFF THE LIST.

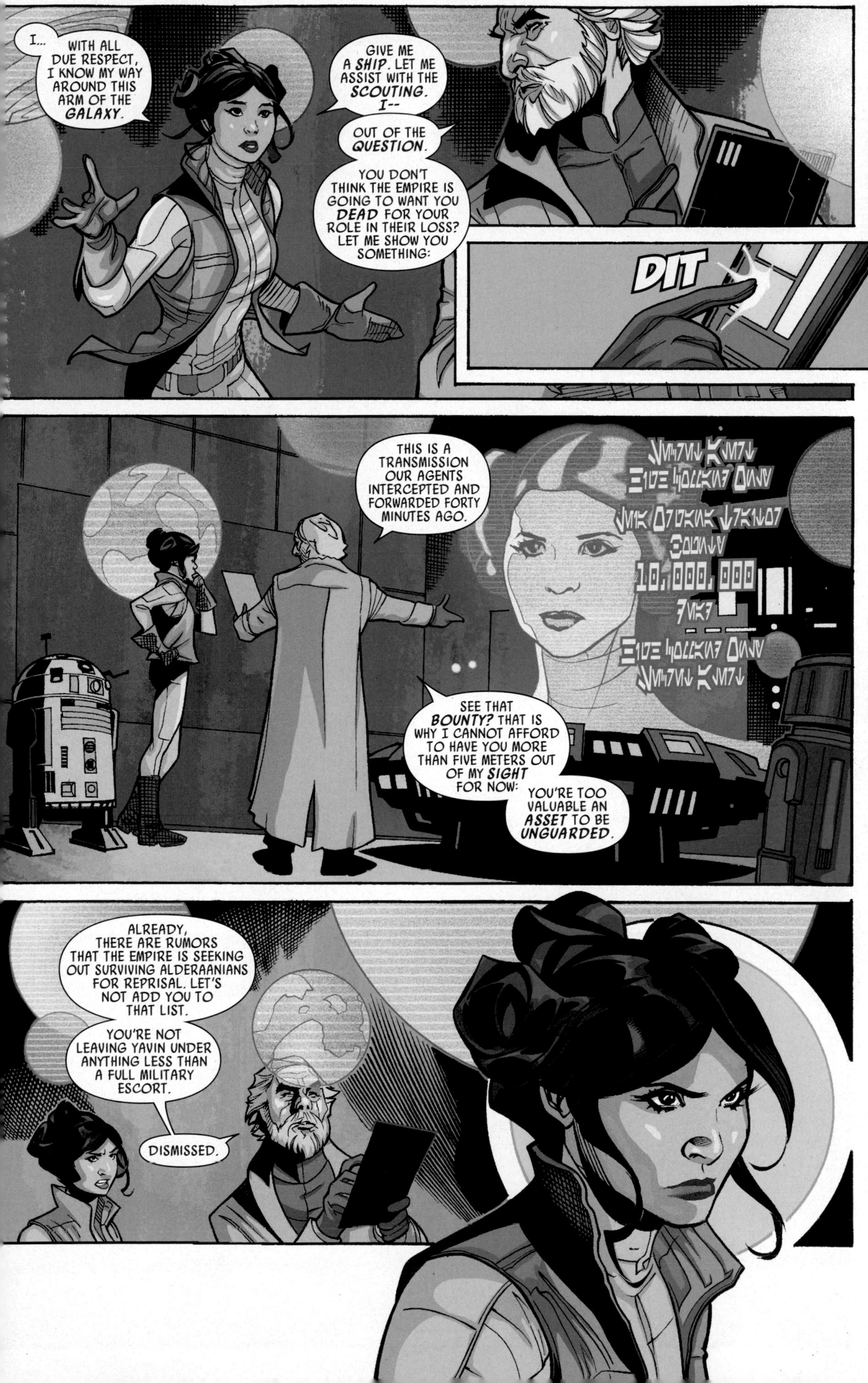
I...
WITH ALL DUE RESPECT, I KNOW MY WAY AROUND THIS ARM OF THE GALAXY.
GIVE ME A SHIP. LET ME ASSIST WITH THE SCOUTING. I--
OUT OF THE QUESTION.
YOU DON'T THINK THE EMPIRE IS GOING TO WANT YOU DEAD FOR YOUR ROLE IN THEIR LOSS? LET ME SHOW YOU SOMETHING:
DIT
THIS IS A TRANSMISSION OUR AGENTS INTERCEPTED AND FORWARDED FORTY MINUTES AGO.
10,000,000
SEE THAT BOUNTY? THAT IS WHY I CANNOT AFFORD TO HAVE YOU MORE THAN FIVE METERS OUT OF MY SIGHT FOR NOW:
YOU'RE TOO VALUABLE AN ASSET TO BE UNGUARDED.
ALREADY, THERE ARE RUMORS THAT THE EMPIRE IS SEEKING OUT SURVIVING ALDERAANIANS FOR REPRISAL. LET'S NOT ADD YOU TO THAT LIST.
YOU'RE NOT LEAVING YAVIN UNDER ANYTHING LESS THAN A FULL MILITARY ESCORT.
DISMISSED.

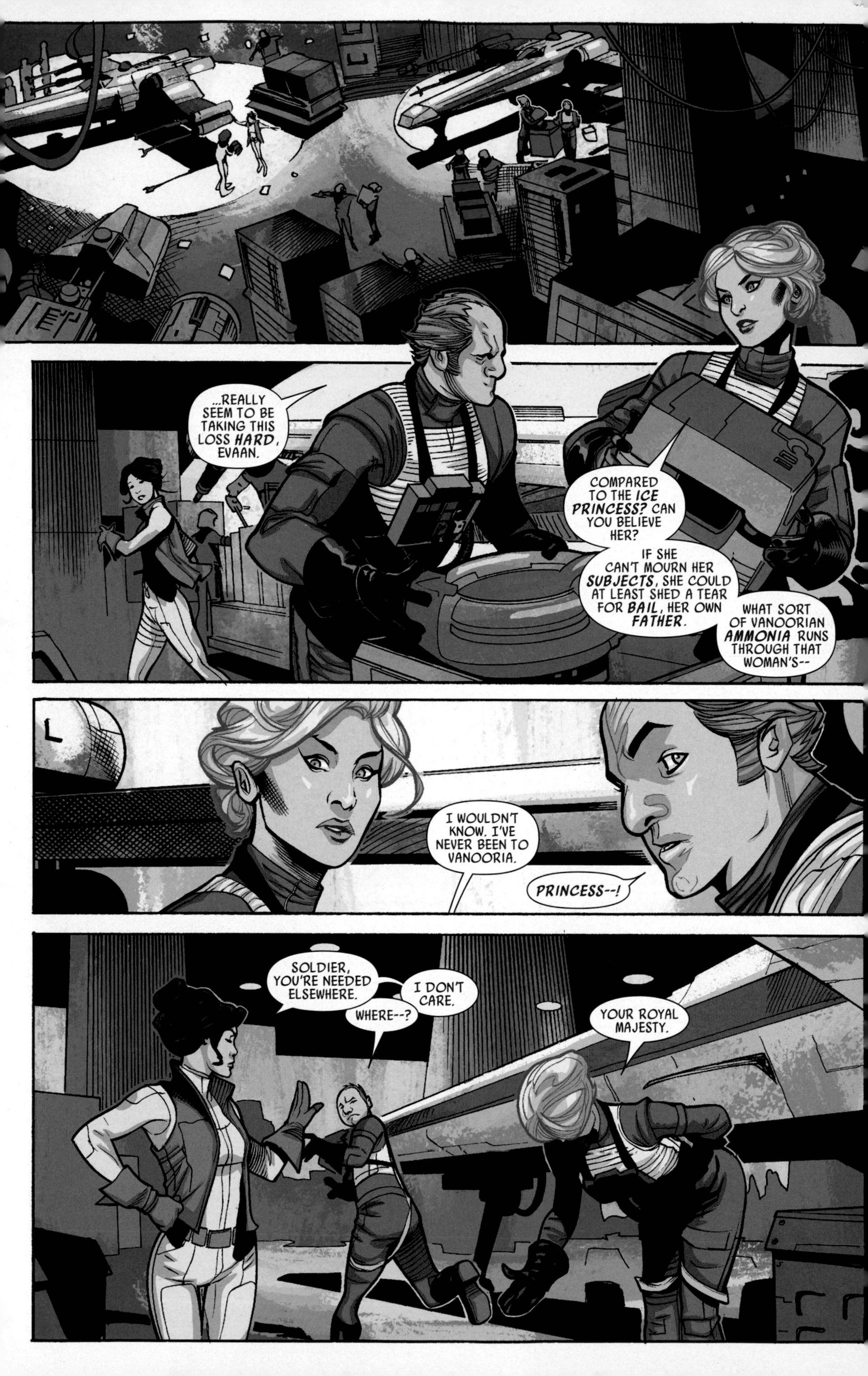
...REALLY SEEM TO BE TAKING THIS LOSS HARD, EVAAN.
COMPARED TO THE ICE PRINCESS? CAN YOU BELIEVE HER?
IF SHE CAN'T MOURN HER SUBJECTS, SHE COULD AT LEAST SHED A TEAR FOR BAIL, HER OWN FATHER.
WHAT SORT OF VANOORIAN AMMONIA RUNS THROUGH THAT WOMAN'S--
I WOULDN'T KNOW. I'VE NEVER BEEN TO VANOORIA.
PRINCESS--!
SOLDIER, YOU'RE NEEDED ELSEWHERE.
WHERE--?
I DON'T CARE.
YOUR ROYAL MAJESTY.

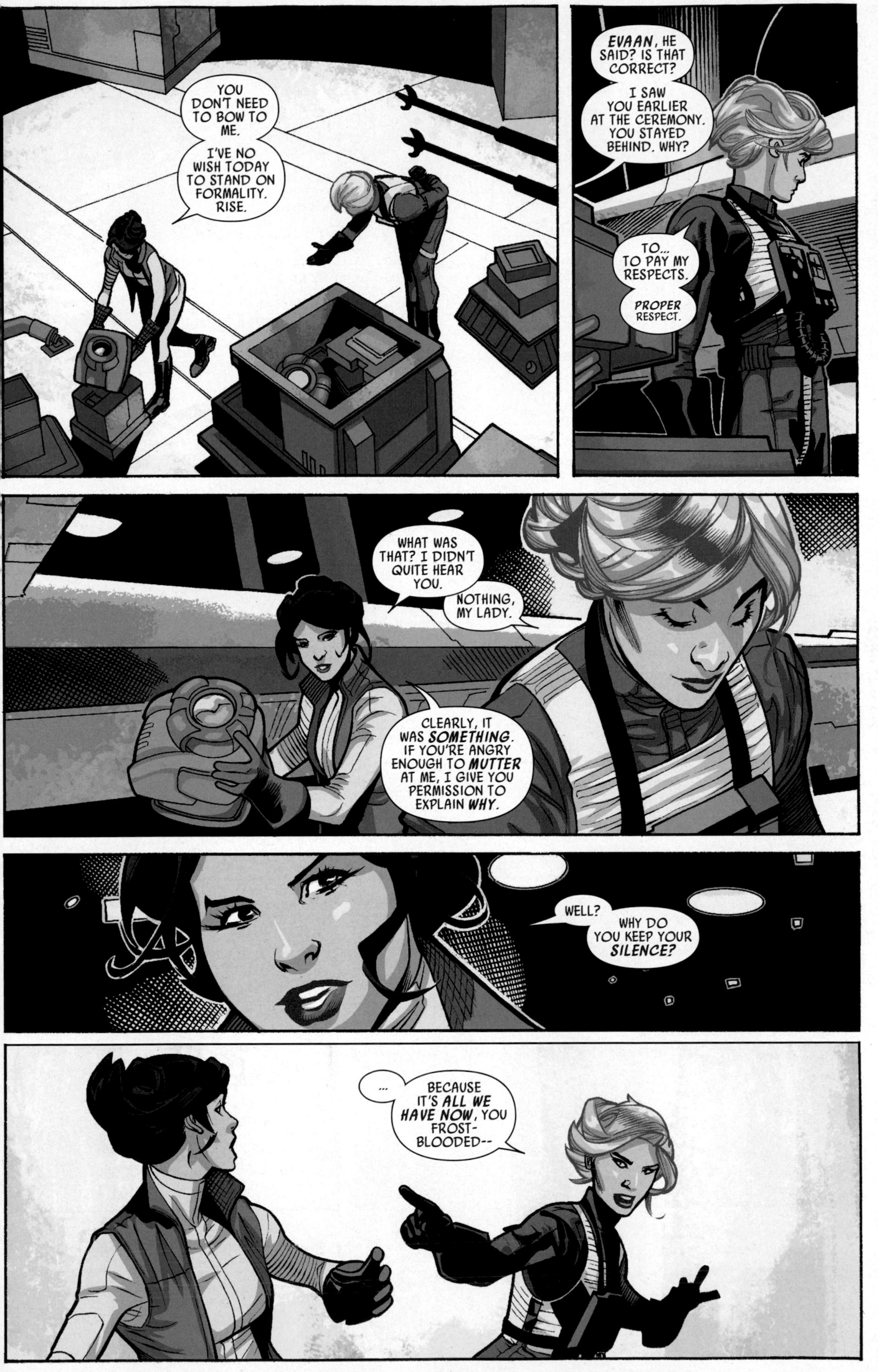
YOU DON'T NEED TO BOW TO ME.
I'VE NO WISH TODAY TO STAND ON FORMALITY. RISE.
EVAAN, HE SAID? IS THAT CORRECT?
I SAW YOU EARLIER AT THE CEREMONY. YOU STAYED BEHIND. WHY?
TO... TO PAY MY RESPECTS.
PROPER RESPECT.
WHAT WAS THAT? I DIDN'T QUITE HEAR YOU.
NOTHING, MY LADY.
CLEARLY, IT WAS SOMETHING. IF YOU'RE ANGRY ENOUGH TO MUTTER AT ME, I GIVE YOU PERMISSION TO EXPLAIN WHY.
WELL?
WHY DO YOU KEEP YOUR SILENCE?
...
BECAUSE IT'S ALL WE HAVE NOW, YOU FROST-BLOODED--

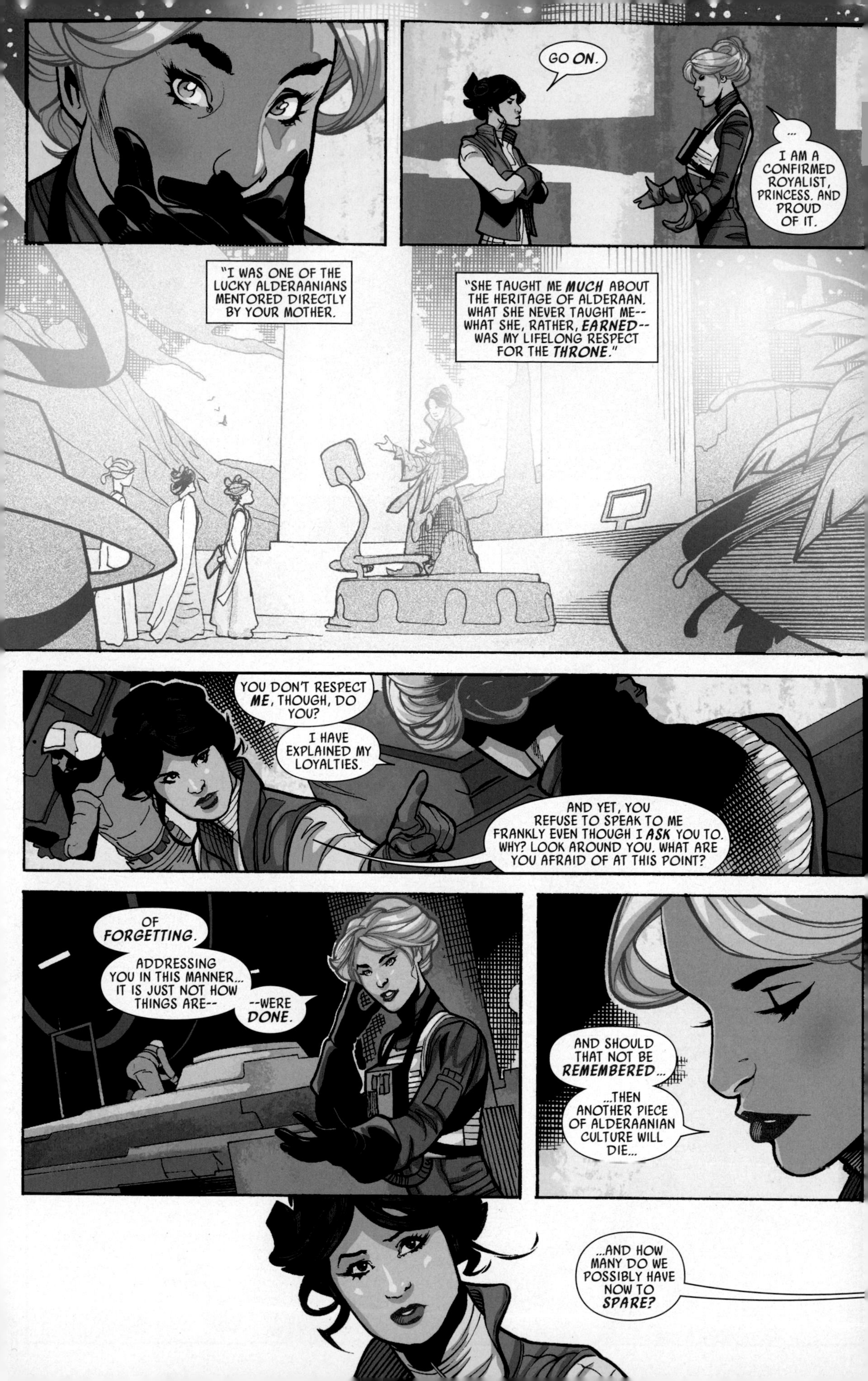
GO ON.
...
I AM A CONFIRMED ROYALIST, PRINCESS. AND PROUD OF IT.
"I WAS ONE OF THE LUCKY ALDERAANIANS MENTORED DIRECTLY BY YOUR MOTHER.
"SHE TAUGHT ME MUCH ABOUT THE HERITAGE OF ALDERAAN. WHAT SHE NEVER TAUGHT ME-- WHAT SHE, RATHER, EARNED-- WAS MY LIFELONG RESPECT FOR THE THRONE."
YOU DON'T RESPECT ME, THOUGH, DO YOU?
I HAVE EXPLAINED MY LOYALTIES.
AND YET, YOU REFUSE TO SPEAK TO ME FRANKLY EVEN THOUGH I ASK YOU TO. WHY? LOOK AROUND YOU. WHAT ARE YOU AFRAID OF AT THIS POINT?
OF FORGETTING.
ADDRESSING YOU IN THIS MANNER... IT IS JUST NOT HOW THINGS ARE--
--WERE DONE.
AND SHOULD THAT NOT BE REMEMBERED...
...THEN ANOTHER PIECE OF ALDERAANIAN CULTURE WILL DIE...
...AND HOW MANY DO WE POSSIBLY HAVE NOW TO SPARE?

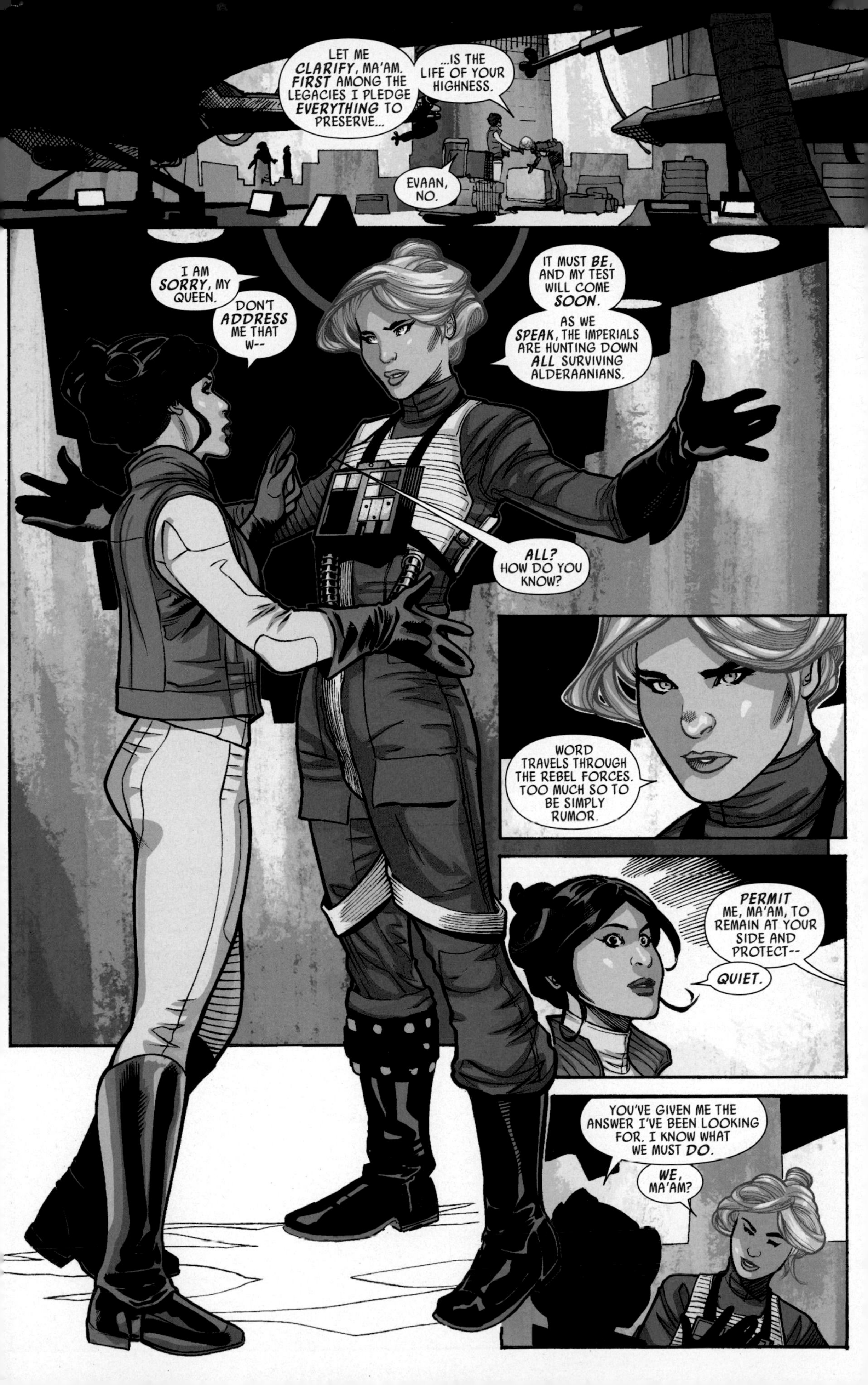
LET ME CLARIFY, MA'AM. FIRST AMONG THE LEGACIES I PLEDGE EVERYTHING TO PRESERVE...
...IS THE LIFE OF YOUR HIGHNESS.
EVAAN, NO.
I AM SORRY, MY QUEEN.
DON'T ADDRESS ME THAT W--
IT MUST BE, AND MY TEST WILL COME SOON.
AS WE SPEAK, THE IMPERIALS ARE HUNTING DOWN ALL SURVIVING ALDERAANIANS.
ALL? HOW DO YOU KNOW?
WORD TRAVELS THROUGH THE REBEL FORCES. TOO MUCH SO TO BE SIMPLY RUMOR.
PERMIT ME, MA'AM, TO REMAIN AT YOUR SIDE AND PROTECT--
QUIET.
YOU'VE GIVEN ME THE ANSWER I'VE BEEN LOOKING FOR. I KNOW WHAT WE MUST DO.
WE, MA'AM?

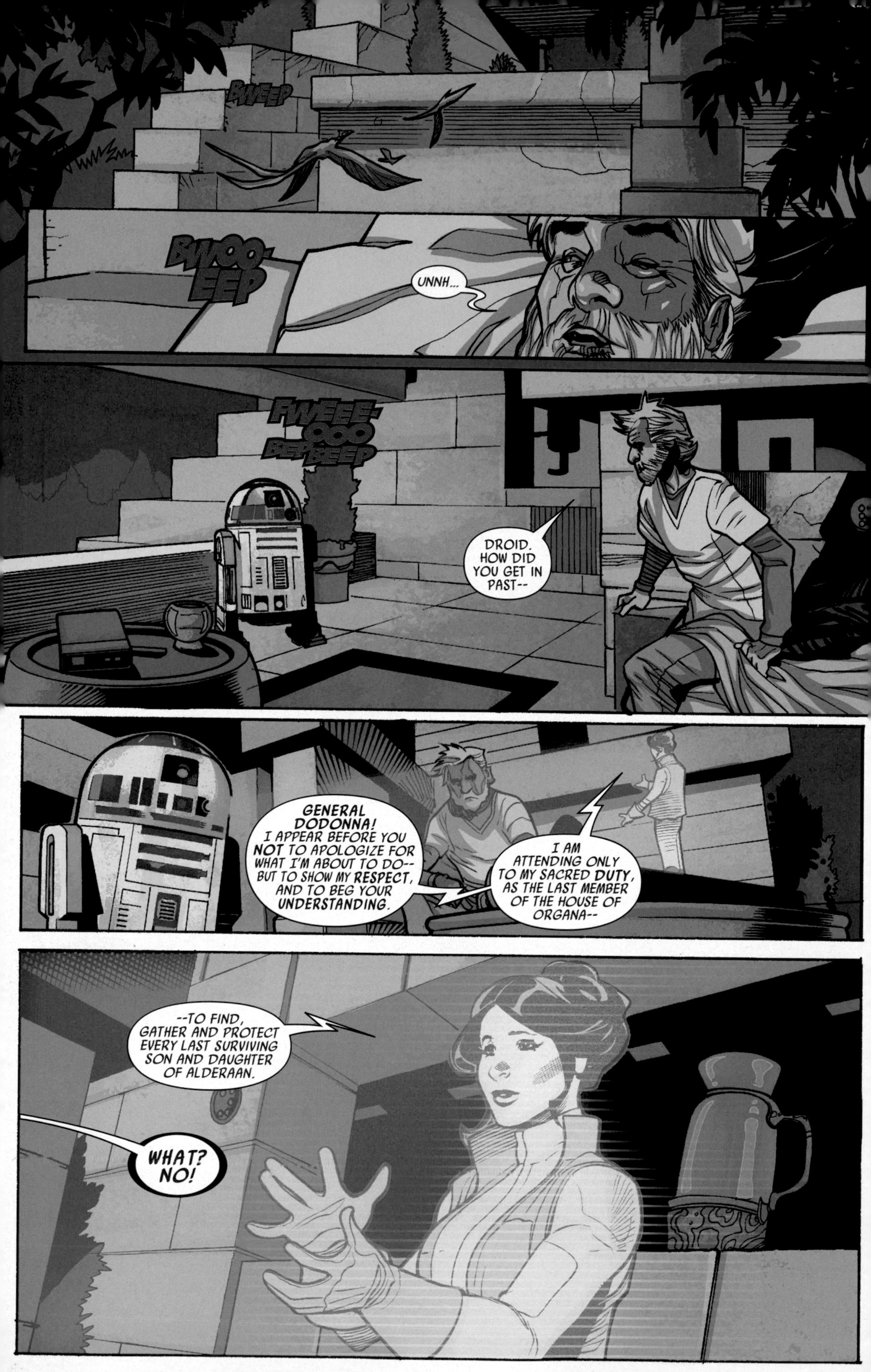
BWEEP
BWOO-EEP
UNNH...
FWEEE-OOO BEP BEEP
DROID. HOW DID YOU GET IN PAST--
GENERAL DODONNA! I APPEAR BEFORE YOU NOT TO APOLOGIZE FOR WHAT I'M ABOUT TO DO-- BUT TO SHOW MY RESPECT, AND TO BEG YOUR UNDERSTANDING.
I AM ATTENDING ONLY TO MY SACRED DUTY, AS THE LAST MEMBER OF THE HOUSE OF ORGANA--
--TO FIND, GATHER AND PROTECT EVERY LAST SURVIVING SON AND DAUGHTER OF ALDERAAN.
WHAT? NO!

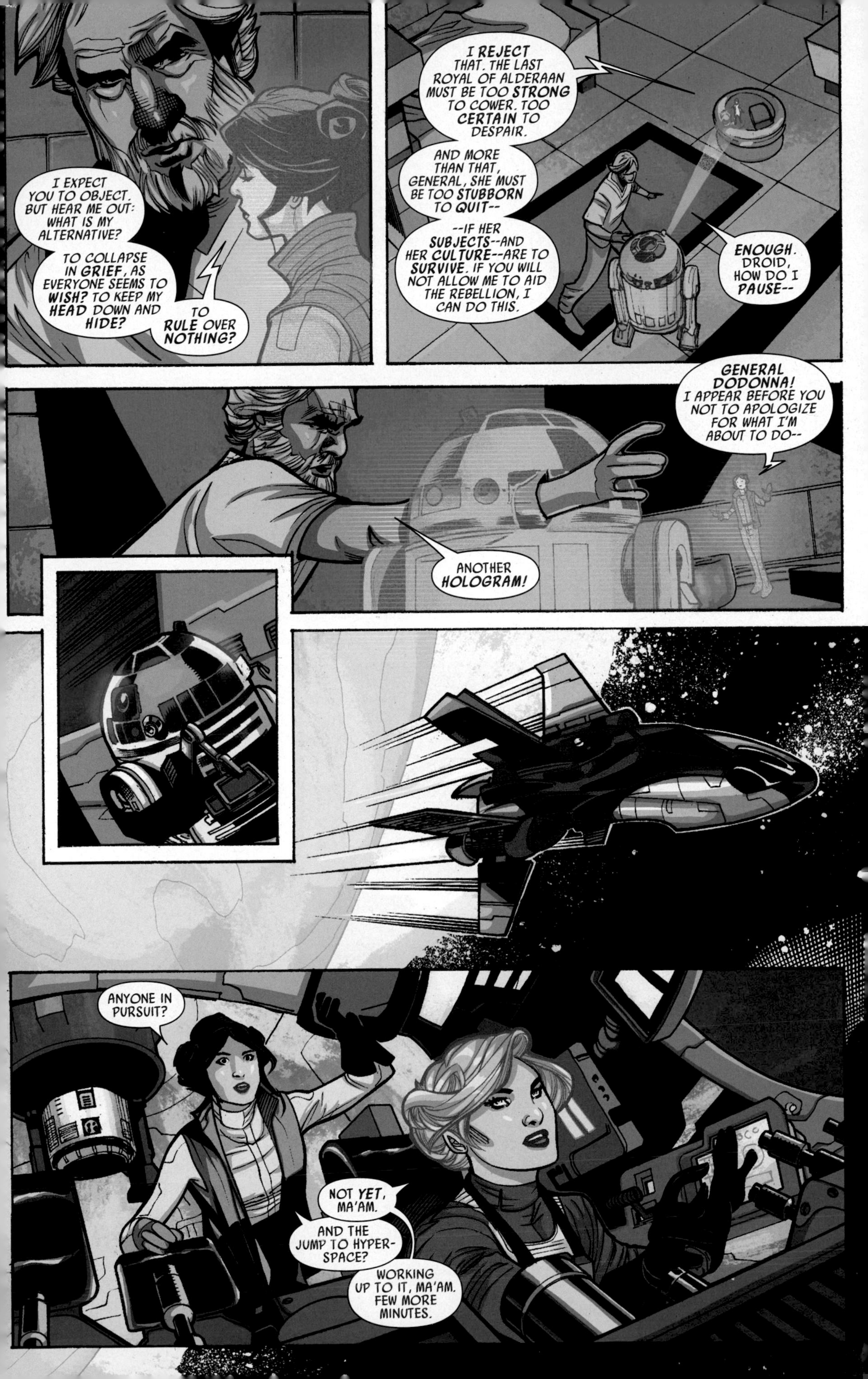
I EXPECT YOU TO OBJECT. BUT HEAR ME OUT: WHAT IS MY ALTERNATIVE?
TO COLLAPSE IN GRIEF, AS EVERYONE SEEMS TO WISH? TO KEEP MY HEAD DOWN AND HIDE?
TO RULE OVER NOTHING?
I REJECT THAT. THE LAST ROYAL OF ALDERAAN MUST BE TOO STRONG TO COWER. TOO CERTAIN TO DESPAIR.
AND MORE THAN THAT, GENERAL, SHE MUST BE TOO STUBBORN TO QUIT--
--IF HER SUBJECTS--AND HER CULTURE--ARE TO SURVIVE. IF YOU WILL NOT ALLOW ME TO AID THE REBELLION, I CAN DO THIS.
ENOUGH. DROID, HOW DO I PAUSE--
GENERAL DODONNA! I APPEAR BEFORE YOU NOT TO APOLOGIZE FOR WHAT I'M ABOUT TO DO--
ANOTHER HOLOGRAM!
ANYONE IN PURSUIT?
NOT YET, MA'AM.
AND THE JUMP TO HYPERSPACE?
WORKING UP TO IT, MA'AM. FEW MORE MINUTES.

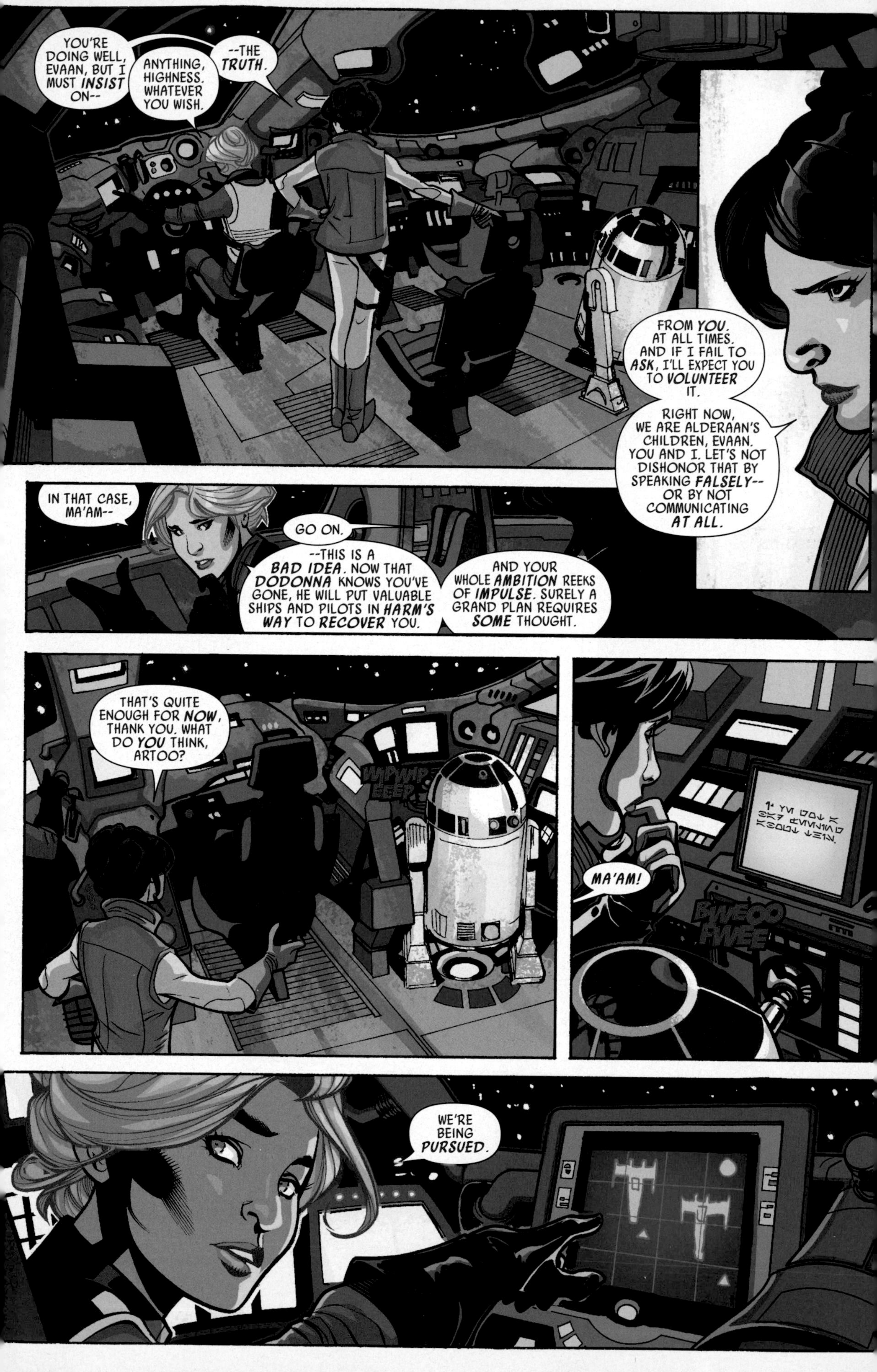
YOU'RE DOING WELL, EVAAN, BUT I MUST INSIST ON--
ANYTHING, HIGHNESS. WHATEVER YOU WISH.
--THE TRUTH.
FROM YOU. AT ALL TIMES. AND IF I FAIL TO ASK, I'LL EXPECT YOU TO VOLUNTEER IT.
RIGHT NOW, WE ARE ALDERAAN'S CHILDREN, EVAAN. YOU AND I. LET'S NOT DISHONOR THAT BY SPEAKING FALSELY-- OR BY NOT COMMUNICATING AT ALL.
IN THAT CASE, MA'AM--
GO ON.
--THIS IS A BAD IDEA. NOW THAT DODONNA KNOWS YOU'VE GONE, HE WILL PUT VALUABLE SHIPS AND PILOTS IN HARM'S WAY TO RECOVER YOU.
AND YOUR WHOLE AMBITION REEKS OF IMPULSE. SURELY A GRAND PLAN REQUIRES SOME THOUGHT.
THAT'S QUITE ENOUGH FOR NOW, THANK YOU. WHAT DO YOU THINK, ARTOO?
WAPWAP EEEP
MA'AM!
BWEOO FWEE
WE'RE BEING PURSUED.

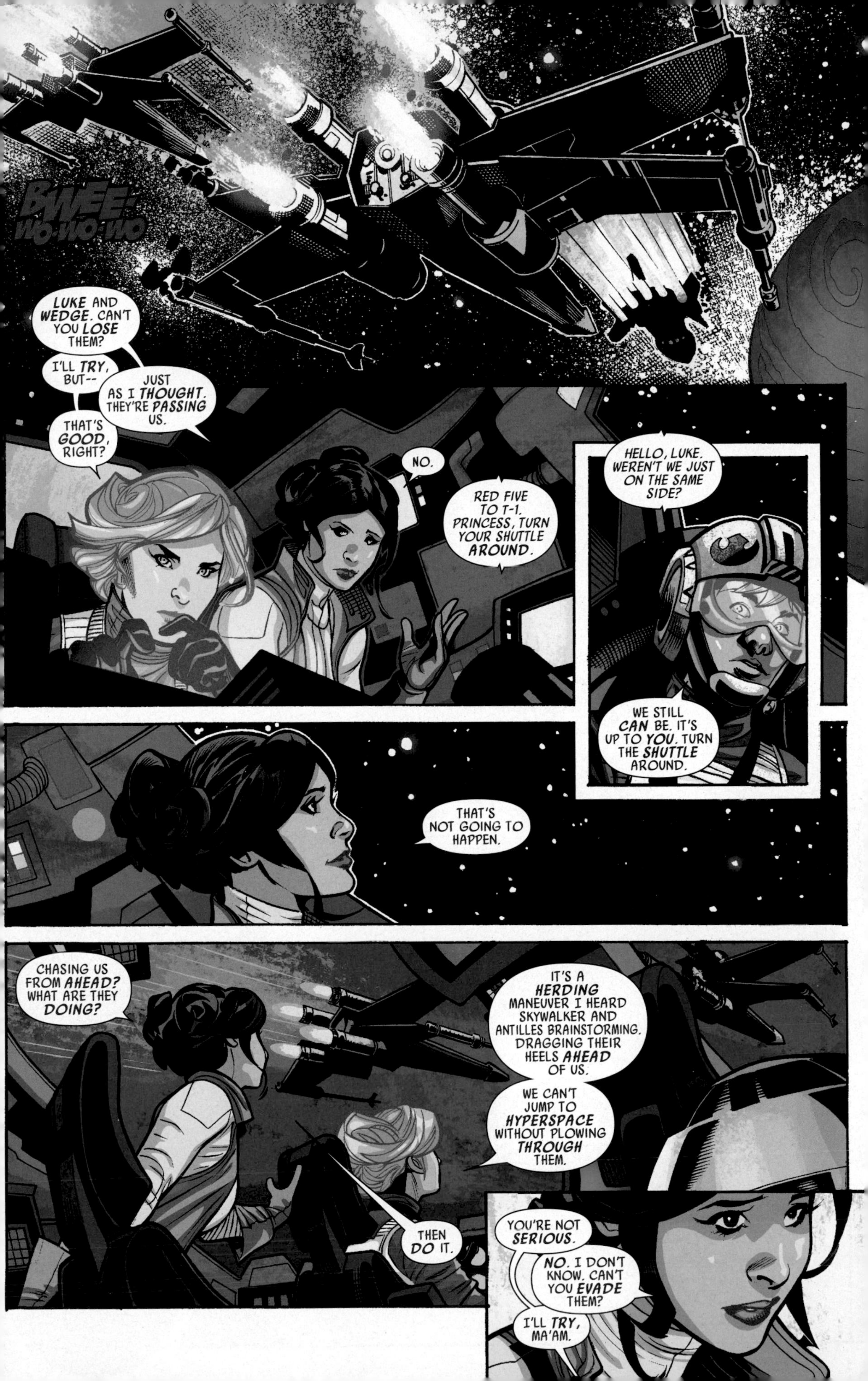
BWEE-WO-WO-WO
LUKE AND WEDGE. CAN'T YOU LOSE THEM?
I'LL TRY, BUT--
JUST AS I THOUGHT. THEY'RE PASSING US.
THAT'S GOOD, RIGHT?
NO.
RED FIVE TO T-1. PRINCESS, TURN YOUR SHUTTLE AROUND.
HELLO, LUKE. WEREN'T WE JUST ON THE SAME SIDE?
WE STILL CAN BE. IT'S UP TO YOU. TURN THE SHUTTLE AROUND.
THAT'S NOT GOING TO HAPPEN.
CHASING US FROM AHEAD? WHAT ARE THEY DOING?
IT'S A HERDING MANEUVER I HEARD SKYWALKER AND ANTILLES BRAINSTORMING. DRAGGING THEIR HEELS AHEAD OF US.
WE CAN'T JUMP TO HYPERSPACE WITHOUT PLOWING THROUGH THEM.
THEN DO IT.
YOU'RE NOT SERIOUS.
NO. I DON'T KNOW. CAN'T YOU EVADE THEM?
I'LL TRY, MA'AM.

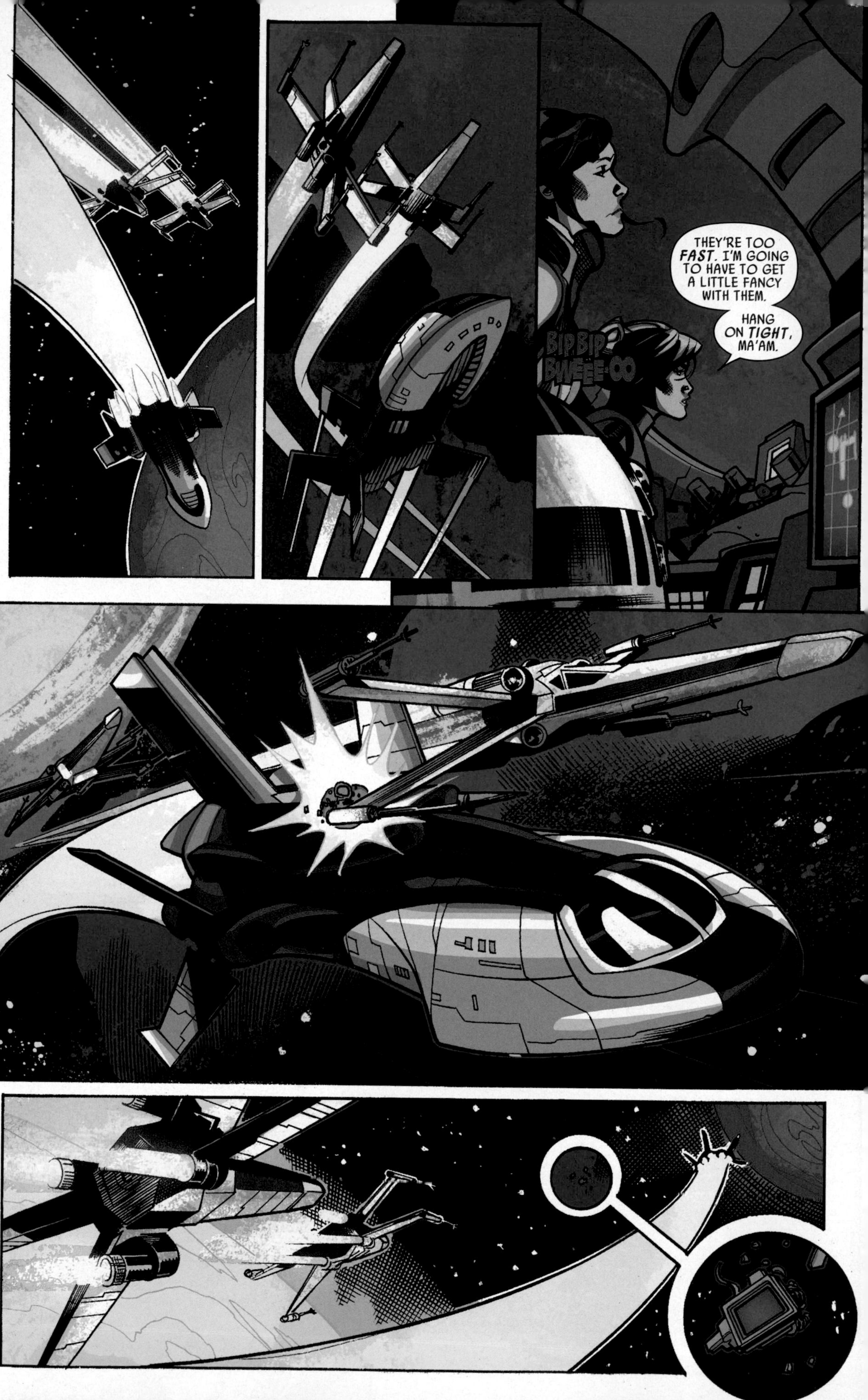
THEY'RE TOO FAST. I'M GOING TO HAVE TO GET A LITTLE FANCY WITH THEM.
HANG ON TIGHT, MA'AM.
BIP BIP BWEEE-OO

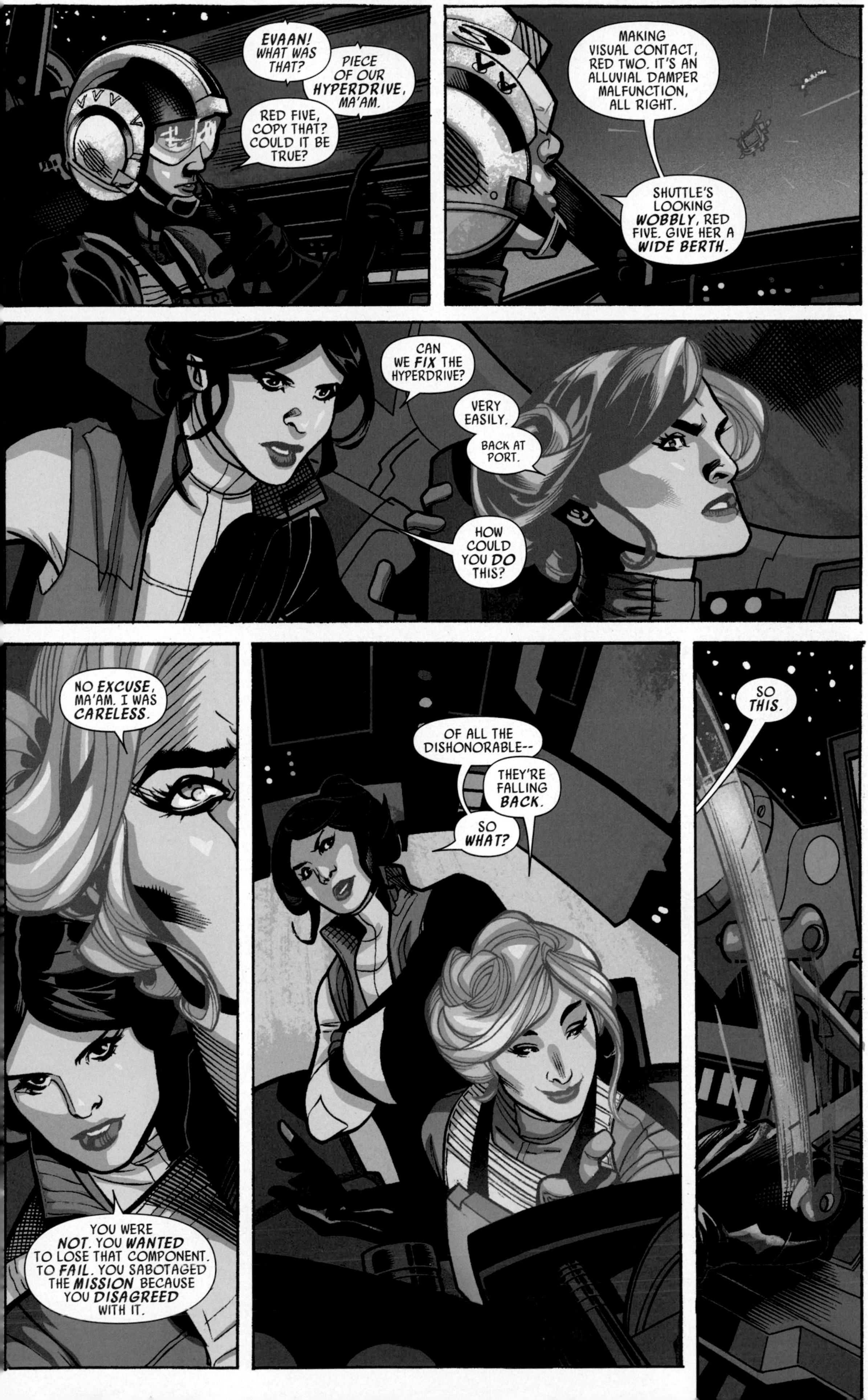
EVAAN! WHAT WAS THAT?
PIECE OF OUR HYPERDRIVE, MA'AM.
RED FIVE, COPY THAT? COULD IT BE TRUE?
MAKING VISUAL CONTACT, RED TWO. IT'S AN ALLUVIAL DAMPER MALFUNCTION, ALL RIGHT.
SHUTTLE'S LOOKING WOBBLY, RED FIVE. GIVE HER A WIDE BERTH.
CAN WE FIX THE HYPERDRIVE?
VERY EASILY.
BACK AT PORT.
HOW COULD YOU DO THIS?
NO EXCUSE, MA'AM. I WAS CARELESS.
YOU WERE NOT. YOU WANTED TO LOSE THAT COMPONENT. TO FAIL. YOU SABOTAGED THE MISSION BECAUSE YOU DISAGREED WITH IT.
OF ALL THE DISHONORABLE--
THEY'RE FALLING BACK.
SO WHAT?
SO THIS.

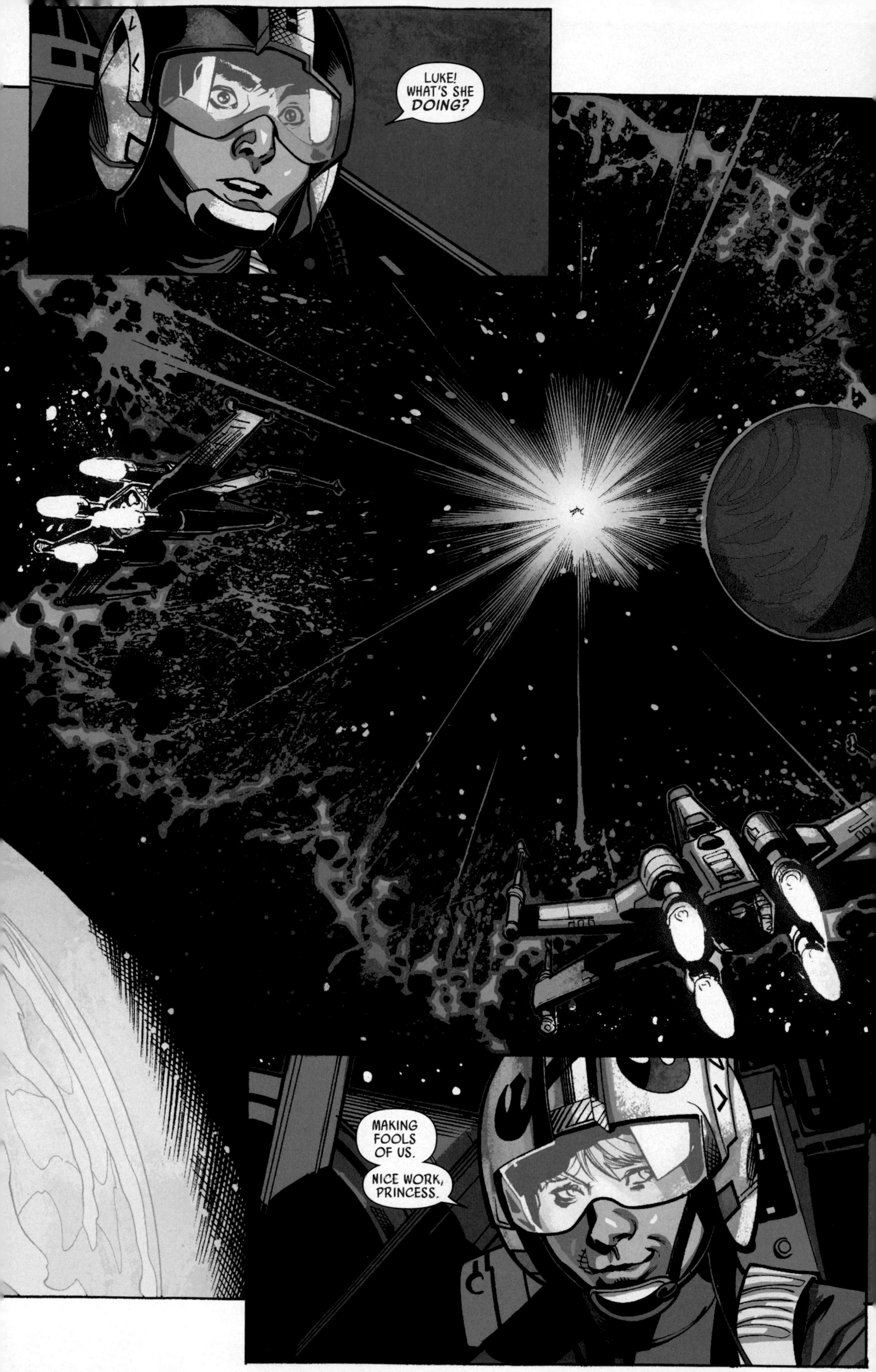
LUKE! WHAT'S SHE DOING?
MAKING FOOLS OF US.
NICE WORK, PRINCESS.

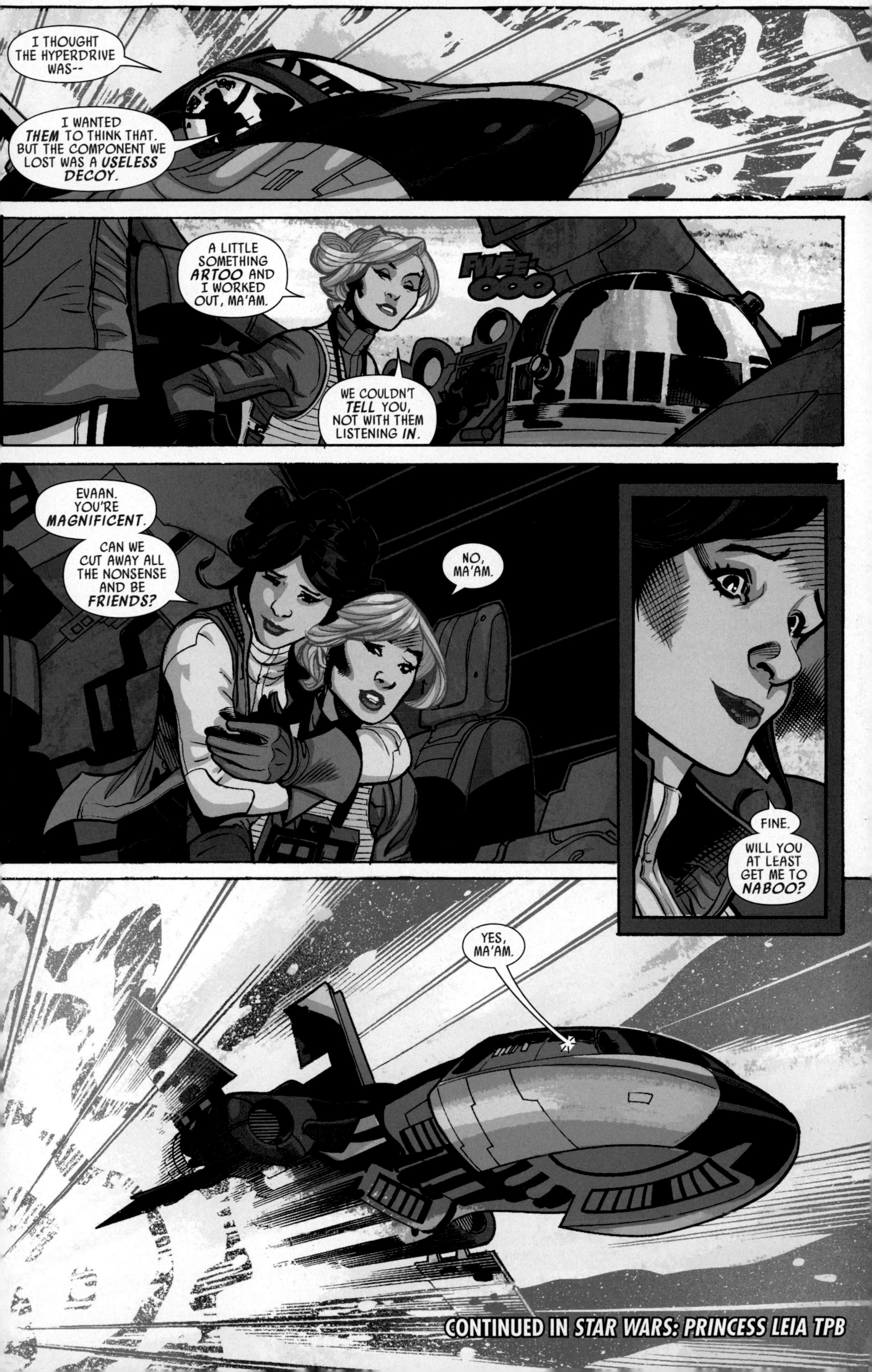
I THOUGHT THE HYPERDRIVE WAS--
I WANTED *THEM* TO THINK THAT. BUT THE COMPONENT WE LOST WAS A *USELESS DECOY*.
A LITTLE SOMETHING *ARTOO* AND I WORKED OUT, MA'AM.
FWEE-OOO
WE COULDN'T *TELL* YOU, NOT WITH THEM LISTENING *IN*.
EVAAN. YOU'RE *MAGNIFICENT*.
CAN WE CUT AWAY ALL THE NONSENSE AND BE *FRIENDS?*
NO, MA'AM.
FINE.
WILL YOU AT LEAST GET ME TO *NABOO?*
YES, MA'AM.
CONTINUED IN *STAR WARS: PRINCESS LEIA TPB*

STAR WARS
PRINCESS LEIA

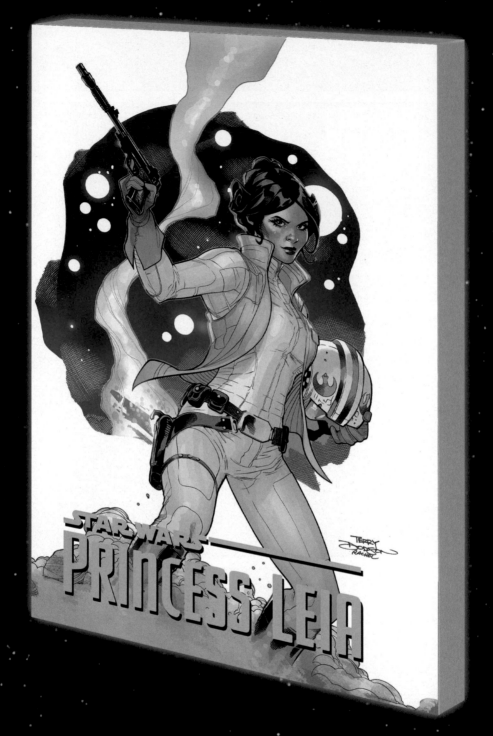

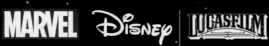

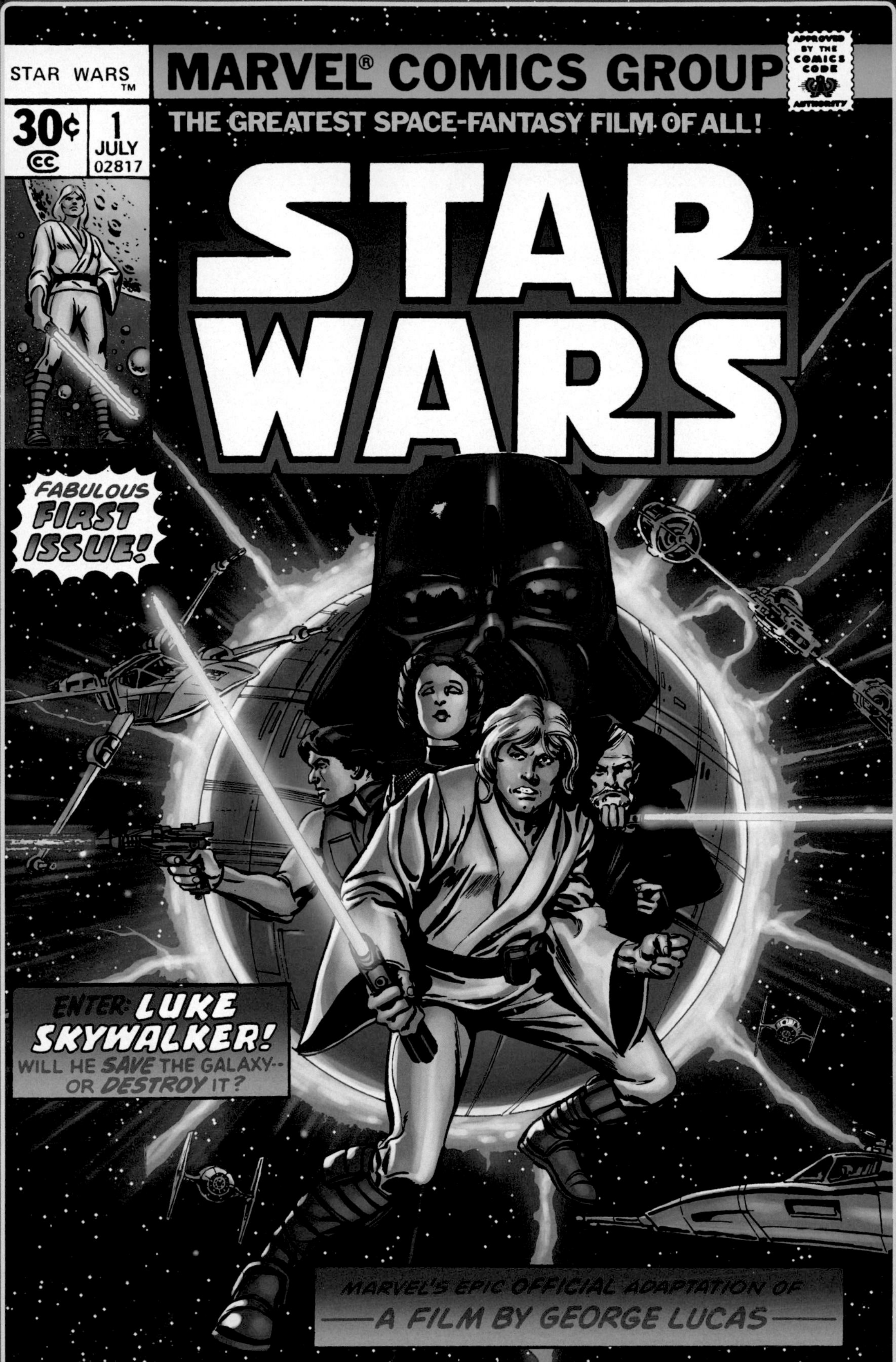
STAR WARS TM
MARVEL® COMICS GROUP
APPROVED BY THE COMICS CODE AUTHORITY
30¢ CC
1 JULY 02817
THE GREATEST SPACE-FANTASY FILM OF ALL!
STAR WARS
FABULOUS FIRST ISSUE!
ENTER: LUKE SKYWALKER!
WILL HE SAVE THE GALAXY-- OR DESTROY IT?
MARVEL'S EPIC OFFICIAL ADAPTATION OF
A FILM BY GEORGE LUCAS

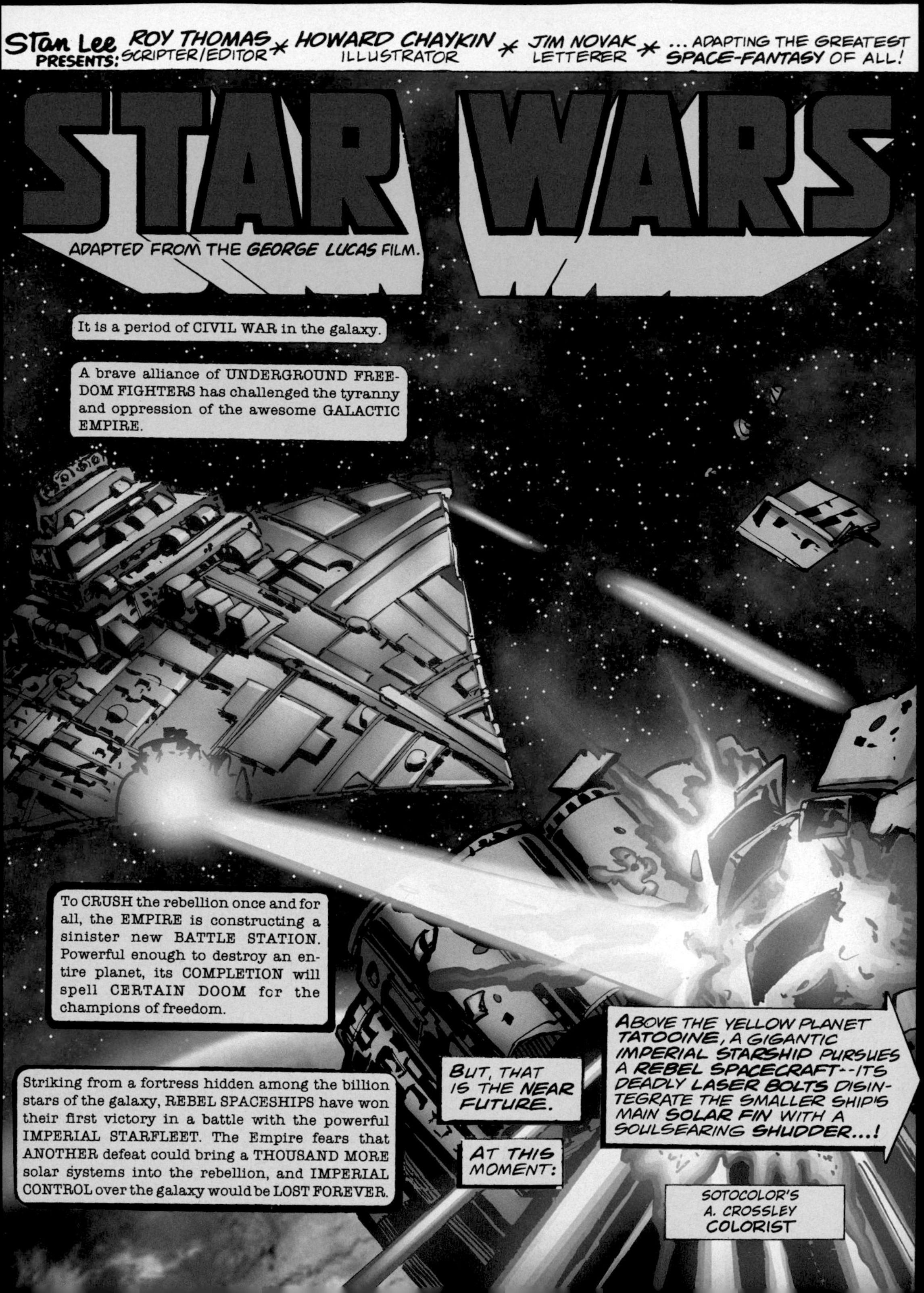

Stan Lee PRESENTS: ROY THOMAS SCRIPTER/EDITOR * HOWARD CHAYKIN ILLUSTRATOR * JIM NOVAK LETTERER * ... ADAPTING THE GREATEST SPACE-FANTASY OF ALL!
STAR WARS
ADAPTED FROM THE GEORGE LUCAS FILM.
It is a period of CIVIL WAR in the galaxy.
A brave alliance of UNDERGROUND FREEDOM FIGHTERS has challenged the tyranny and oppression of the awesome GALACTIC EMPIRE.
To CRUSH the rebellion once and for all, the EMPIRE is constructing a sinister new BATTLE STATION. Powerful enough to destroy an entire planet, its COMPLETION will spell CERTAIN DOOM for the champions of freedom.
Striking from a fortress hidden among the billion stars of the galaxy, REBEL SPACESHIPS have won their first victory in a battle with the powerful IMPERIAL STARFLEET. The Empire fears that ANOTHER defeat could bring a THOUSAND MORE solar systems into the rebellion, and IMPERIAL CONTROL over the galaxy would be LOST FOREVER.
BUT, THAT IS THE NEAR FUTURE.
AT THIS MOMENT:
ABOVE THE YELLOW PLANET TATOOINE, A GIGANTIC IMPERIAL STARSHIP PURSUES A REBEL SPACECRAFT--ITS DEADLY LASER BOLTS DISINTEGRATE THE SMALLER SHIP'S MAIN SOLAR FIN WITH A SOULSEARING SHUDDER...!
SOTOCOLOR'S A. CROSSLEY COLORIST

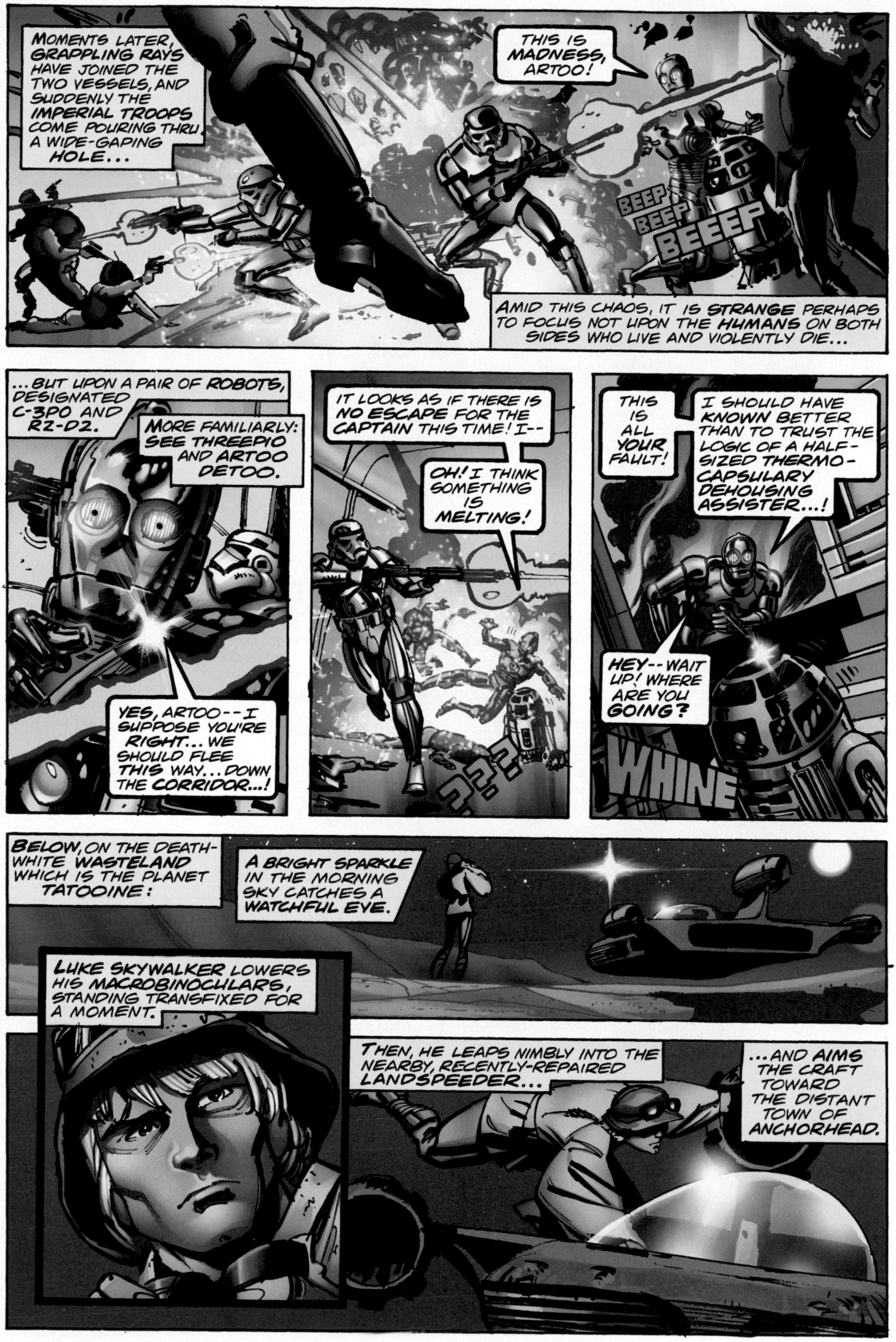
MOMENTS LATER, GRAPPLING RAYS HAVE JOINED THE TWO VESSELS, AND SUDDENLY THE IMPERIAL TROOPS COME POURING THRU A WIDE-GAPING HOLE...
THIS IS MADNESS, ARTOO!
BEEP BEEP BEEEP
AMID THIS CHAOS, IT IS STRANGE PERHAPS TO FOCUS NOT UPON THE HUMANS ON BOTH SIDES WHO LIVE AND VIOLENTLY DIE...
...BUT UPON A PAIR OF ROBOTS, DESIGNATED C-3PO AND R2-D2.
MORE FAMILIARLY: SEE THREEPIO AND ARTOO DETOO.
YES, ARTOO--I SUPPOSE YOU'RE RIGHT... WE SHOULD FLEE THIS WAY... DOWN THE CORRIDOR...!
IT LOOKS AS IF THERE IS NO ESCAPE FOR THE CAPTAIN THIS TIME! I--
OH! I THINK SOMETHING IS MELTING!
THIS IS ALL YOUR FAULT!
I SHOULD HAVE KNOWN BETTER THAN TO TRUST THE LOGIC OF A HALF-SIZED THERMO-CAPSULARY DEHOUSING ASSISTER...!
HEY--WAIT UP! WHERE ARE YOU GOING?
WHINE
BELOW, ON THE DEATH-WHITE WASTELAND WHICH IS THE PLANET TATOOINE:
A BRIGHT SPARKLE IN THE MORNING SKY CATCHES A WATCHFUL EYE.
LUKE SKYWALKER LOWERS HIS MACROBINOCULARS, STANDING TRANSFIXED FOR A MOMENT.
THEN, HE LEAPS NIMBLY INTO THE NEARBY, RECENTLY-REPAIRED LANDSPEEDER...
...AND AIMS THE CRAFT TOWARD THE DISTANT TOWN OF ANCHORHEAD.

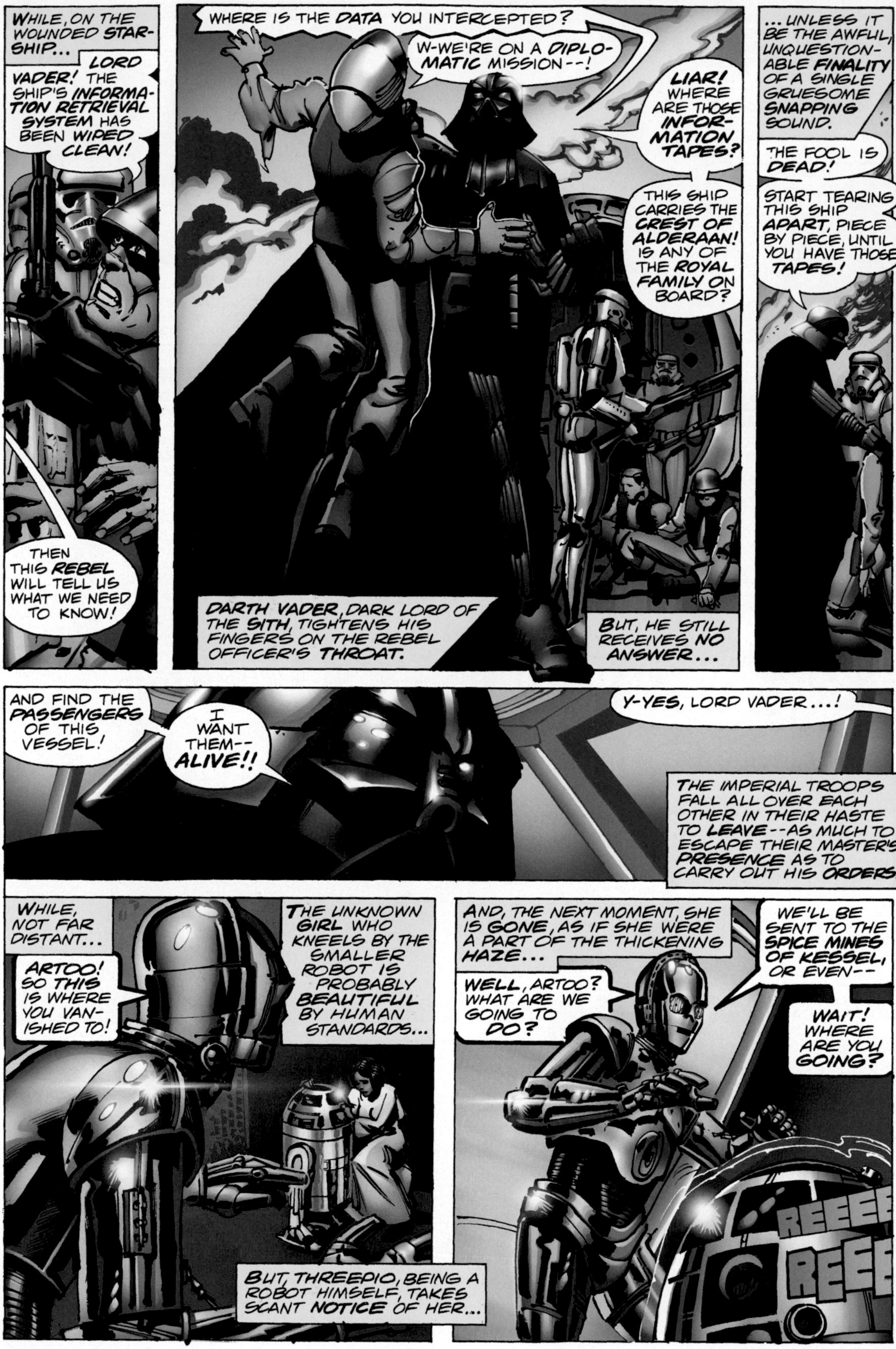
WHILE, ON THE WOUNDED STAR-SHIP...
LORD VADER! THE SHIP'S INFORMATION RETRIEVAL SYSTEM HAS BEEN WIPED CLEAN!
THEN THIS REBEL WILL TELL US WHAT WE NEED TO KNOW!
WHERE IS THE DATA YOU INTERCEPTED?
W-WE'RE ON A DIPLOMATIC MISSION--!
LIAR! WHERE ARE THOSE INFORMATION TAPES?
THIS SHIP CARRIES THE CREST OF ALDERAAN! IS ANY OF THE ROYAL FAMILY ON BOARD?
DARTH VADER, DARK LORD OF THE SITH, TIGHTENS HIS FINGERS ON THE REBEL OFFICER'S THROAT.
BUT, HE STILL RECEIVES NO ANSWER...
...UNLESS IT BE THE AWFUL, UNQUESTIONABLE FINALITY OF A SINGLE GRUESOME SNAPPING SOUND.
THE FOOL IS DEAD!
START TEARING THIS SHIP APART, PIECE BY PIECE, UNTIL YOU HAVE THOSE TAPES!
AND FIND THE PASSENGERS OF THIS VESSEL!
I WANT THEM--ALIVE!!
Y-YES, LORD VADER...!
THE IMPERIAL TROOPS FALL ALL OVER EACH OTHER IN THEIR HASTE TO LEAVE--AS MUCH TO ESCAPE THEIR MASTER'S PRESENCE AS TO CARRY OUT HIS ORDERS.
WHILE, NOT FAR DISTANT...
ARTOO! SO THIS IS WHERE YOU VANISHED TO!
THE UNKNOWN GIRL WHO KNEELS BY THE SMALLER ROBOT IS PROBABLY BEAUTIFUL BY HUMAN STANDARDS...
BUT, THREEPIO, BEING A ROBOT HIMSELF, TAKES SCANT NOTICE OF HER...
AND, THE NEXT MOMENT, SHE IS GONE, AS IF SHE WERE A PART OF THE THICKENING HAZE...
WELL, ARTOO? WHAT ARE WE GOING TO DO?
WE'LL BE SENT TO THE SPICE MINES OF KESSEL, OR EVEN--
WAIT! WHERE ARE YOU GOING?

MISSION? **WHAT** MISSION? WHAT ARE YOU **TALKING** ABOUT?

HEY! YOU'RE NOT PERMITTED TO GO NEAR THOSE EMERGENCY LIFEPODS!

DON'T YOU CALL ME A MINDLESS PHILOSOPHER, YOU OVERWEIGHT GLOBE OF GREASE!

TWANG!

NEXT, AS A NEW AND **CLOSER** EXPLOSION SENDS DUST AND DEBRIS AND **FLAMES** THRU THE SUB-HALLWAY...

...**THREEPIO** FINDS THAT EVEN A **ROBOT** CAN CHANGE HIS MIND.

THEN, AS THE **SAFETY DOOR** SNAPS SHUT BEHIND HIM--

I'M GOING TO **REGRET** THIS.

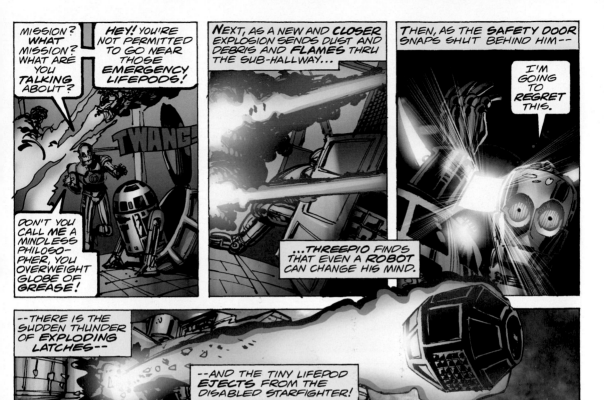

--THERE IS THE SUDDEN THUNDER OF **EXPLODING LATCHES**--

--AND THE TINY LIFEPOD **EJECTS** FROM THE DISABLED STARFIGHTER!

...AS, BACK ABOARD...

THERE'S ONE OF THEM!

SET WEAPONS FOR **STUN!**

I'VE SET MINE TO **KILL!**

ZZZZ

THEN, THE YOUNG GIRL STARTS TO **FLEE** ONCE MORE--

--BUT, UNFORTUNATELY, **NOT** AT THE LIGHT-SPEED OF A **PARALYSIS RAY.**

OHHH

FSS

SHE'LL BE ALL RIGHT.

REPORT TO **LORD VADER!**

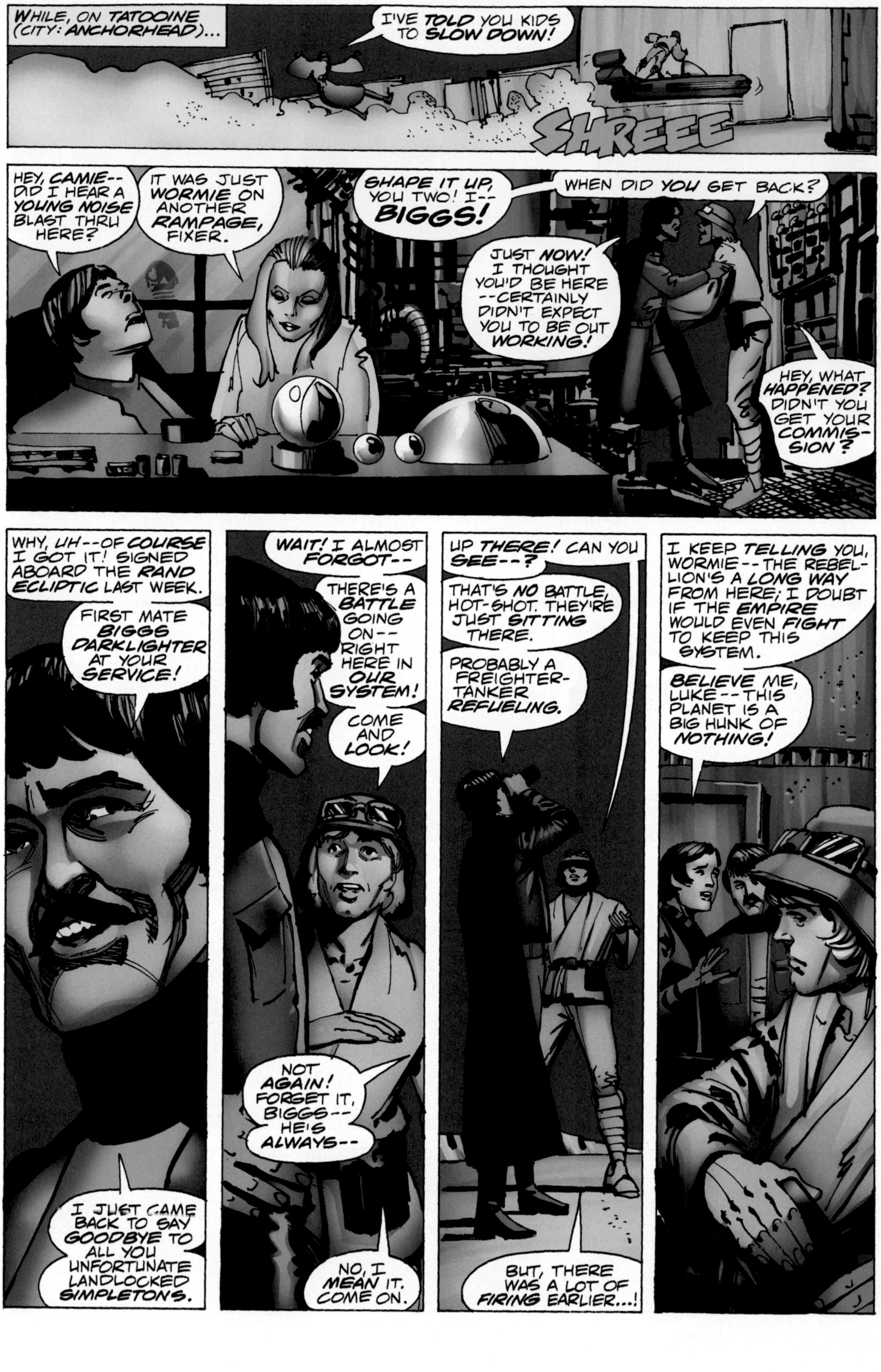

WHILE, ON TATOOINE (CITY: ANCHORHEAD)...
I'VE TOLD YOU KIDS TO SLOW DOWN!
SHREEE
HEY, CAMIE-- DID I HEAR A YOUNG NOISE BLAST THRU HERE?
IT WAS JUST WORMIE ON ANOTHER RAMPAGE, FIXER.
SHAPE IT UP, YOU TWO! I-- BIGGS!
WHEN DID YOU GET BACK?
JUST NOW! I THOUGHT YOU'D BE HERE --CERTAINLY DIDN'T EXPECT YOU TO BE OUT WORKING!
HEY, WHAT HAPPENED? DIDN'T YOU GET YOUR COMMIS-SION?
WHY, UH--OF COURSE I GOT IT! SIGNED ABOARD THE RAND ECLIPTIC LAST WEEK.
FIRST MATE BIGGS DARKLIGHTER AT YOUR SERVICE!
I JUST CAME BACK TO SAY GOODBYE TO ALL YOU UNFORTUNATE LANDLOCKED SIMPLETONS.
WAIT! I ALMOST FORGOT--
THERE'S A BATTLE GOING ON-- RIGHT HERE IN OUR SYSTEM!
COME AND LOOK!
NOT AGAIN! FORGET IT, BIGGS-- HE'S ALWAYS--
NO, I MEAN IT. COME ON.
UP THERE! CAN YOU SEE--?
THAT'S NO BATTLE, HOT-SHOT. THEY'RE JUST SITTING THERE.
PROBABLY A FREIGHTER-TANKER REFUELING.
BUT, THERE WAS A LOT OF FIRING EARLIER...!
I KEEP TELLING YOU, WORMIE--THE REBEL-LION'S A LONG WAY FROM HERE; I DOUBT IF THE EMPIRE WOULD EVEN FIGHT TO KEEP THIS SYSTEM.
BELIEVE ME, LUKE--THIS PLANET IS A BIG HUNK OF NOTHING!

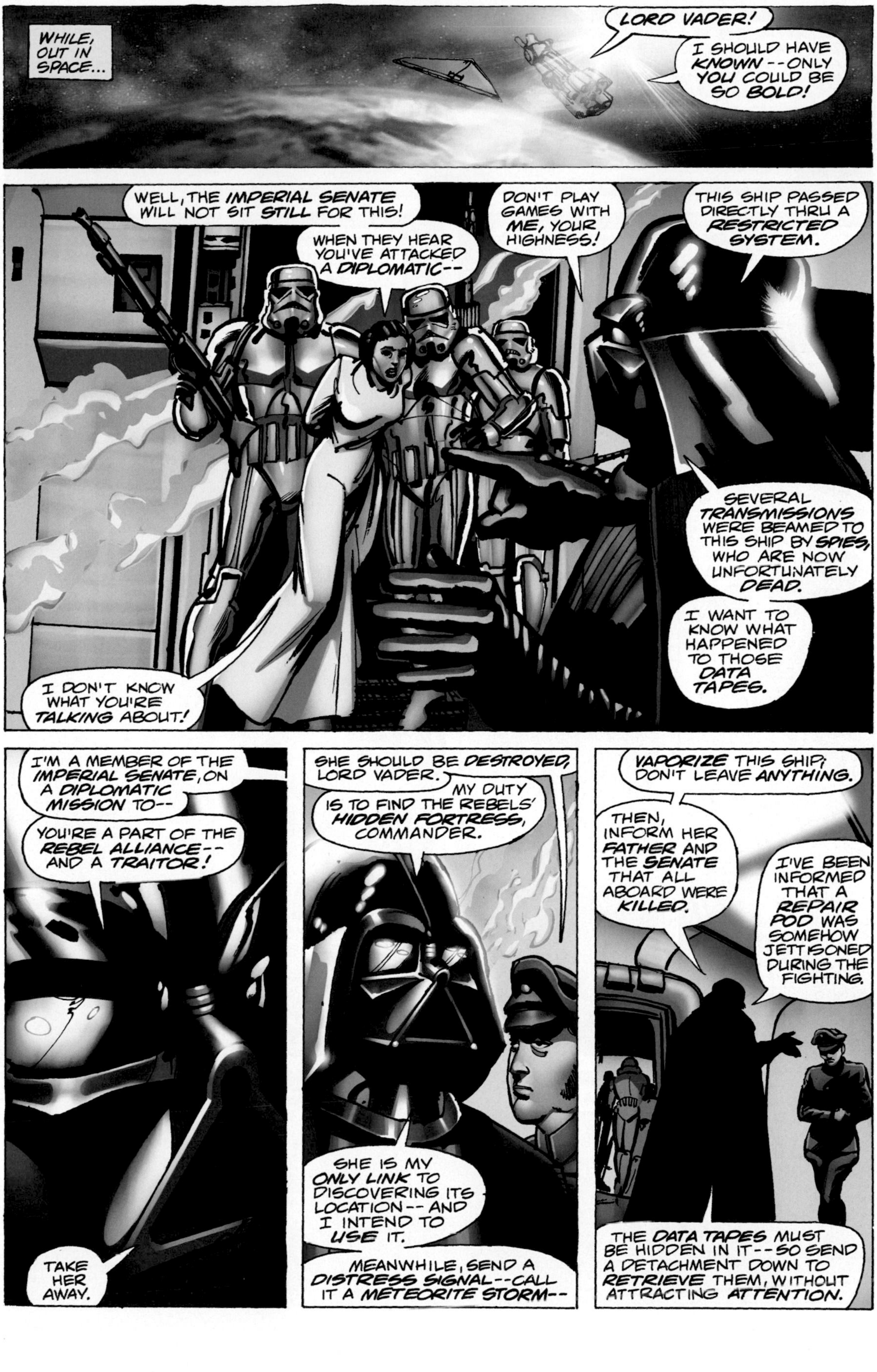

WHILE, OUT IN SPACE...
LORD VADER!
I SHOULD HAVE KNOWN--ONLY YOU COULD BE SO BOLD!
WELL, THE IMPERIAL SENATE WILL NOT SIT STILL FOR THIS!
WHEN THEY HEAR YOU'VE ATTACKED A DIPLOMATIC--
DON'T PLAY GAMES WITH ME, YOUR HIGHNESS!
THIS SHIP PASSED DIRECTLY THRU A RESTRICTED SYSTEM.
SEVERAL TRANSMISSIONS WERE BEAMED TO THIS SHIP BY SPIES, WHO ARE NOW UNFORTUNATELY DEAD.
I WANT TO KNOW WHAT HAPPENED TO THOSE DATA TAPES.
I DON'T KNOW WHAT YOU'RE TALKING ABOUT!
I'M A MEMBER OF THE IMPERIAL SENATE, ON A DIPLOMATIC MISSION TO--
YOU'RE A PART OF THE REBEL ALLIANCE-- AND A TRAITOR!
TAKE HER AWAY.
SHE SHOULD BE DESTROYED, LORD VADER.
MY DUTY IS TO FIND THE REBELS' HIDDEN FORTRESS, COMMANDER.
SHE IS MY ONLY LINK TO DISCOVERING ITS LOCATION-- AND I INTEND TO USE IT.
MEANWHILE, SEND A DISTRESS SIGNAL--CALL IT A METEORITE STORM--
VAPORIZE THIS SHIP; DON'T LEAVE ANYTHING.
THEN, INFORM HER FATHER AND THE SENATE THAT ALL ABOARD WERE KILLED.
I'VE BEEN INFORMED THAT A REPAIR POD WAS SOMEHOW JETTISONED DURING THE FIGHTING.
THE DATA TAPES MUST BE HIDDEN IN IT--SO SEND A DETACHMENT DOWN TO RETRIEVE THEM, WITHOUT ATTRACTING ATTENTION.

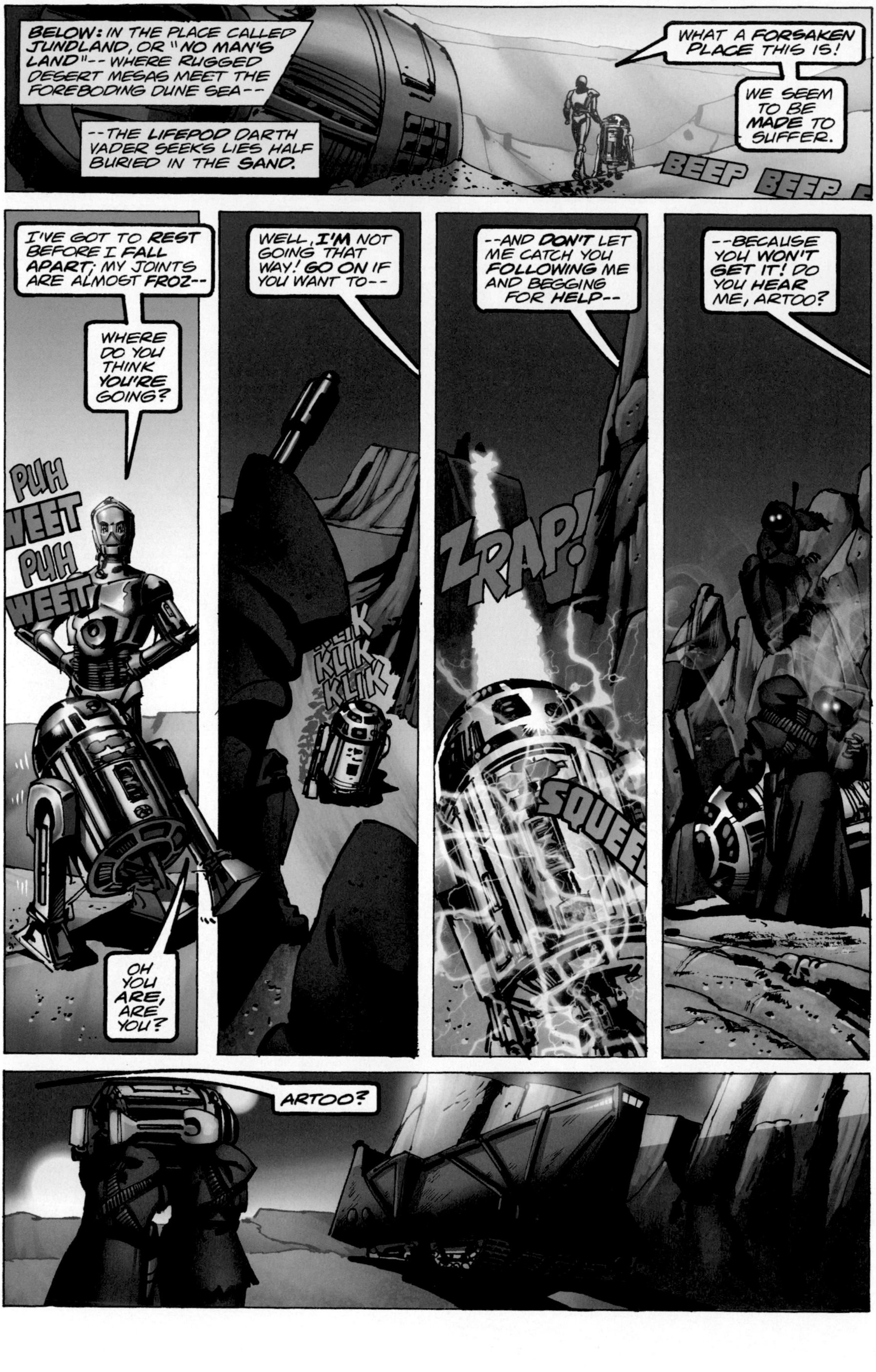
BELOW: IN THE PLACE CALLED JUNDLAND, OR "NO MAN'S LAND"-- WHERE RUGGED DESERT MESAS MEET THE FOREBODING DUNE SEA--
--THE LIFEPOD DARTH VADER SEEKS LIES HALF BURIED IN THE SAND.
WHAT A FORSAKEN PLACE THIS IS!
WE SEEM TO BE MADE TO SUFFER.
BEEP BEEP
I'VE GOT TO REST BEFORE I FALL APART; MY JOINTS ARE ALMOST FROZ--
WHERE DO YOU THINK YOU'RE GOING?
PUH WEET PUH WEET
OH YOU ARE, ARE YOU?
WELL, I'M NOT GOING THAT WAY! GO ON IF YOU WANT TO--
KLIK KLIK
--AND DON'T LET ME CATCH YOU FOLLOWING ME AND BEGGING FOR HELP--
ZRAP!
--BECAUSE YOU WON'T GET IT! DO YOU HEAR ME, ARTOO?
ARTOO?

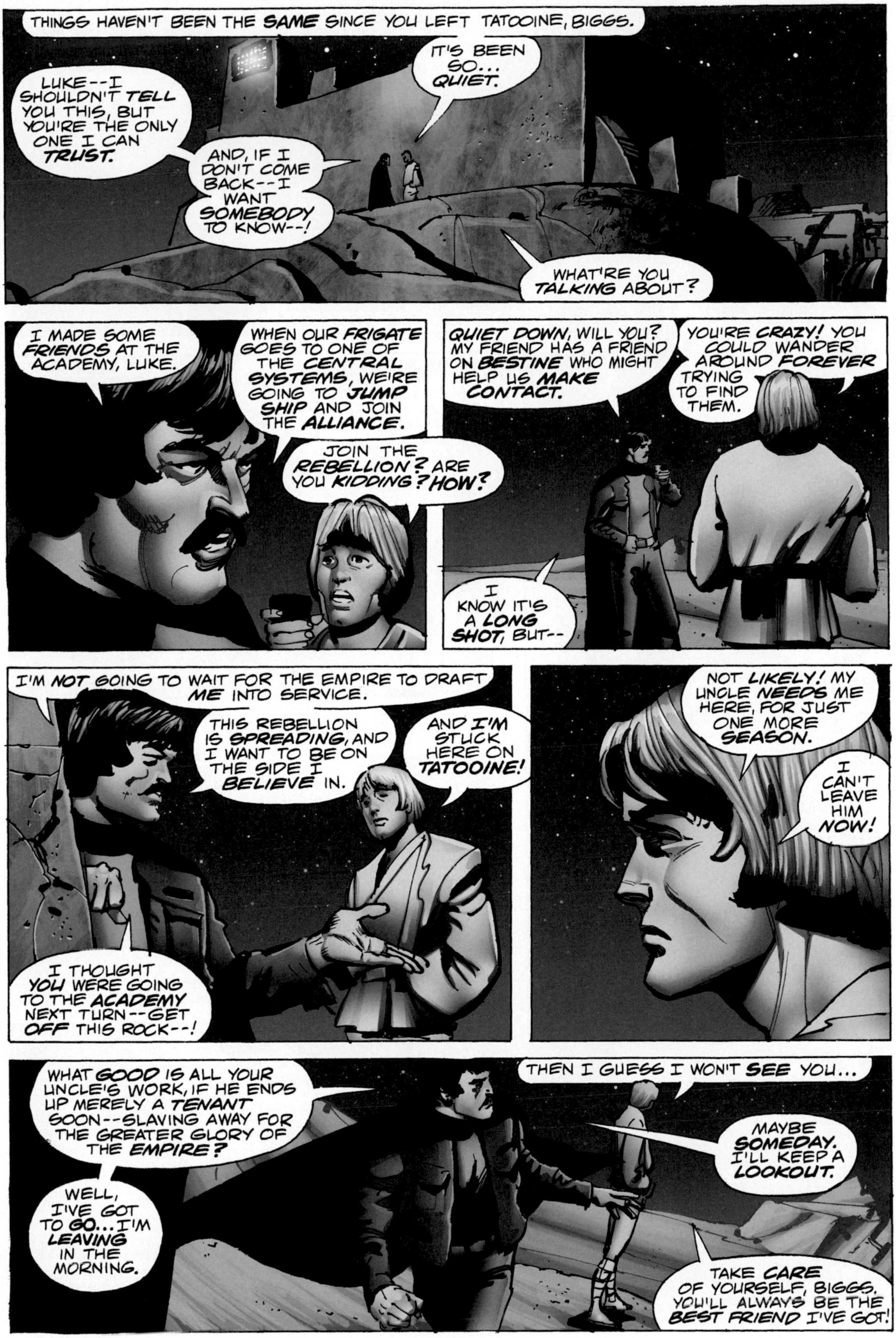
THINGS HAVEN'T BEEN THE SAME SINCE YOU LEFT TATOOINE, BIGGS.
IT'S BEEN SO... QUIET.
LUKE--I SHOULDN'T TELL YOU THIS, BUT YOU'RE THE ONLY ONE I CAN TRUST.
AND, IF I DON'T COME BACK--I WANT SOMEBODY TO KNOW--!
WHAT'RE YOU TALKING ABOUT?
I MADE SOME FRIENDS AT THE ACADEMY, LUKE.
WHEN OUR FRIGATE GOES TO ONE OF THE CENTRAL SYSTEMS, WE'RE GOING TO JUMP SHIP AND JOIN THE ALLIANCE.
JOIN THE REBELLION? ARE YOU KIDDING? HOW?
QUIET DOWN, WILL YOU? MY FRIEND HAS A FRIEND ON BESTINE WHO MIGHT HELP US MAKE CONTACT.
YOU'RE CRAZY! YOU COULD WANDER AROUND FOREVER TRYING TO FIND THEM.
I KNOW IT'S A LONG SHOT, BUT--
I'M NOT GOING TO WAIT FOR THE EMPIRE TO DRAFT ME INTO SERVICE.
THIS REBELLION IS SPREADING, AND I WANT TO BE ON THE SIDE I BELIEVE IN.
AND I'M STUCK HERE ON TATOOINE!
I THOUGHT YOU WERE GOING TO THE ACADEMY NEXT TURN--GET OFF THIS ROCK--!
NOT LIKELY! MY UNCLE NEEDS ME HERE, FOR JUST ONE MORE SEASON.
I CAN'T LEAVE HIM NOW!
WHAT GOOD IS ALL YOUR UNCLE'S WORK, IF HE ENDS UP MERELY A TENANT SOON--SLAVING AWAY FOR THE GREATER GLORY OF THE EMPIRE?
WELL, I'VE GOT TO GO...I'M LEAVING IN THE MORNING.
THEN I GUESS I WON'T SEE YOU...
MAYBE SOMEDAY. I'LL KEEP A LOOKOUT.
TAKE CARE OF YOURSELF, BIGGS. YOU'LL ALWAYS BE THE BEST FRIEND I'VE GOT!

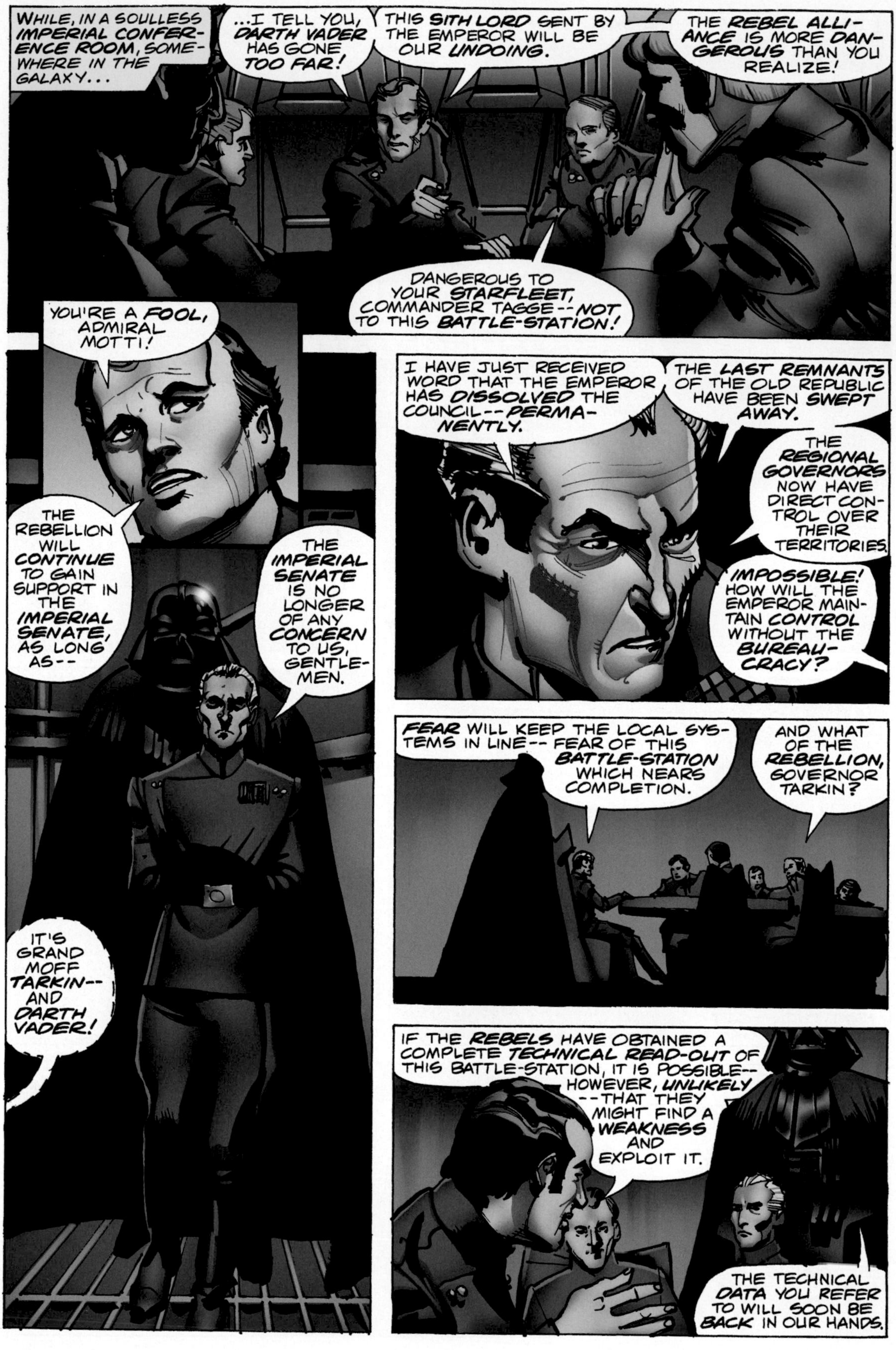

WHILE, IN A SOULLESS IMPERIAL CONFERENCE ROOM, SOMEWHERE IN THE GALAXY...
...I TELL YOU, DARTH VADER HAS GONE TOO FAR!
THIS SITH LORD SENT BY THE EMPEROR WILL BE OUR UNDOING.
THE REBEL ALLIANCE IS MORE DANGEROUS THAN YOU REALIZE!
DANGEROUS TO YOUR STARFLEET, COMMANDER TAGGE--NOT TO THIS BATTLE-STATION!
YOU'RE A FOOL, ADMIRAL MOTTI!
THE REBELLION WILL CONTINUE TO GAIN SUPPORT IN THE IMPERIAL SENATE, AS LONG AS--
THE IMPERIAL SENATE IS NO LONGER OF ANY CONCERN TO US, GENTLEMEN.
IT'S GRAND MOFF TARKIN--AND DARTH VADER!
I HAVE JUST RECEIVED WORD THAT THE EMPEROR HAS DISSOLVED THE COUNCIL--PERMANENTLY.
THE LAST REMNANTS OF THE OLD REPUBLIC HAVE BEEN SWEPT AWAY.
THE REGIONAL GOVERNORS NOW HAVE DIRECT CONTROL OVER THEIR TERRITORIES.
IMPOSSIBLE! HOW WILL THE EMPEROR MAINTAIN CONTROL WITHOUT THE BUREAUCRACY?
FEAR WILL KEEP THE LOCAL SYSTEMS IN LINE--FEAR OF THIS BATTLE-STATION WHICH NEARS COMPLETION.
AND WHAT OF THE REBELLION, GOVERNOR TARKIN?
IF THE REBELS HAVE OBTAINED A COMPLETE TECHNICAL READ-OUT OF THIS BATTLE-STATION, IT IS POSSIBLE--HOWEVER, UNLIKELY--THAT THEY MIGHT FIND A WEAKNESS AND EXPLOIT IT.
THE TECHNICAL DATA YOU REFER TO WILL SOON BE BACK IN OUR HANDS.

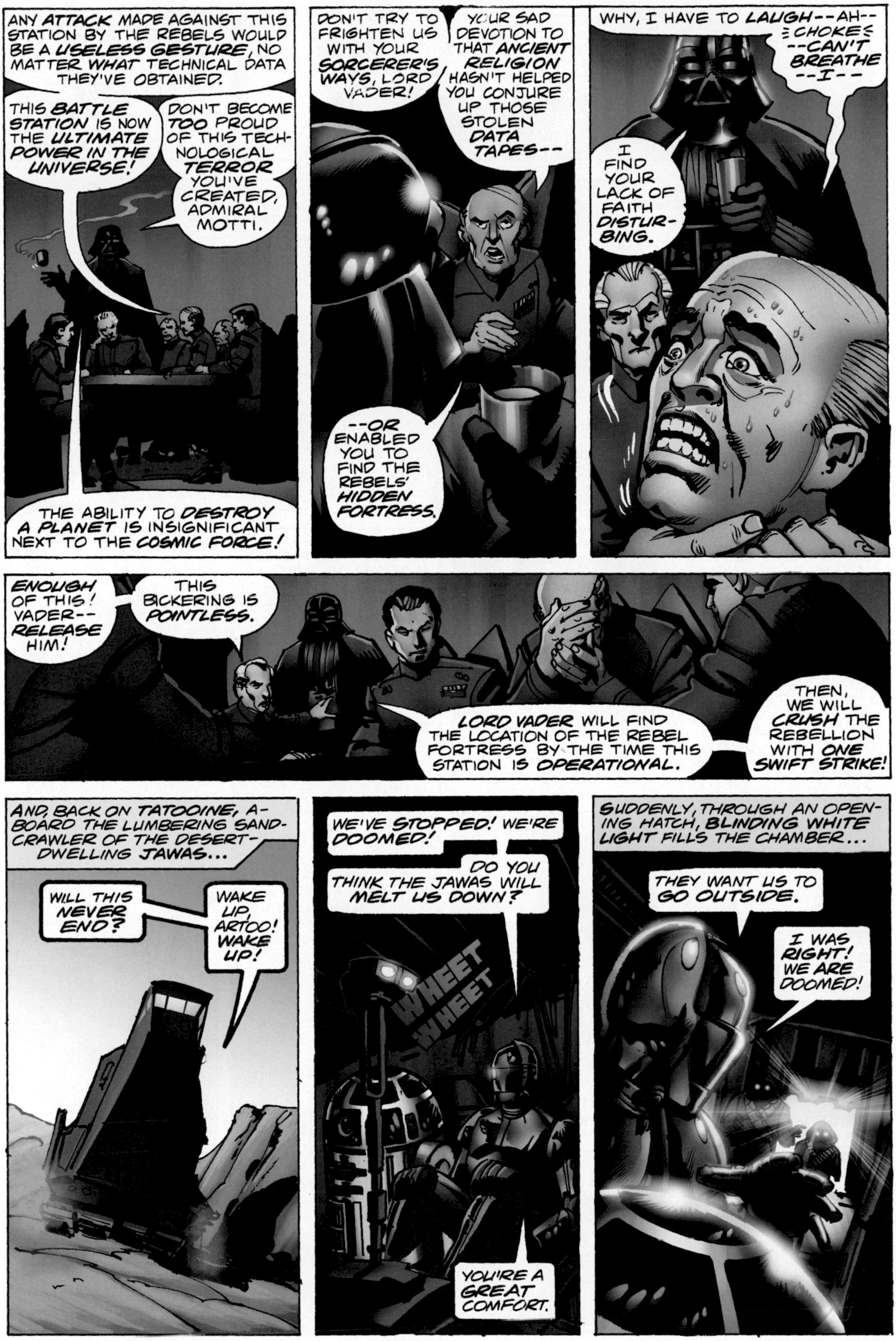
ANY ATTACK MADE AGAINST THIS STATION BY THE REBELS WOULD BE A USELESS GESTURE, NO MATTER WHAT TECHNICAL DATA THEY'VE OBTAINED.
THIS BATTLE STATION IS NOW THE ULTIMATE POWER IN THE UNIVERSE!
DON'T BECOME TOO PROUD OF THIS TECHNOLOGICAL TERROR YOU'VE CREATED, ADMIRAL MOTTI.
THE ABILITY TO DESTROY A PLANET IS INSIGNIFICANT NEXT TO THE COSMIC FORCE!
DON'T TRY TO FRIGHTEN US WITH YOUR SORCERER'S WAYS, LORD VADER!
YOUR SAD DEVOTION TO THAT ANCIENT RELIGION HASN'T HELPED YOU CONJURE UP THOSE STOLEN DATA TAPES--
--OR ENABLED YOU TO FIND THE REBELS' HIDDEN FORTRESS.
WHY, I HAVE TO LAUGH--AH-- CHOKE --CAN'T BREATHE --I--
I FIND YOUR LACK OF FAITH DISTURBING.
ENOUGH OF THIS! VADER-- RELEASE HIM!
THIS BICKERING IS POINTLESS.
LORD VADER WILL FIND THE LOCATION OF THE REBEL FORTRESS BY THE TIME THIS STATION IS OPERATIONAL.
THEN, WE WILL CRUSH THE REBELLION WITH ONE SWIFT STRIKE!
AND, BACK ON TATOOINE, ABOARD THE LUMBERING SANDCRAWLER OF THE DESERT-DWELLING JAWAS...
WILL THIS NEVER END?
WAKE UP, ARTOO! WAKE UP!
WE'VE STOPPED! WE'RE DOOMED!
DO YOU THINK THE JAWAS WILL MELT US DOWN?
WHEET WHEET
YOU'RE A GREAT COMFORT.
SUDDENLY, THROUGH AN OPENING HATCH, BLINDING WHITE LIGHT FILLS THE CHAMBER...
THEY WANT US TO GO OUTSIDE.
I WAS RIGHT! WE ARE DOOMED!

LUKE-- TELL YOUR UNCLE *OWEN* THAT IF HE GETS A *TRANS-LATOR* TO BE SURE IT SPEAKS *"BOCCE"!*

IT LOOKS LIKE WE DON'T HAVE MUCH OF A *CHOICE*, AUNT BERU, BUT I'LL *REMIND* HIM.

YES, THIS R2-D2 MODEL WILL DO FINE; THAT *OTHER* ONE OVER THERE LOOKS READY FOR THE *JUNKHEAP.*

SAVE YOUR SALES PITCH! *YOU*--ROBOT--DO YOU KNOW *ETIQUETTE* AND *PROTOCOL?*

DO I KNOW *PROTOCOL!* WHY, IT'S MY *PRIMARY* FUNCTION!

I AM WELL VERSED IN THE *CUSTOMS* AND--

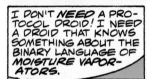

I DON'T *NEED* A PRO-TOCOL DROID! I NEED A DROID THAT KNOWS SOMETHING ABOUT THE *BINARY* LANGUAGE OF *MOISTURE* VAPOR-ATORS.

VAPORATORS! SIR, MY *FIRST* JOB WAS PRO-GRAMMING BINARY *LOAD LIFTERS*, A VERY SIMILAR--

DO YOU SPEAK *"BOCCE"?*

IT'S LIKE A SEC-OND LANGUAGE FOR ME, SIR. I'M AS FLUENT AS--

SHUT UP!

I'LL TAKE *THIS* ONE.

SHUTTING UP, SIR.

LUKE, TAKE THEM TO THE *GARAGE* AND CLEAN THEM UP.

BUT I WAS GOING INTO *TOSHI* STATION TO--

AFTER YOU'VE FINISHED YOUR *CHORES!*

UNCLE OWEN-- *THIS* R2 UNIT HAS A *BAD MOTIVATOR*, LOOK!

SPROING!

IF I MIGHT SAY SO, SIR, *THIS* R2 UNIT IS IN *TOP* CONDITION --A REAL *BARGAIN.*

THEN WE'LL TAKE *IT*--AS A *REPLACE-MENT.*

I'LL TAKE CARE OF THE *JAWAS*, LUKE. *RUN* ALONG.

BLEEP!

DON'T YOU *FORGET* THIS, ARTOO!

WHY I STICK MY *NECK* OUT FOR YOU IS BE-YOND MY *CAPACITY* TO--

BEEP BEEP BEEP

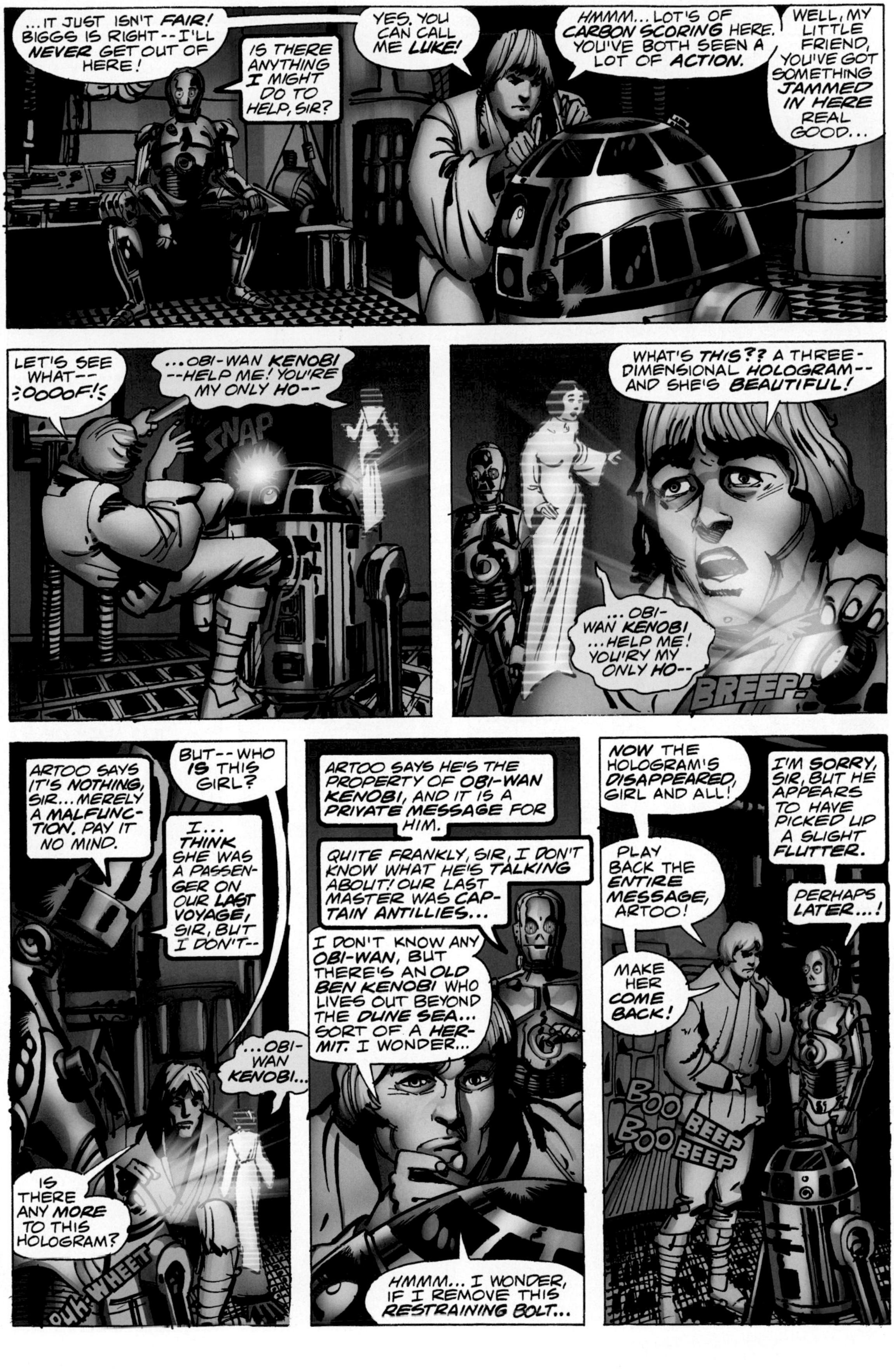
...IT JUST ISN'T FAIR! BIGGS IS RIGHT--I'LL NEVER GET OUT OF HERE!
IS THERE ANYTHING I MIGHT DO TO HELP, SIR?
YES, YOU CAN CALL ME LUKE!
HMMM... LOT'S OF CARBON SCORING HERE. YOU'VE BOTH SEEN A LOT OF ACTION.
WELL, MY LITTLE FRIEND, YOU'VE GOT SOMETHING JAMMED IN HERE REAL GOOD...
LET'S SEE WHAT-- OOOOF!
...OBI-WAN KENOBI --HELP ME! YOU'RE MY ONLY HO--
SNAP
WHAT'S THIS?? A THREE-DIMENSIONAL HOLOGRAM--AND SHE'S BEAUTIFUL!
...OBI-WAN KENOBI ...HELP ME! YOU'RY MY ONLY HO--
BREEP!
ARTOO SAYS IT'S NOTHING, SIR... MERELY A MALFUNCTION. PAY IT NO MIND.
BUT--WHO IS THIS GIRL?
I... THINK SHE WAS A PASSENGER ON OUR LAST VOYAGE, SIR, BUT I DON'T--
...OBI-WAN KENOBI...
IS THERE ANY MORE TO THIS HOLOGRAM?
OOH-WHEET
ARTOO SAYS HE'S THE PROPERTY OF OBI-WAN KENOBI, AND IT IS A PRIVATE MESSAGE FOR HIM.
QUITE FRANKLY, SIR, I DON'T KNOW WHAT HE'S TALKING ABOUT! OUR LAST MASTER WAS CAPTAIN ANTILLIES...
I DON'T KNOW ANY OBI-WAN, BUT THERE'S AN OLD BEN KENOBI WHO LIVES OUT BEYOND THE DUNE SEA... SORT OF A HERMIT. I WONDER...
HMMM... I WONDER, IF I REMOVE THIS RESTRAINING BOLT...
NOW THE HOLOGRAM'S DISAPPEARED, GIRL AND ALL!
PLAY BACK THE ENTIRE MESSAGE, ARTOO!
MAKE HER COME BACK!
I'M SORRY, SIR, BUT HE APPEARS TO HAVE PICKED UP A SLIGHT FLUTTER.
PERHAPS LATER...!
BOO BOO BEEP BEEP

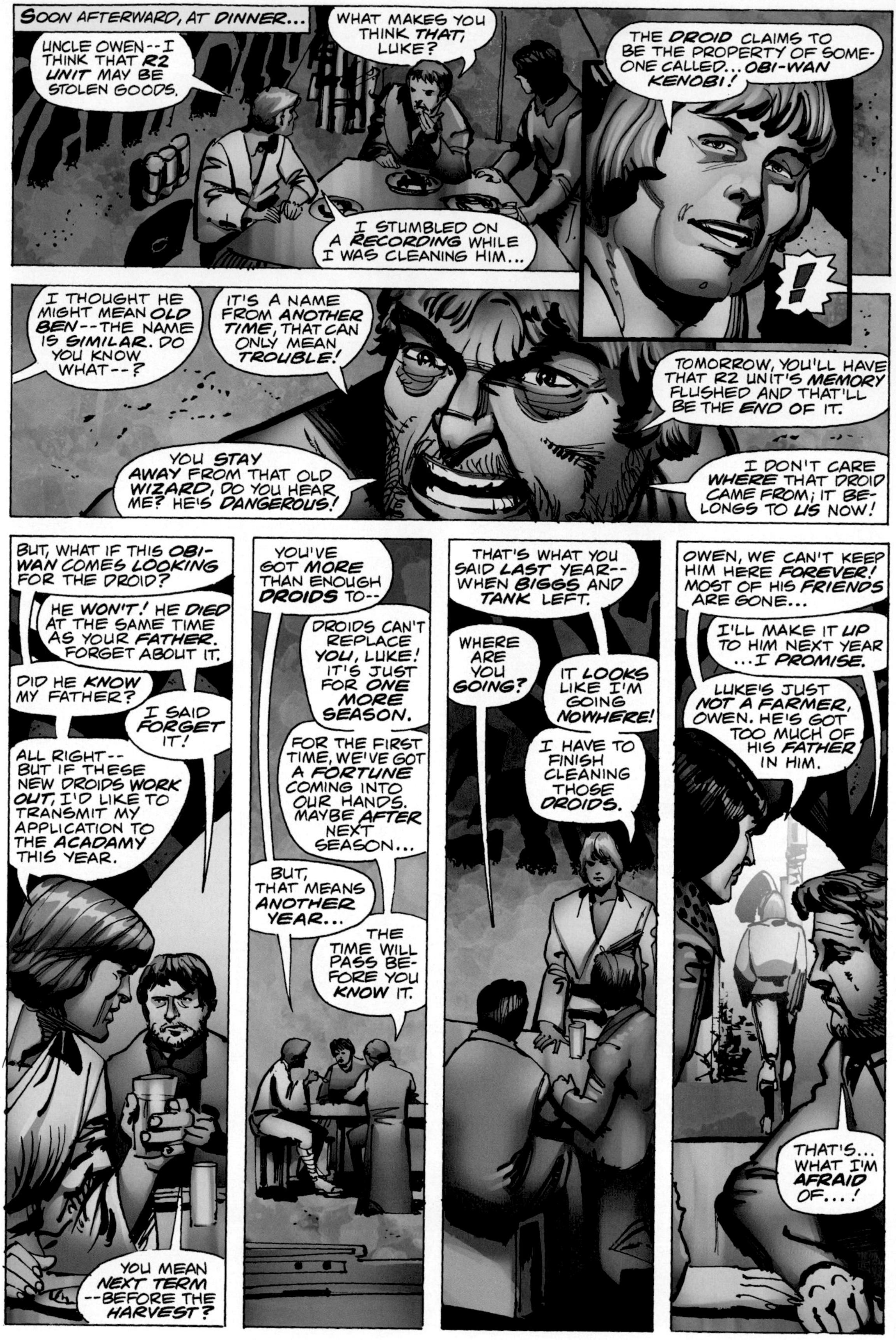
SOON AFTERWARD, AT DINNER...
UNCLE OWEN--I THINK THAT R2 UNIT MAY BE STOLEN GOODS.
WHAT MAKES YOU THINK THAT, LUKE?
I STUMBLED ON A RECORDING WHILE I WAS CLEANING HIM...
THE DROID CLAIMS TO BE THE PROPERTY OF SOMEONE CALLED... OBI-WAN KENOBI!
!
I THOUGHT HE MIGHT MEAN OLD BEN--THE NAME IS SIMILAR. DO YOU KNOW WHAT--?
IT'S A NAME FROM ANOTHER TIME, THAT CAN ONLY MEAN TROUBLE!
TOMORROW, YOU'LL HAVE THAT R2 UNIT'S MEMORY FLUSHED AND THAT'LL BE THE END OF IT.
YOU STAY AWAY FROM THAT OLD WIZARD, DO YOU HEAR ME? HE'S DANGEROUS!
I DON'T CARE WHERE THAT DROID CAME FROM; IT BELONGS TO US NOW!
BUT, WHAT IF THIS OBI-WAN COMES LOOKING FOR THE DROID?
HE WON'T! HE DIED AT THE SAME TIME AS YOUR FATHER. FORGET ABOUT IT.
DID HE KNOW MY FATHER?
I SAID FORGET IT!
ALL RIGHT--BUT IF THESE NEW DROIDS WORK OUT, I'D LIKE TO TRANSMIT MY APPLICATION TO THE ACADAMY THIS YEAR.
YOU MEAN NEXT TERM--BEFORE THE HARVEST?
YOU'VE GOT MORE THAN ENOUGH DROIDS TO--
DROIDS CAN'T REPLACE YOU, LUKE! IT'S JUST FOR ONE MORE SEASON.
FOR THE FIRST TIME, WE'VE GOT A FORTUNE COMING INTO OUR HANDS. MAYBE AFTER NEXT SEASON...
BUT, THAT MEANS ANOTHER YEAR...
THE TIME WILL PASS BEFORE YOU KNOW IT.
THAT'S WHAT YOU SAID LAST YEAR--WHEN BIGGS AND TANK LEFT.
WHERE ARE YOU GOING?
IT LOOKS LIKE I'M GOING NOWHERE!
I HAVE TO FINISH CLEANING THOSE DROIDS.
OWEN, WE CAN'T KEEP HIM HERE FOREVER! MOST OF HIS FRIENDS ARE GONE...
I'LL MAKE IT UP TO HIM NEXT YEAR ...I PROMISE.
LUKE'S JUST NOT A FARMER, OWEN. HE'S GOT TOO MUCH OF HIS FATHER IN HIM.
THAT'S... WHAT I'M AFRAID OF...!

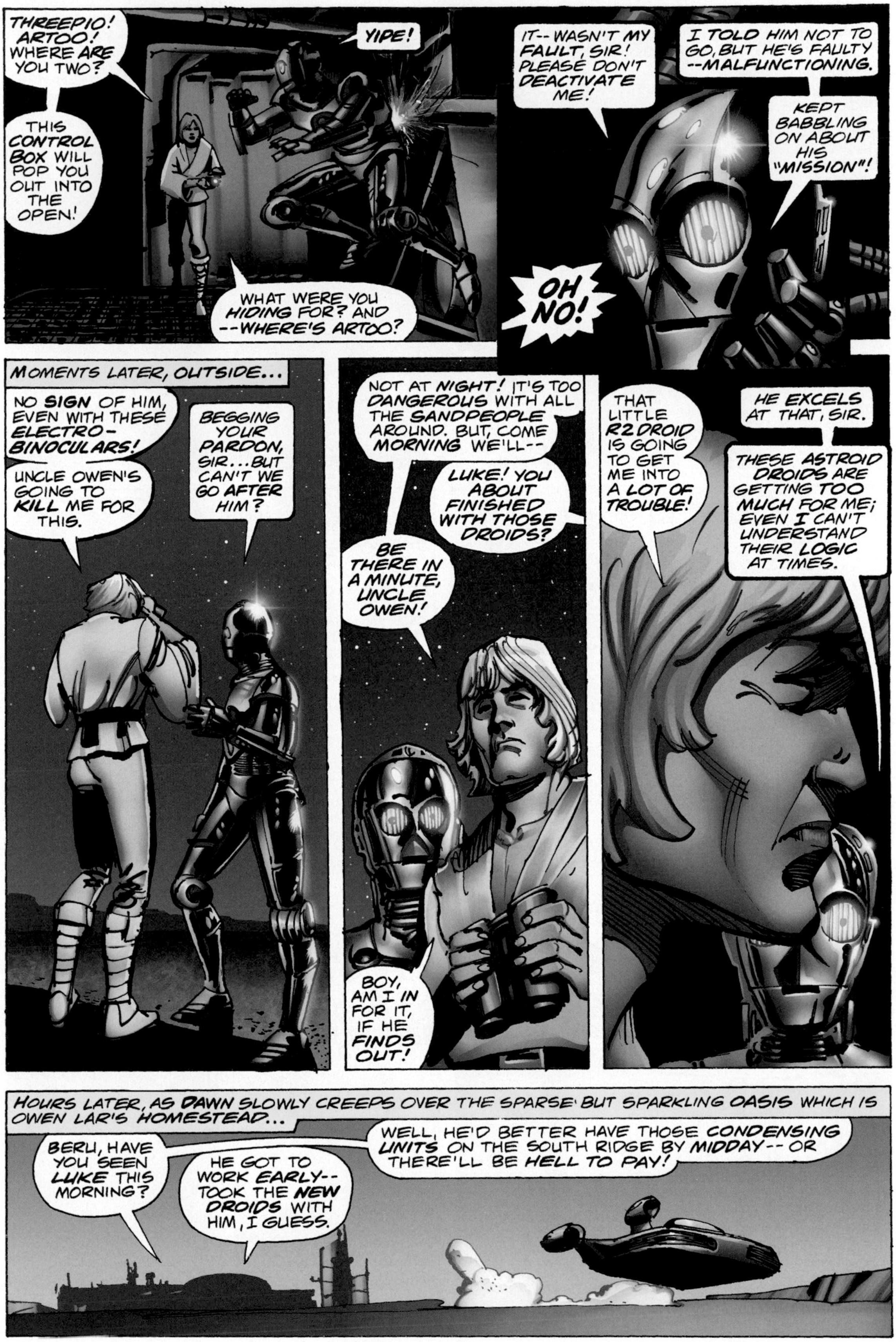
THREEPIO! ARTOO! WHERE ARE YOU TWO?
THIS CONTROL BOX WILL POP YOU OUT INTO THE OPEN!
YIPE!
WHAT WERE YOU HIDING FOR? AND --WHERE'S ARTOO?
IT--WASN'T MY FAULT, SIR! PLEASE DON'T DEACTIVATE ME!
I TOLD HIM NOT TO GO, BUT HE'S FAULTY --MALFUNCTIONING.
KEPT BABBLING ON ABOUT HIS "MISSION"!
OH NO!
MOMENTS LATER, OUTSIDE...
NO SIGN OF HIM, EVEN WITH THESE ELECTRO-BINOCULARS!
UNCLE OWEN'S GOING TO KILL ME FOR THIS.
BEGGING YOUR PARDON, SIR...BUT CAN'T WE GO AFTER HIM?
NOT AT NIGHT! IT'S TOO DANGEROUS WITH ALL THE SANDPEOPLE AROUND. BUT, COME MORNING WE'LL--
LUKE! YOU ABOUT FINISHED WITH THOSE DROIDS?
BE THERE IN A MINUTE, UNCLE OWEN!
BOY, AM I IN FOR IT, IF HE FINDS OUT!
THAT LITTLE R2 DROID IS GOING TO GET ME INTO A LOT OF TROUBLE!
HE EXCELS AT THAT, SIR.
THESE ASTROID DROIDS ARE GETTING TOO MUCH FOR ME; EVEN I CAN'T UNDERSTAND THEIR LOGIC AT TIMES.
HOURS LATER, AS DAWN SLOWLY CREEPS OVER THE SPARSE BUT SPARKLING OASIS WHICH IS OWEN LAR'S HOMESTEAD...
BERU, HAVE YOU SEEN LUKE THIS MORNING?
HE GOT TO WORK EARLY--TOOK THE NEW DROIDS WITH HIM, I GUESS.
WELL, HE'D BETTER HAVE THOSE CONDENSING UNITS ON THE SOUTH RIDGE BY MIDDAY-- OR THERE'LL BE HELL TO PAY!

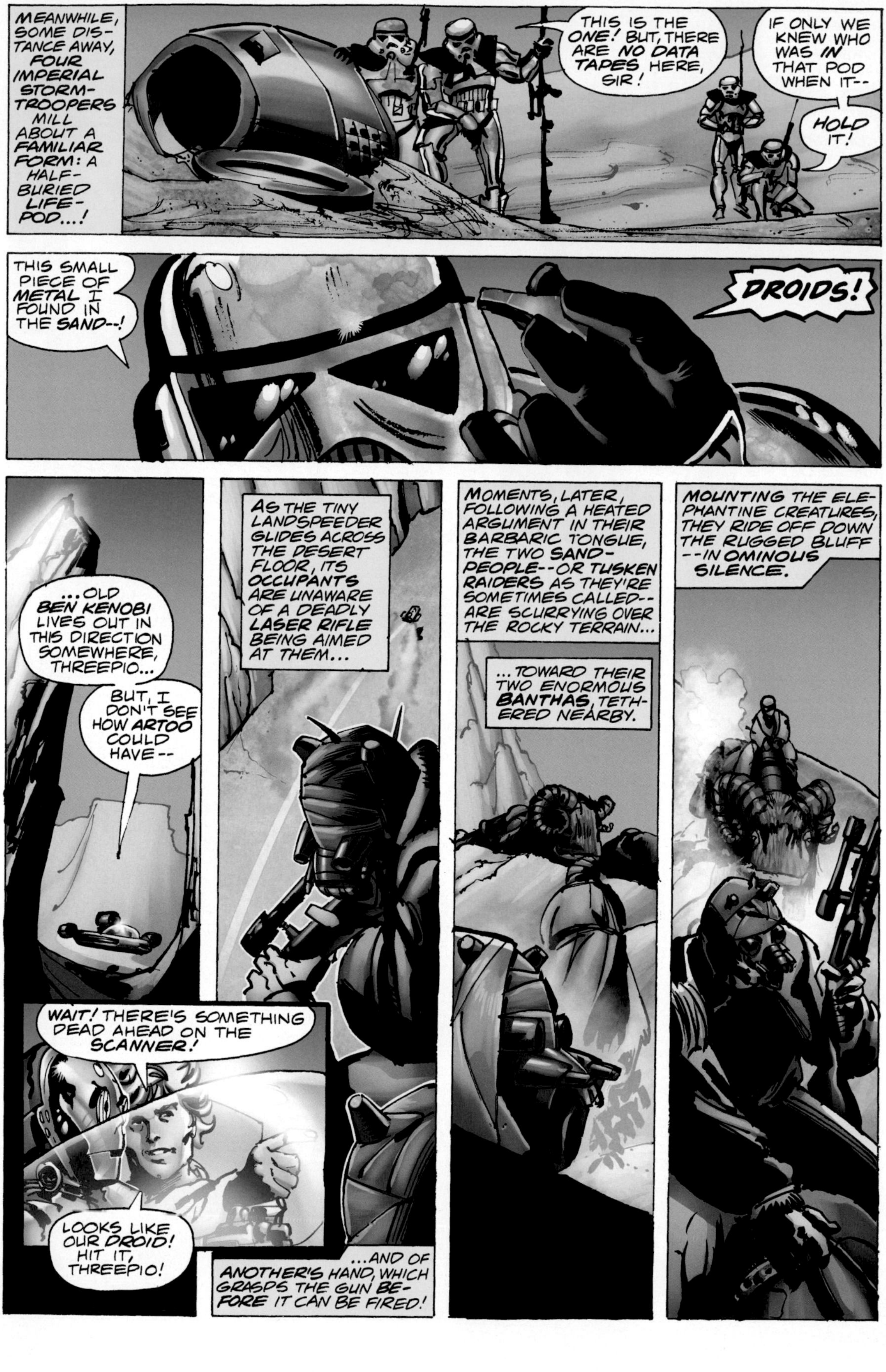
MEANWHILE, SOME DISTANCE AWAY, FOUR IMPERIAL STORM-TROOPERS MILL ABOUT A FAMILIAR FORM: A HALF-BURIED LIFE-POD...!
THIS IS THE ONE! BUT, THERE ARE NO DATA TAPES HERE, SIR!
IF ONLY WE KNEW WHO WAS IN THAT POD WHEN IT--
HOLD IT!
THIS SMALL PIECE OF METAL I FOUND IN THE SAND--!
DROIDS!
...OLD BEN KENOBI LIVES OUT IN THIS DIRECTION SOMEWHERE, THREEPIO...
BUT, I DON'T SEE HOW ARTOO COULD HAVE--
WAIT! THERE'S SOMETHING DEAD AHEAD ON THE SCANNER!
LOOKS LIKE OUR DROID! HIT IT, THREEPIO!
AS THE TINY LANDSPEEDER GLIDES ACROSS THE DESERT FLOOR, ITS OCCUPANTS ARE UNAWARE OF A DEADLY LASER RIFLE BEING AIMED AT THEM...
...AND OF ANOTHER'S HAND, WHICH GRASPS THE GUN BEFORE IT CAN BE FIRED!
MOMENTS, LATER, FOLLOWING A HEATED ARGUMENT IN THEIR BARBARIC TONGUE, THE TWO SAND-PEOPLE--OR TUSKEN RAIDERS AS THEY'RE SOMETIMES CALLED--ARE SCURRYING OVER THE ROCKY TERRAIN...
...TOWARD THEIR TWO ENORMOUS BANTHAS, TETHERED NEARBY.
MOUNTING THE ELEPHANTINE CREATURES, THEY RIDE OFF DOWN THE RUGGED BLUFF--IN OMINOUS SILENCE.

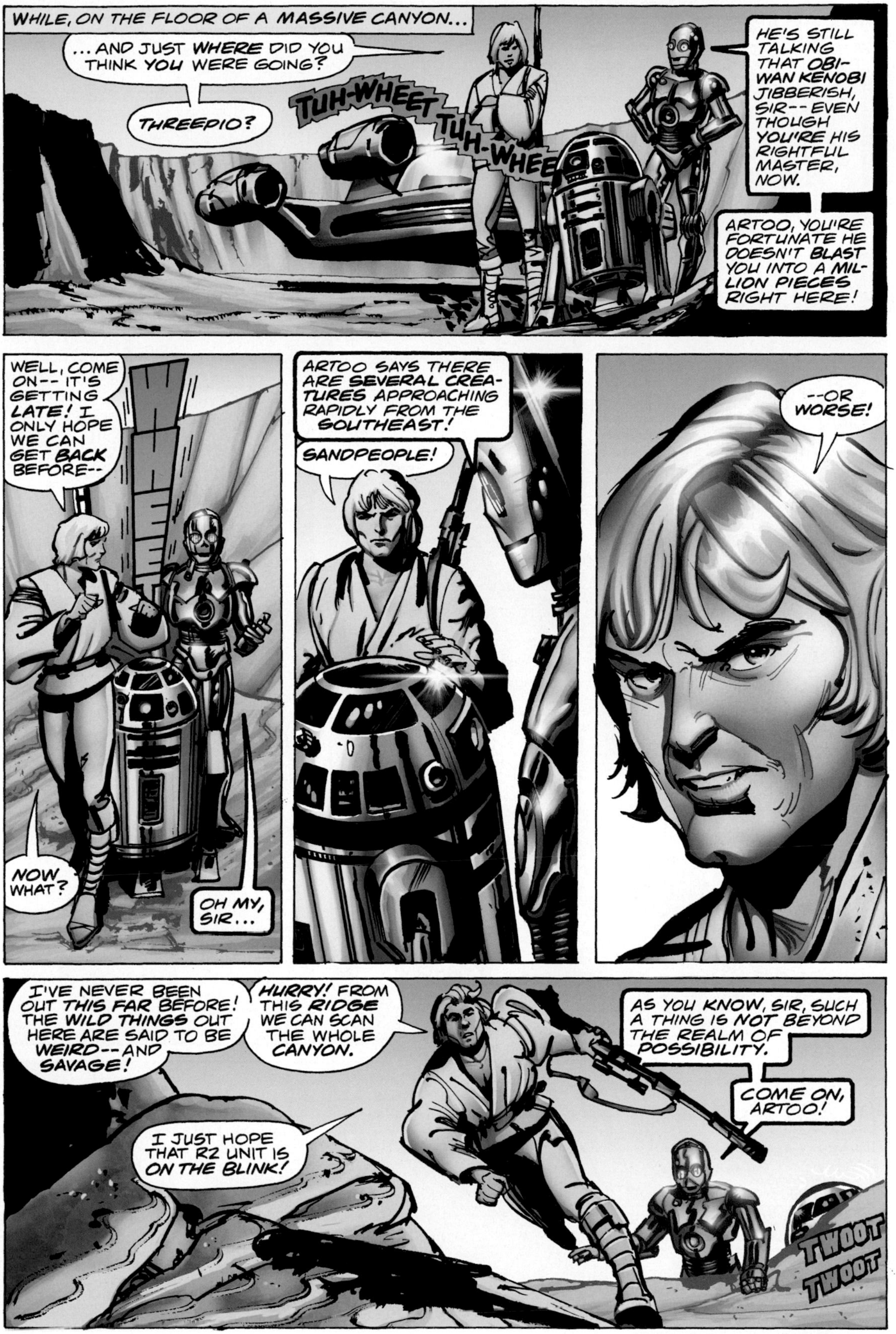
WHILE, ON THE FLOOR OF A MASSIVE CANYON...
...AND JUST WHERE DID YOU THINK YOU WERE GOING?
THREEPIO?
TUH-WHEET TUH-WHEE
HE'S STILL TALKING THAT OBI-WAN KENOBI JIBBERISH, SIR-- EVEN THOUGH YOU'RE HIS RIGHTFUL MASTER, NOW.
ARTOO, YOU'RE FORTUNATE HE DOESN'T BLAST YOU INTO A MILLION PIECES RIGHT HERE!
WELL, COME ON-- IT'S GETTING LATE! I ONLY HOPE WE CAN GET BACK BEFORE--
WHEET
NOW WHAT?
OH MY, SIR...
ARTOO SAYS THERE ARE SEVERAL CREATURES APPROACHING RAPIDLY FROM THE SOUTHEAST!
SANDPEOPLE!
--OR WORSE!
I'VE NEVER BEEN OUT THIS FAR BEFORE! THE WILD THINGS OUT HERE ARE SAID TO BE WEIRD--AND SAVAGE!
HURRY! FROM THIS RIDGE WE CAN SCAN THE WHOLE CANYON.
AS YOU KNOW, SIR, SUCH A THING IS NOT BEYOND THE REALM OF POSSIBILITY.
COME ON, ARTOO!
I JUST HOPE THAT R2 UNIT IS ON THE BLINK!
TWOOT TWOOT

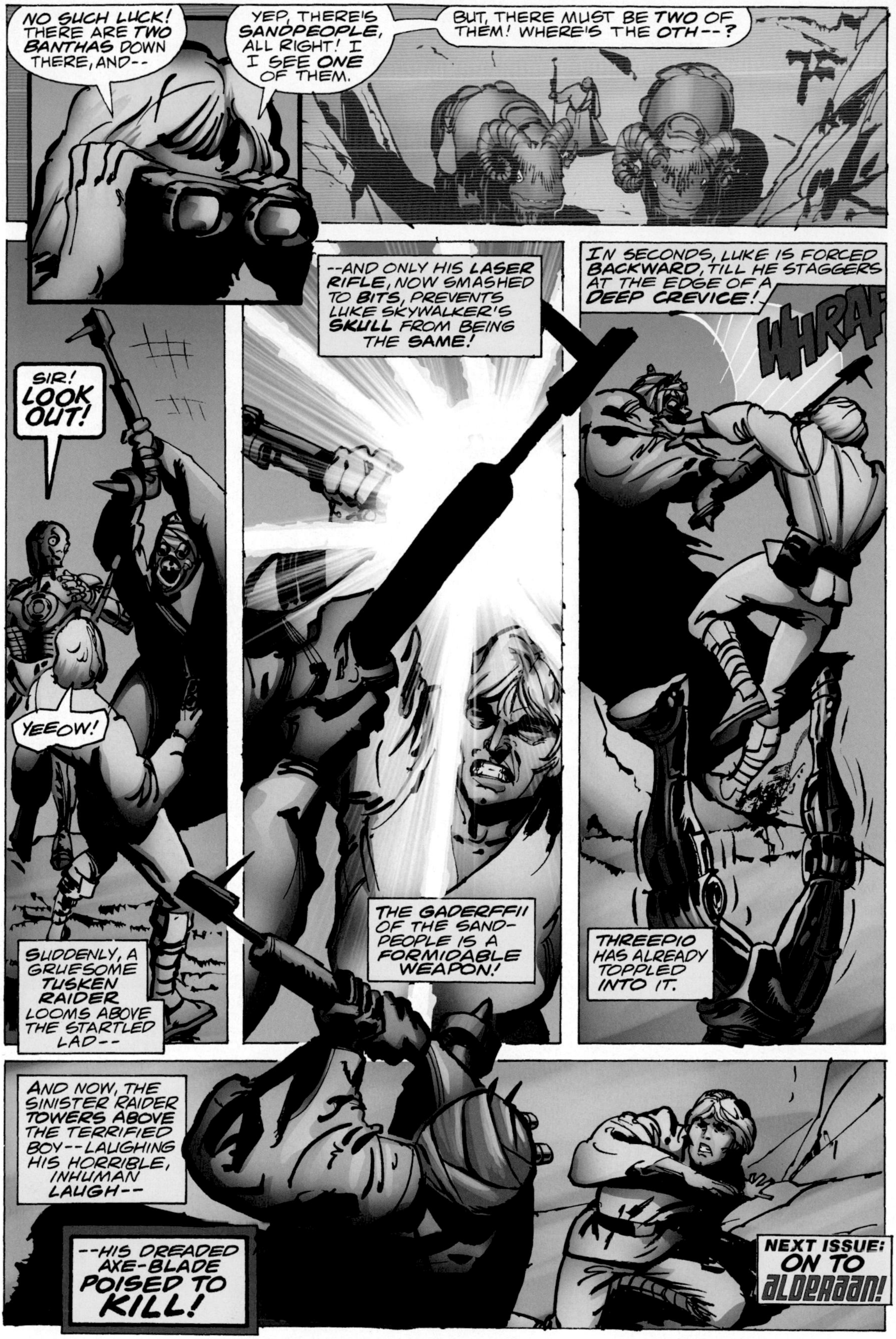
NO SUCH LUCK! THERE ARE TWO BANTHAS DOWN THERE, AND--
YEP, THERE'S SANDPEOPLE, ALL RIGHT! I I SEE ONE OF THEM.
BUT, THERE MUST BE TWO OF THEM! WHERE'S THE OTH--?
SUDDENLY, A GRUESOME TUSKEN RAIDER LOOMS ABOVE THE STARTLED LAD--
SIR! LOOK OUT!
YEEOW!
--AND ONLY HIS LASER RIFLE, NOW SMASHED TO BITS, PREVENTS LUKE SKYWALKER'S SKULL FROM BEING THE SAME!
THE GADERFFII OF THE SAND-PEOPLE IS A FORMIDABLE WEAPON!
IN SECONDS, LUKE IS FORCED BACKWARD, TILL HE STAGGERS AT THE EDGE OF A DEEP CREVICE!
WHRAP
THREEPIO HAS ALREADY TOPPLED INTO IT.
AND NOW, THE SINISTER RAIDER TOWERS ABOVE THE TERRIFIED BOY--LAUGHING HIS HORRIBLE, INHUMAN LAUGH--
--HIS DREADED AXE-BLADE POISED TO KILL!
NEXT ISSUE: ON TO ALDERAAN!

CONTINUED IN *STAR WARS: EPISODE IV — A NEW HOPE HC*

RETURN TO THE ORIGINAL MARVEL YEARS
WITH THESE DELUXE CLASSIC COLLECTIONS!

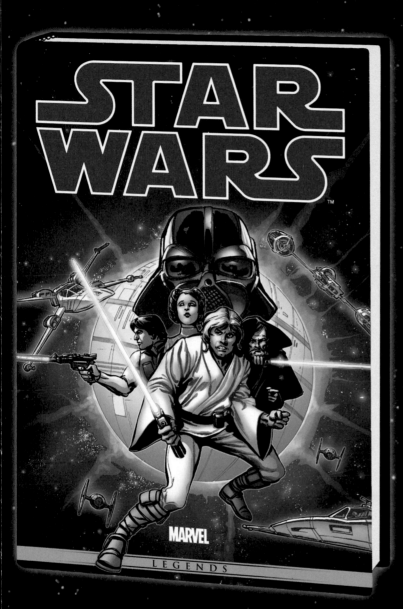

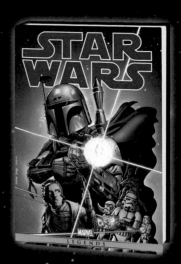

STAR WARS:
THE ORIGINAL MARVEL YEARS
OMNIBUS VOL. 2
978-0-7851-9342-5

STAR WARS: THE ORIGINAL MARVEL YEARS
OMNIBUS VOL. 1
978-0-7851-9106-3

STAR WARS:
THE ORIGINAL MARVEL YEARS
OMNIBUS VOL. 3
978-0-7851-9346-3

AVAILABLE NOW WHEREVER BOOKS ARE SOLD

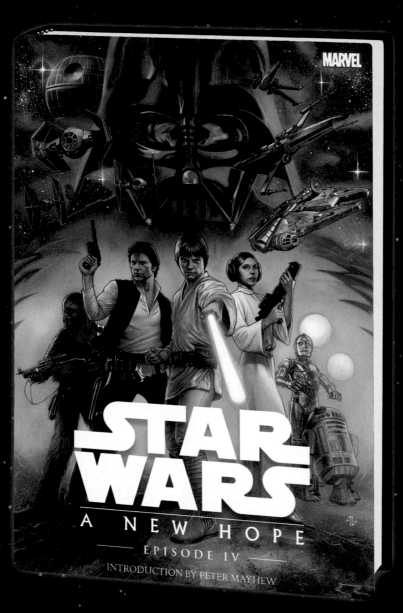

Y FAR, FAR AWAY!
F THE BIGGEST MOVIES IN HISTORY,
ERED INTERIORS!

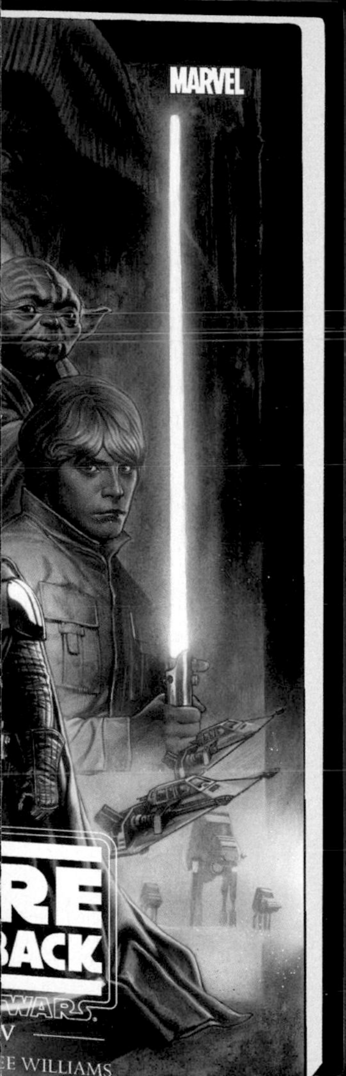
MARVEL
RE
BACK
V
EE WILLIAMS

PIRE STRIKES BACK HC

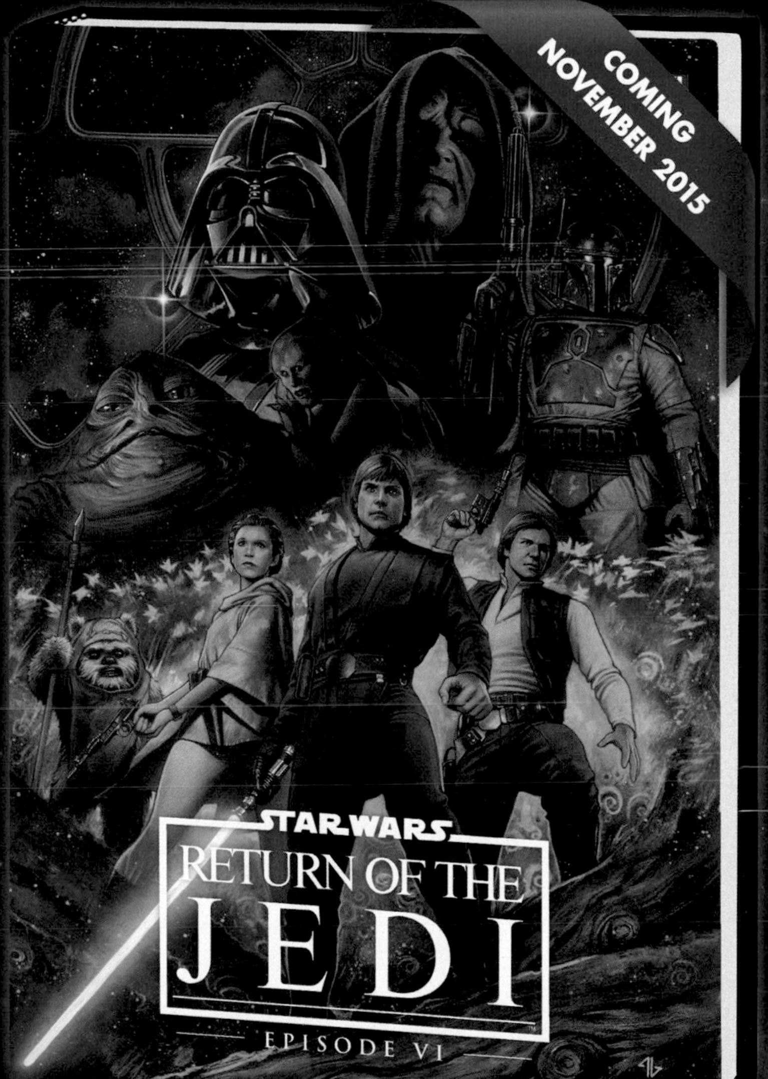
COMING
NOVEMBER 2015
STAR WARS
RETURN OF THE
JEDI
EPISODE VI

STAR WARS: EPISODE VI – RETURN OF THE JEDI HC
978-0-7851-9369-2

AN EPIC JOURNEY FROM THE BEGINNINGS OF THE OLD REPUBLIC TO THE RISE OF THE EMPIRE AND BEYOND!

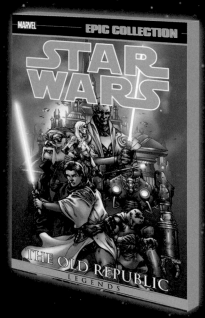

MARVEL
EPIC COLLECTION
STAR WARS
THE OLD REPUBLIC
LEGENDS

STAR WARS LEGENDS EPIC COLLECTION: THE OLD REPUBLIC VOL. 1 TPB
978-0-7851-9717-1

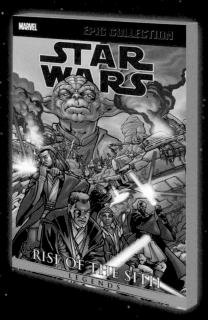

MARVEL
EPIC COLLECTION
STAR WARS
RISE OF THE SITH
LEGENDS

STAR WARS LEGENDS EPIC COLLECTION: RISE OF THE SITH VOL. 1 TPB
978-0-7851-9722-5

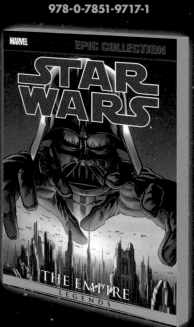

MARVEL
EPIC COLLECTION
STAR WARS
THE EMPIRE
LEGENDS

STAR WARS LEGENDS EPIC COLLECTION: THE EMPIRE VOL. 1 TPB
978-0-7851-9398-2

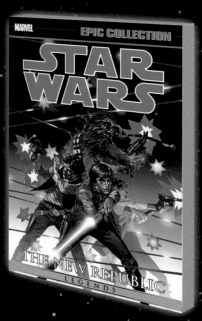

MARVEL
EPIC COLLECTION
STAR WARS
THE NEW REPUBLIC
LEGENDS

STAR WARS LEGENDS EPIC COLLECTION: THE NEW REPUBLIC VOL. 1 TPB
978-0-7851-9716-4

AVAILABLE NOW WHEREVER BOOKS ARE SOLD

MARVEL Disney LUCASFILM